Lecture Notes in Computer Science 10452

Commenced Publication in 1973
Founding and Former Series Editors:
Gerhard Goos, Juris Hartmanis, and Jan van Leeuwen

More information about this series at http://www.springer.com/series/7408

Tim Menzies · Justyna Petke (Eds.)

Search Based Software Engineering

9th International Symposium, SSBSE 2017
Paderborn, Germany, September 9–11, 2017
Proceedings

 Springer

Editors
Tim Menzies ⓘ
North Carolina State University
Morgantown, WV
USA

Justyna Petke ⓘ
Department of Computer Science
University College London
London
UK

ISSN 0302-9743   ISSN 1611-3349 (electronic)
Lecture Notes in Computer Science
ISBN 978-3-319-66298-5   ISBN 978-3-319-66299-2 (eBook)
DOI 10.1007/978-3-319-66299-2

Library of Congress Control Number: 2017949514

LNCS Sublibrary: SL2 – Programming and Software Engineering

Printed on acid-free paper

This Springer imprint is published by Springer Nature
The registered company is Springer International Publishing AG
The registered company address is: Gewerbestrasse 11, 6330 Cham, Switzerland

Preface

On behalf of the SSBSE 2017 Program Committee, we are pleased to present the proceedings of the 9th International Symposium on Search Based Software Engineering.

This year SSBSE was hosted in Paderborn, Germany, continuing to bring together international researchers to exchange and discuss ideas and to celebrate the latest progress in this rapidly advancing field.

It was a privilege for us to serve as program chairs and we believe that the quality of the program reflects the excellent efforts of the authors, reviewers, keynote speakers, tutorial presenters, and organizers.

First and foremost we are grateful for the widespread participation and support from the SBSE community. This year, SSBSE attracted a large number of submissions–the technical track alone attracted 26 submissions from 14 countries, which is an increase compared with last year.

We would like to thank all the authors for their high-quality contributions. We had a triple-blind review process in place for the main track. Each submission was reviewed by at least three Program Committee members and followed by an online discussion. At the end of the review process:

- 12 papers were accepted to the research track (7 long and 5 short)
- 4 papers were accepted to the challenge track,
- 2 papers were accepted to the student track.

We would like to thank the Program Committee members for providing timely, detailed, and constructive feedback, and for actively participating in the online discussions.

We also wish to thank the general chair, Lars Grunske, who brought SSBSE to Paderborn and put on, together with his team, such an enjoyable event. Special thanks are also due to:

- The track chairs of our specialist tracks:

  - David R. White and Tanja E.J. Vos for organizing an exciting challenge track;
  - Claire Le Goues for chairing the student and short paper tracks.
    Dr. Le Goues deserves additional credit for proposing to change the name from graduate to student track, allowing more participation from students; they are a vital part of any research field.

- Also, we especially thank Matheus Paixao (web chair) and Gregory Gay (publicity chair) for their precious help in reaching out to the community.

In addition to our technical sessions, covering a wide range of topics, SSBSE 2017 attendees had the opportunity to hear

- State-of-the-art reports from two esteemed keynote speakers: Myra B. Cohen and Joachim Wegener.
- Technical tutorials from: Gordon Fraser, Antonio J. Nebro, Dimo Brockhoff, and Hermann Kaindl.
- Journal first invited talk sessions.

We hope that, with these proceedings, anyone who did not have the chance to be with us in Paderborn, will have the opportunity to follow the latest advances of the SBSE community.

June 2017

Tim Menzies
Justyna Petke

Organization

Organizing Committee

General Chair

Lars Grunske   Humboldt University of Berlin, Germany

Program Chairs

Tim Menzies   North Carolina State University, USA
Justyna Petke   University College London, UK

Student and Short Papers Track Chair

Claire Le Goues   Carnegie Mellon University, USA

SSBSE Challenge Track Chairs

David R. White   University College London, UK
Tanja E.J. Vos   Open University, Netherlands

Publicity Chair

Gregory Gay   University of South Carolina, USA

Web Chair

Matheus Paixao   University College London, UK

Proceedings Chair

Sinem Getir   Humboldt University of Berlin, Germany

Local Arrangements Chair

Uwe Pohlmann   University of Paderborn, Germany

Steering Committee

Andrea Arcuri   Westerdals, Norway
Claire Le Goues   Carnegie Mellon University, USA
Federica Sarro   University College London, UK
Gregory Gay   University of South Carolina, USA
Gordon Fraser   University of Sheffield, UK
Jerffeson Teixeira de Souza   Ceará State University, Brazil
Márcio de Oliveira Barros   Federal University of the State of Rio de Janeiro, Brazil
Marouane Kessentini   University of Michigan, USA

| Mohamed Wiem | University of Michigan, USA |
| Shin Yoo | Korea Advanced Institute of Science and Technology, South Korea |

Program Committee

Aldeida Aleti	Monash University, Australia
Alessandro Marchetto	Fondazione Bruno Kessler, Italy
Andrea Arcuri	Westerdals, Norway
Anne Koziolek	Karlsruhe Institute of Technology, Germany
Federica Sarro	University College London, UK
Francisco Chicano	University of Malaga, Spain
Giuliano Antoniol	École Polytechnique de Montréal, Canada
Gregory Gay	University of South Carolina, USA
Guenther Ruhe	University of Calgary, Canada
Hadi Hemmati	University of Manitoba, Canada
Jerffeson Teixeira de Souza	Ceará State University, Brazil
Juan Pablo Galeotti	University of Buenos Aires, Argentina
Leandro Minku	University of Leicester, UK
Leonardo Bottaci	University of Hull, UK
Márcio de Oliveira Barros	Federal University of the State of Rio de Janeiro, Brazil
Mark Harman	University College London, UK
Marouane Kessentini	University of Michigan, USA
Massimiliano Di Penta	University of Sannio, Italy
Muhammad Zohaib Iqbal	National University of Computer & Emerging Sciences, Pakistan
Pasqualina Potena	SICS Swedish ICT, Sweden
Phil McMinn	University of Sheffield, UK
Shin Yoo	Korea Advanced Institute of Science and Technology, South Korea
Thelma E. Colanzi	State University of Maring, Brazil

Challenge Track Program Committee

Alexandru Marginean	University College London, UK
Jonathan M. Aitken	University of Sheffield, UK
Christopher Simons	University of West England, UK
Sarah Thomson	University of Stirling, UK
Héctor Menéndez	University College London, UK
Sevil Sen	University of York, UK
Tanja E.J. Vos	Technical University of Valencia, Spain
Gordon Fraser	University of Sheffield, UK
José Raúl Romero	University of Cordoba, Spain
Shaukat Ali	Simula Research Laboratory, Norway
Inmaculada Medina-Bulo	University of Cadiz, Spain

Student and Short Papers Program Committee

Gordon Fraser	University of Sheffield, UK
Pasqualina Potena	SICS Swedish ICT, Sweden
Thelma E. Colanzi	State University of Maring, Brazil
Celso Camilo-Junior	Universidade Federal de Gois, Brazil
Aldeida Aleti	Monash University, Australia
David R. White	University College London, UK
Simon Poulding	Blekinge Institute of Technology, Sweden
Christopher Timperley	Carnegie Mellon University, USA
Gregory Kapfhammer	Allegheny College, USA
Gregory Gay	University of South Carolina, USA
Anne Koziolek	Karlsruhe Institute of Technology, Germany
Phil McMinn	University of Sheffield, UK
Jonathan Dorn	University of Virginia, USA
Eric Schulte	GrammaTech, USA

Additional Reviewers

Assunção, Wesley K.G.	Jilani, Atif	Petrozziello, Alessio
Guimaraes, Carlos	Karim, Rezaul	

Sponsoring Institutions

Keynotes

The Grass isn't Always Greener: A Changing Neighborhood and Varying Landscape

Myra B. Cohen

University of Nebraska-Lincoln, NE, USA
myra@cse.unl.edu

Abstract. Search based software engineering has been used to solve many problems in software engineering and as such many different search based algorithms have been utilized for optimizing problems across the full software lifecycle. Solutions range from simple greedy to local heuristic search to evolutionary, population based techniques. Choosing the algorithm to use for a particular problem is a key design decision. However, an equally important decision, and one that is often less explored, is the design of the search neighborhood and the choice of its transformation operators. In this talk I will discuss some of our experience with varying the neighborhoods and transformation operators for problems such as software test generation and reverse engineering system models. I will show how this important design decision can have a large impact on the quality of a search algorithm for different variants of the same problem, because it fundamentally alters the search landscape. I will also show that while one neighborhood may be superior solving one variation of a problem, it may not work well at all for another variant of the same problem.

Biography: Myra Cohen is a Susan J. Rosowski Professor at the University of Nebraska-Lincoln where she has been a member of the Laboratory for Empirically Based Software Quality Research and Development, ESQuaReD since 2004. Her research expertise is in combinatorial testing and software testing of highly configurable software, software product lines, graphical user interfaces, and self-adaptive software. She regularly utilizes search based software engineering techniques in her research and teaches a graduate course on this topic. She has been a program committee member of many highly regarded software engineering conferences such as ICSE, FSE, ASE, ISSTA and ICST. She was the program co-chair of SSBSE in 2011, the GECCO SBSE track in 2010 and ISSRE in 2013. She was the general chair of ASE in 2015.

Industrial Applications of Evolutionary Testing

Joachim Wegener

Berner & Mattner Systemtechnik GmbH, Berlin, Germany

Abstract. Test case design could be easily interpreted as the search of the tester for an error-sensitive set of test cases. The application of search techniques to find an adequate set of test cases automatically is straight forward if an appropriate transformation of the testing goals into a fitness function could be defined. Therefore, numerous publications on evolutionary testing were published during the last two decades from researchers all over the world. Nevertheless, evolutionary testing has not found its way into industrial practice. Industrial applications are mostly limited to experimental case studies. The keynote will present successful applications of evolutionary testing in industrial practice and will discuss the success factors. Most successful applications are from the test of embedded systems, since here often very complex implementations are required in order to realize single, well tangible system tasks. But also the aspects hindering a broader application of evolutionary testing in practice shall be discussed. The time is right for a wider introduction.

Biography: Dr. Joachim Wegener studied computer science at the Technical University Berlin and received his PhD from Humboldt University Berlin. His thesis work, Evolutionary Testing of real-time systems temporal behavior gained him the Best Dissertation in Software Engineering award of the Ernst-Denert-Foundation and the German Computer Society, 2002. Joachim Wegener began his professional career as a scientist at Daimler AG Research and Technology. For DaimlerChrysler research and advanced development he led the software analysis and testing group as well as a group on advanced techniques in software engineering. Since 2007 he works for Berner Mattner Systemtechnik GmbH a subsidiary of the Assystem group specialized on embedded systems development services and products. At Berner Mattner, Joachim Wegener is responsible for the departments in Berlin, Brunswick, Cologne and Wolfsburg as well as the product development. He is one of the international leading industrial researchers in evolutionary and systematic testing and has more than ninety publications. He is the inventor of the successful classification tree editors CTE, CTE XL and TESTONA with several thousand users worldwide.

Tutorials

Algorithms for Multiobjective Optimization and How to Benchmark Them

Dimo Brockhoff

Inria Saclay - Île-de-France, Palaiseau, France
dimo.brockhoff@inria.fr

Abstract. Multiobjective optimization problems, in which two or more objective functions are to be optimized simultaneously, appear in many application domains. The field of search based software engineering is no exception. Various algorithms for multiobjective optimization have been proposed in recent years, with the effect that the ultimate practical question when solving a concrete problem became increasingly difficult: which of the many available algorithm shall I actually use? To contribute to the answer of this question, we revisit several common multiobjective optimization algorithms in this talk and discuss their strengths and weaknesses from a more theoretical perspective. In addition, we look at the latest developments on how to benchmark (multiobjective) algorithms and showcase the performance of some common (and not so common) algorithms on the 55 unconstrained numerical blackbox functions of the biobjective BBOB test suite.

Biography: Dimo Brockhoff received his diploma in computer science from University of Dortmund, Germany in 2005 and his PhD (Dr. sc. ETH) from ETH Zurich, Switzerland in 2009. Later, he held two postdoctoral research positions in France at Inria Saclay Ile-de-France (2009-2010) and at Ecole Polytechnique (2010-2011) before joining Inria in November 2011 as a permanent researcher. After working at Inrias Lille - Nord Europe research center for about five years, he has been back to the Saclay - Ile-de-France center since October 2016 to become member of the new Randomized Optimization team. His research interests are focused on evolutionary multiobjective optimization (EMO), in particular on theoretical aspects of indicator-based search, and on the benchmarking of blackbox algorithms in general. Dimo has been involved in the co-organization of several special issues and workshops around these topics such as the SIMCO and SAMCO workshops at the Lorentz center in the Netherlands in 2013 and 2016 and the Blackbox Optimization Benchmarking workshops at CEC 2015 and at GECCO 2013, 2015, and 2016.

Search-based Unit Test Generation with EvoSuite

Gordon Fraser

Computer Science, University of Sheffield, UK
Gordon.Fraser@sheffield.ac.uk

Abstract. EvoSuite automatically generates test cases with assertions for classes written in Java code, using a search-based approach that evolves whole test suites towards satisfying a coverage criterion. For the produced test suites, EvoSuite suggests possible oracles by adding small and effective sets of assertions that concisely summarize the current behavior; these assertions allow the developer to detect deviations from expected behavior, and to capture the current behavior in order to protect against future defects breaking this behaviour. In this tutorial, we will discuss how to use of the EvoSuite search-based test generation infrastructure to apply search-based test generation, and how to build on EvoSuite to develop new techniques using, or extending, search-based testing.

Biography: Gordon Fraser is a Senior Lecturer in Computer Science at the University of Sheffield, UK. He received his Ph.D. from Graz University of Technology, Austria, in 2007, and worked as a post-doc researcher at Saarland University, Germany. He has published on improving software quality and programmer productivity at all major software engineering venues (e.g., TSE, TOSEM, ICSE, ISSTA, FSE, ASE, ICST). He is chair of the steering committees of the International Conference on Software Testing, Verification, and Validation (ICST) and the Symposium on Search-Based Software Engineering (SSBSE). He has been programme chair of several testing-related conferences (ICST, TAP, TAIC PART, SSBSE) and workshops, is a regular member of many programme and organising committees in the field (e.g., ICSE, FSE, ASE, ISSTA), and is editorial board member of the IEEE Transactions on Software Engineering (TSE) and Software Testing, Verification, and Reliability (STVR) journals. He is a founder and one of the core developers of the EvoSuite search-based unit test generator.

Optimization Search for GUIs and Cyberphysical Systems

Hermann Kaindl

Institute of Computer Technology Wien - TU Wien, Austria
hermann.kaindl@tuwien.ac.at

Abstract. This tutorial presents and contrasts two different optimization search approaches studied by this proposer for automated GUI generation and for feature interactions in cyberphysical automotive systems. Providing several GUIs tailored for multiple devices (desktop PCs, tablet PCs and smartphones) is desirable but expensive, and it takes time. Our new approach just requires a device specification with a few parameters for automated GUI tailoring in the course of designtime generation from the same highlevel interaction design model. This tailoring is implemented as heuristic optimization search.

With increasing numbers of features in automotive systems, feature interaction (FI) becomes more and more relevant regarding safety and emissions. Our new approach for optimization of feature interactions integrates an optimization objective (minimize CO_2 emission) with both soft and hard constraints (e.g., related to certain temperatures). In the course of iterations of hillclimbing optimization at runtime, the integrating objective function is dynamically adapted for heuristic coordination of FIs.

These approaches will be contrasted primarily in terms of the very different application domains and, more fundamentally, regarding designtime vs. runtime optimization with their very different requirements.

Biography: Hermann Kaindl joined the Institute of Computer Technology at TU Wien in Vienna, Austria, in early 2003 as a full professor. Prior to moving to academia, he was a senior consultant with the division of program and systems engineering at Siemens Austria. There he has gained more than 24 years of industrial experience in software development and humancomputer interaction. He has published five books and more than 220 papers in refereed journals, books and conference proceedings, and he has previously run more than 50 tutorials. He is a Senior Member of the IEEE and a Distinguished Scientist Member of the ACM, and he is on the executive board of the Austrian Society for Artificial Intelligence. In the past, Hermann Kaindl published his basic research on Heuristic Search in Artificial Intelligence in the AIJ, several IEEE Transactions, and in many Conference Proceedings of IJCAIs, AAAIs and ECAIs.

Multi-objective Optimization with the jMetal Framework. Applications to SBSE

Antonio J. Nebro

University of Malaga, Malaga, Spain
antonio@lcc.uma.es

Abstract. jMetal is a Java-based framework for multi-objective optimization with metaheuristics which has become popular in some disciplines, including Search Based Software Engineering (SBSE). In this tutorial, we give a practical overview of the main jMetal components (algorithms, encodings, problems, operators, experiments, quality indicators), focusing on how to configure and run some of the included algorithms and also on how to incorporate new solution representations and problems. We give examples of classical algorithms but also more modern techniques, including preference-based metaheuristics. Some SBSE problems will be used as case studies.

Biography: Antonio J. Nebro received his M.S. and Ph.D. degrees in Computer Science from the University of Malaga, Spain, in 1992 and 1999, respectively. He is currently an Associate Professor of Computer Science at the University of Malaga, Spain. His current research activity is related to multi-objective optimization techniques, parallelism and Big Data, and the application of these techniques to real-world problems of the domains of bioinformatics and civil engineering. He has coauthored 30 articles published in international journals, 28 of which are indexed in JCR, 15 book chapters and more than 30 articles in international conferences. His H index is 30, and his papers have more than 3250 citations. He is one of the designers and main developer of the jMetal framework for multi-objective optimization with metaheuristics.

Journal-First Presentations

A Systematic Mapping Study of Search-based Software Engineering for Software Product Lines

Roberto E. Lopez-Herrejon, Lukas Linsbauer, and Alexander Egyed

Abstract. Context: Search-Based Software Engineering (SBSE) is an emerging discipline that focuses on the application of search-based optimization techniques to software engineering problems. Software Product Lines (SPLs) are families of related software systems whose members are distinguished by the set of features each one provides. SPL development practices have proven benefits such as improved software reuse, better customization, and faster time to market. A typical SPL usually involves a large number of systems and features, a fact that makes them attractive for the application of SBSE techniques which are able to tackle problems that involve large search spaces.

Objective: The main objective of our work is to identify the quantity and the type of research on the application of SBSE techniques to SPL problems. More concretely, the SBSE techniques that have been used and at what stage of the SPL life cycle, the type of case studies employed and their empirical analysis, and the fora where the research has been published. **Method**: A systematic mapping study was conducted with five research questions and assessed 77 publications from 2001, when the term SBSE was coined, until 2014.

Results: The most common application of SBSE techniques found was testing followed by product configuration, with genetic algorithms and multi-objective evolutionary algorithms being the two most commonly used techniques. Our study identified the need to improve the robustness of the empirical evaluation of existing research, a lack of extensive and robust tool support, and multiple avenues worthy of further investigation. **Conclusions**: Our study attested the great synergy existing between both fields, corroborated the increasing and ongoing interest in research on the subject, and revealed challenging open research questions.

Inf. Softw. Technol. 61, C (May 2015), 33–51

Technical Debt Reduction Using Search Based Automated Refactoring

Michael Mohan, Des Greer, and Paul McMullan

Abstract. Software refactoring has been recognized as a valuable process during software development and is often aimed at repaying technical debt. Technical debt arises when a software product has been built or amended without full care for structure and extensibility. Refactoring is useful to keep technical debt low and if it can be automated there are obvious efficiency benefits. Using a combination of automated refactoring techniques, software metrics and meta-heuristic searches, an automated refactoring tool can improve the structure of a software system without affecting its functionality. In this paper, four different refactoring approaches are compared using an automated software refactoring tool. Weighted sums of metrics are used to form different fitness functions that drive the search process towards certain aspects of software quality. Metrics are combined to measure coupling, abstraction and inheritance and a fourth fitness function is proposed to measure reduction in technical debt. The 4 functions are compared against each other using 3 different searches on 6 different open source programs. Four out of the 6 programs show a larger improvement in the technical debt function after the search based refactoring process. The results show that the technical debt function is useful for assessing improvement in quality.

Journal of Systems and Software 120 (2016): 183–194

Contents

Challenge Papers

Student Papers

Long Research Papers

Many Independent Objective (MIO) Algorithm for Test Suite Generation

Andrea Arcuri[1,2(✉)]

[1] Faculty of Technology, Westerdals Oslo ACT, Oslo, Norway
arcand@westerdals.no
[2] University of Luxembourg, Luxembourg City, Luxembourg

Abstract. Automatically generating test suites is intrinsically a multi-objective problem, as any of the testing targets (e.g., statements to execute or mutants to kill) is an objective on its own. Test suite generation has peculiarities that are quite different from other more regular optimisation problems. For example, given an existing test suite, one can add more tests to cover the remaining objectives. One would like the smallest number of small tests to cover many objectives as possible, but that is a secondary goal compared to covering those targets in the first place. Furthermore, the amount of objectives in software testing can quickly become unmanageable, in the order of (tens/hundreds of) thousands, especially for system testing of industrial size systems. Traditional multi-objective optimisation algorithms can already start to struggle with just four or five objectives to optimize. To overcome these issues, different techniques have been proposed, like for example the Whole Test Suite (WTS) approach and the Many-Objective Sorting Algorithm (MOSA). However, those techniques might not scale well to very large numbers of objectives and limited search budgets (a typical case in system testing). In this paper, we propose a novel algorithm, called Many Independent Objective (MIO) algorithm. This algorithm is designed and tailored based on the specific properties of test suite generation. An empirical study, on a set of artificial and actual software, shows that the MIO algorithm can achieve higher coverage compared to WTS and MOSA, as it can better exploit the peculiarities of test suite generation.

Keywords: Test generation · SBSE · SBST · MOO

1 Introduction

Test case generation can be modelled as an optimisation problem, and so different kinds of search algorithms can be used to address it [9]. There can be different objectives to optimise, like for example branch coverage or the detection of mutants in the system under test (SUT). When aiming at maximising these metrics, often the sought solutions are not single test cases, as a single test cannot cover all the objectives in the SUT. Often, the final solutions are sets of test cases, usually referred as *test suites*.

© Springer International Publishing AG 2017
T. Menzies and J. Petke (Eds.): SSBSE 2017, LNCS 10452, pp. 3–17, 2017.
DOI: 10.1007/978-3-319-66299-2_1

There are many different kinds of search algorithms that can be used for generating test suites. The most famous is perhaps the Genetic Algorithms (GA), which is often the first choice when addressing a new software engineering problem for the first time. But it can well happen that on specific problems other search algorithms could be better. Therefore, when investigating a new problem, it is not uncommon to evaluate and compare different algorithms. On average, no search algorithm can be best on all possible problems [13]. It is not uncommon that, even on non-trivial tasks, simpler algorithms like $(1 + 1)$ Evolutionary Algorithm (EA) or Hill Climbing (HC) can give better results than GA (e.g., as in [1]).

A major factor affecting the performance of a search algorithm is the so called *search budget*, i.e., for how long the search can be run, usually the longer the better. But the search budget is also strongly related to the tradeoff between the *exploitation* and *exploration* of the search landscape. If the budget is low, then a population-based algorithm like GA (which puts more emphasis on the exploration) is likely to perform worse than a single, more focused individual-based algorithm like HC or $(1 + 1)$ EA. On the other hand, if the search budget is large enough, the exploration made by the GA can help it to escape from the so called local optima in which HC and $(1 + 1)$ EA can easily get stuck in.

To obtain even better results, then one has to design specialised search algorithms that try to exploit the specific properties of the addressed problem domain. In the case of test suite generation, there are at least the following peculiarities:

- testing targets can be sought *independently*. Given an existing test suite, to cover the remaining testing targets (e.g., lines and branches), you can create and add new tests without the need to modify the existing ones in the suite. At the end of the search, one wants a minimised test suite, but that is a secondary objective compared to code coverage.
- testing targets can be strongly related (e.g., two nested branches), as well as being completely independent (e.g., code in two different top-level functions with no shared state).
- some testing targets can be *infeasible*, i.e., impossible to cover. There can be different reasons for it, e.g., dead code, defensive programming or the testing tool not handling all kinds of SUT inputs (e.g., files or network connections). Detecting whether a target is feasible or not is an undecidable problem.
- for non-trivial software, there can be a very large number of objectives. This is specially true not only for system-level testing, but also for unit testing when mutation score is one of the coverage criteria [7]. Traditional multi-objective algorithms are ill suited to tackle large numbers of objectives [10].

In this paper, we propose a novel search algorithm that exploits such characteristics and, as such, it is specialised for test suite generation (and any problem sharing those properties). We call it the Many Independent Objective (MIO) algorithm. We carried out an empirical study to compare the MIO algorithm with the current state-of-the-art, namely the Whole Test Suite [6] approach and the Many-Objective Sorting Algorithm [11]. On a set of artificial software with different characteristics (clear gradients, plateaus, deceptive local optima and infeasible targets), in most cases MIO achieves higher coverage. This was also confirmed with unit test experiments on three numerical functions.

2 Background

2.1 Whole Test Suite (WTS)

The Whole Test Suite [6] approach was introduced as an algorithm to generate whole test suites. Before that, typical test case generators were targeting only single objectives, like specific lines or branches, using heuristics like the *branch distance* and the *approach level* (as for example done in [8]).

In the WTS approach, a GA is used, where an individual in the GA population is a set of test cases. Mutation and crossover operators can modify both the set composition (i.e., remove or add new tests) and its content (e.g., modify the tests). As fitness function, the sum of all branch distances in the SUT is used. At the end of the search, the best solution in the population is given as output test suite. To avoid losing good tests during the search, the WTS can also be extended to use an *archive* of best tests seen so far [12].

2.2 Many-Objective Sorting Algorithm (MOSA)

The Many-Objective Sorting Algorithm (MOSA) [11] was introduced to overcome some of the limitations of WTS. In MOSA, each testing target (e.g., lines) is an objective to optimize. MOSA is an extension of NSGA-II [5], a very popular multi-objective algorithm. In MOSA, the population is composed of tests, not test suites. When a new target is covered, the test covering it gets stored in an archive, and such target is not used any more in the fitness function. A final output test suite is composed by the best tests found during the search and that are stored in the archive.

In NSGA-II, selection is based on ranks (from 1 on, where 1 is the best): an individual that subsumes many other individuals gets a better rank, and so it is more likely to be selected for reproduction. One of the main differences of MOSA compared to NSGA-II is the use of the *preference sorting criterion*: to avoid losing the best individuals for a given testing target, for each uncovered testing target the best individual gets the best rank (0 in MOSA), regardless of its subsuming relations with the other tests.

3 The MIO Algorithm

3.1 Core Algorithm

Both WTS and MOSA have been shown to provide good results, at least for unit test generation [6,11,12]. However, both algorithms have intrinsic limitations, like for example:

- population-based algorithms like WTS and MOSA do put more emphasis on the exploration of the search landscape, which is not ideal in constrained situations of limited search budgets, like for example in system-level testing where each test case execution can be computationally expensive. Letting the user to tune the population size parameter is not a viable option, unless it is done automatically (but even then, it has side effects, as we will see in the empirical study).
- although once a target is covered it is not used any more for the fitness function, the individuals optimised for it would still be in the population. They will die out eventually after a few generations, but, until then, their presence in the population can hamper the search if those covered targets are unrelated to the remaining non-covered targets.
- in the presence of infeasible targets, some tests can get good fitness score (e.g., a close to 0 branch distance) although they will never cover those infeasible targets. Those not useful tests might end up taking over a large part of the population.
- there can be a very large number of objectives to cover, even in the order of hundreds of thousands (e.g., in the system-level testing of industrial systems). A fixed size population would simple not work well: if too small, then there would not be enough diverse genetic material in the first generation; if too large, not only convergence would be drastically slowed down, but also the computational cost could sky-rock (e.g., NSGA-II has a quadratic complexity based on the population size).

To avoid these limitations, we have designed a novel evolutionary algorithm that we call the Many Independent Objective (MIO) algorithm. In a nutshell, MIO combines the simplicity and effectiveness of $(1 + 1)$ EA with a dynamic population, dynamic exploration/exploitation tradeoff and feedback-directed target selection.

The MIO algorithm maintains an archive of tests. In the archive, *for each* testing target we keep a different population of tests of size up to n (e.g., $n = 10$). Therefore, given z objectives/targets, there can be up to $n \times z$ tests in the archive at the same time.

At the beginning of the search, the archive will be empty, and so a new test will be randomly generated. From the second step on, MIO will decide to either sample a new test at random (probability P_r), or will choose (details later) one existing test in the archive (probability $1 - P_r$), copy it, and mutate it. Every time a new test is sampled/mutated, its fitness is calculated, and it will be saved in the archive if needed (details later). At this point, we need to define how tests are saved in the archive, and how MIO samples from the archive.

When a test is evaluated, a copy of it might be saved in 0 or more of the z populations in the archive, based on its fitness value. For each target, there will be a heuristics score h in $[0, 1]$, where 1 means that the target is covered, whereas 0 is the worst possible heuristics value. For example, if the heuristics is the branch distance d, this can be mapped into $[0, 1]$ by using $h = 1/(1 + d)$

(where $h = 0$ if a branch was never reached and so the branch distance d was not calculated).

For each target k, a test is saved in population T_k, with $|T_k| \leq n$, if either:

- if $h_k = 0$, the test is not added regardless of the following conditions.
- if the target is covered, i.e. $h_k = 1$, the test is added and that population is shrunk to one single individual, and it will never expand again (i.e., it will be always $|T_k| = 1$). A new test can *replace* the one in T_k only if it is *shorter* (which will depend on the problem domain, e.g. size measured in sequence of function calls in unit testing) or, if it is of the same size, then replace the current test only if the new test has better coverage on the other targets (i.e., sum of all the heuristics values on all targets).
- if the population is not full (i.e., $|T_k| < n$), then the test is added. Otherwise, if full (i.e., $|T_k| = n$), the test might replace the worst in the population, but only if not worse than it (but not necessarily better). This means no worse heuristic value or, if the same, no larger size.

The idea is that, for each target, we keep a population of candidate tests for it, for which we have at least some heuristics value. But once a target k is covered, we just need to store the best test, and discard the rest. Note: if a discarded test in T_k was good for another target j, then it would be still stored in T_j anyway, so it is not lost.

When MIO needs to sample one test from the archive instead of generating one at random, it will do the following:

- choose one target k at random where $|T_k| > 0$ and k is not covered (i.e., no test has $h_k = 1$). If all non-empty populations are for covered targets, then just choose k randomly among them.
- choose one test randomly from T_k.

By using this approach, we aim at sampling tests that have non-zero heuristics (and so guidance) for targets that are not covered yet.

3.2 Exploration/Exploitation Control

In the MIO algorithm, the two main parameters for handling the tradeoff between exploration and exploitation of the search landscape are the probability P_r of sampling at random and the population size n per target. Exploration is good at the beginning of the search, but, at the end, a more focused exploitation can bring better results. Like in Simulated Annealing, we use an approach in which we gradually reduce the amount of exploration during the search.

We define with F the percentage of time after which a focused search should start. This means that, for some parameters like P_r and n, we define two values: one for the start of the search (e.g., $P_r = 0.5$ and $n = 10$), and one for when the focused phase begins (i.e., $P_r = 0$ and $n = 1$). These values will linearly increase/decrease based on the passing of time. For example, if $F = 0.5$ (i.e., the focused search starts after 50% of the search budget is used), then after 30% of the search, the value P_r would decrease from 0.5 to 0.2.

Note, when during the search decreasing n leads to some cases with $|T| > n$, then those populations are shrunk by removing the worst individuals in it. Once the focused search begins (i.e., $P_r = 0$ and $n = 1$), then MIO starts to resemble a parallel $(1 + 1)$ EA.

When dealing with many objectives, even if there is a clear gradient to cover them in the fitness landscape, there might be simply not enough time left to cover all of them. In software testing, the final user is only interested in tests that do cover targets, and not in tests that are heuristically close to cover them (e.g., close to solve complex constraints in some branch predicates, but not there yet). Therefore, between a test suite A that is close to but does not cover 100 targets, and another one B which does cover 1 target and is very far from covering the remaining 99, the final user would likely prefer B over A.

To take this insight into account, MIO tries to focus on just few targets at a time, instead of spreading its resources thin among all the left uncovered targets. For example, in MIO there is an extra parameter m which controls how many mutations and fitness evaluations should be done on the same individual before sampling a new one. Like P_r and n, m varies over time, like starting from 1 and then increasing up to 10 when the focused search begins.

3.3   Feedback-Directed Sampling

When dealing with many objectives and limited resources, it might not be possible to cover all of them. As discussed in Sect. 3.2, the final user is only interested in the actually covered targets, and not on how close we are to cover them. Therefore, it makes sense to try to focus on targets that we have higher chances to cover. This is helpful also when dealing with infeasible targets for which any heuristics will just plateau at a certain point.

To handle these cases, we use a simple but yet very effective technique that we call Feedback-Directed Sampling (FDS). The sampling algorithm from the archive discussed in Sect. 3.1 is modified as follow. Instead of choosing the target k randomly among the non-covered/non-empty ones, each of these targets will have a counter c_k. Every time a test is sampled from a population T_k, then c_k is increased by 1. Every time a new *better* individual is added to T_k (or replace one of its existing tests), then the counter c_k is reset to 0. When we sample from k from non-covered/non-empty ones, then, instead of choosing k at random, we choose the k with the lowest c_k.

As long as we get improvements for a target k, the higher chances will be that we sample from T_k, as c_k gets reset more often. On the other hand, for infeasible targets, their c will never be reset once they reach their plateau, and so they will be sampled less often. Similarly, more complex targets will be sampled less often, and so the search concentrates on the easier targets that are not covered yet. However, this is not an issue because, once an easy target k is covered, we do not sample from T_k any more (recall Sect. 3.1), unless also *all* the other targets are either covered or with empty T.

4   Empirical Study

To evaluate the performance of the MIO algorithm, we compared it with random search, MOSA and WTS. We used two different case studies: (1) a set of artificial problems with varying, specific characteristics; (2) three numerical functions.

In this paper, we aim at answering the following research questions:

RQ1: On which kinds of problem does MIO perform better than Random, MOSA and WTS?

RQ2: What is the impact of tuning parameters for exploration vs. exploitation of the search landscape in MIO and MOSA?

RQ3: How do the analysed algorithms fare on actual software?

4.1   Artificial Software

In this paper, we designed four different kinds of artificial problems. In all of them, there are z targets, and the search algorithm can be run for up to b fitness evaluations. A test is defined by two components: an id (e.g., think about it like the name of a method to call in unit testing) and a numeric integer value $x \in [0, r]$ (e.g., think about it like the input to a method call). Each target k is independent, and can be covered only by a test with $id = k$. The artificial problems will differ based on their fitness landscape. Given $g \in [0, r]$ the single global optimum chosen at random, and given the normalising function $\rho(d) = 1/(1 + d)$ for distances, then we have four different cases for each target:

Gradient: $h_k = \rho(|x - g|)$. This represents the simplest case where the search algorithm has a direct gradient from x toward the global optimum g.

Plateau: $h_k = \rho(g - x)$ if $g \geq x$, else $h_k = \rho(0.1 \times r)$. In this case, we have one side of the search landscape (before the value of the global optimum g) with a clear gradient. However, the other side is a plateau with a relatively good fitness value (note that $0 \leq |g - x| \leq r$).

Deceptive: $h_k = \rho(g - x)$ if $g \geq x$, else $h_k = \rho(1 + r - x)$. This is similar to the *Plateau* case, where one side of the search landscape has a clear gradient toward g. However, the other side has a deceptive gradient toward leaving g and reach the maximum value r.

Infeasible: like *Gradient*, but with a certain number of the z targets having a constant $h_k = \rho(1)$ and no global optimum.

We implemented the four search algorithms in which, when a test is sampled, its id and x values are chosen at random within the given valid ranges. Mutations on x is done by adding/subtracting 2^i, where i is chosen randomly in $[0, 10]$. We consider mutating id as a *disruptive* operation, and, as such, we only mutate it with low probability 0.01. Mutating id means changing both id and x at random (think about mutating a function call with string inputs into another one that requires integers, where the strings x would have no meaning as integers). All the analysed search algorithms use the same random sampling, mutation operation and archive to store the best tests found so far.

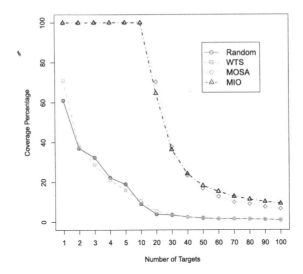

Fig. 1. Coverage results on the *Gradient* problem type, with varying number of targets z.

For the MIO algorithm, we used $F = 0.5$, $P_r = 0.5$, $n = 10$ and max mutations 10. For MOSA, we used the same settings as in [11], i.e. population size 50 and tournament selection size 10. WTS uses the same population size as MOSA, with up to 50 test cases in the same test suite (i.e., one individual). A randomly sampled test suite in WTS will have size randomly chosen between 1 and 50. WTS also has mutation operators to add a new test (probability $1/3$) in a test suite, remove one test at random (probability $1/3$), or modify one (probability $1/3$) like in MIO and MOSA. WTS also uses a crossover operator with probability 70% to combine test suites.

For each problem type but *Infeasible*, we created problems having a variable number of z targets, in particular $z \in \{1, 2, 3, 4, 5, 10, 20, 30, 40, 50, 60, 70, 80, 90, 100\}$, i.e., 15 different values in total, ranging from 1 to 100. We used $r = 1000$. We ran each of the four search algorithms 100 times with budget $b = 1000$. As the optima g are randomised, we make sure that the search algorithms run on the same problem instances. In the case of the *Infeasible* type, we used 10 *Gradient* targets, on which we added a different number of infeasible targets in $\{0, 1, 2, 3, 4, 5, 10, 20, 30, 40, 50, 60, 70, 80, 90, 100\}$, i.e., 16 values in total, with z ranging from $(10 + 0) = 10$ to $(10 + 100) = 110$. Figure 1 shows the results for the *Gradient* type, Fig. 2 for *Plateau*, Fig. 3 for *Deceptive*, and Fig. 4 for *Infeasible*.

The *Gradient* case (Fig. 1) is the simplest, where the four search algorithms obtain their highest coverage. MIO and MOSA have very similar performance, which is higher than the one of Random and WTS. However, on the more difficult case of *Plateau* (Fig. 2), MIO starts to have a clear advantage over MOSA. For example, from $z = 30$ on, MOSA becomes equivalent to Random and WTS,

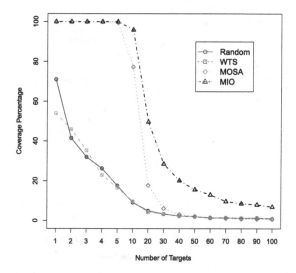

Fig. 2. Coverage results on the *Plateau* problem type, with varying number of targets z.

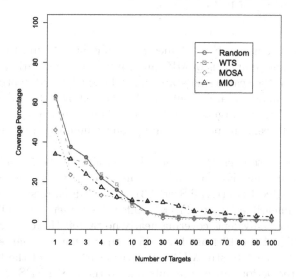

Fig. 3. Coverage results on the *Deceptive* problem type, with varying number of targets z.

covering nearly no target. However, in that particular case, MIO can still achieve around 20% coverage (i.e., 6 targets). Even for large numbers of targets (i.e., 100 when taking into account that the search budget b is only 1000), still MIO can cover some targets, whereas the other algorithms do not.

The *Deceptive* case (Fig. 3) is of particular interest: for low numbers of z targets (i.e., up to 10), both MIO and MOSA perform worse than Random. From 10 targets on, MOSA is equivalent to Random and WTS, whereas MIO

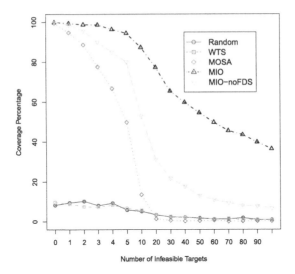

Fig. 4. Coverage results on the *Infeasible* problem type, with varying number of infeasible targets on top of 10 *Gradient* ones.

has better results. This can be explained by taking into account two contrasting factors: (1) the more emphasis of MIO and MOSA on exploitation compared to the exploration of the search landscape is not beneficial in deceptive landscape areas, whereas a random search would not be affected by it; (2) MIO does better handle large numbers of targets (Fig. 1), even when there is no gradient (Fig. 2). The value $z = 10$ seems to be the turning point where (2) starts to have more weight than (1).

The *Infeasible* case (Fig. 4) is where MIO obtains the best results compared to the other algorithms. For this case, we also ran a further version of MIO in which we deactivated FDS (recall Sect. 3.3), as we wanted to study its impact in the presence of infeasible targets. From 20 infeasible targets on, MOSA, Random and WTS become equivalent, covering nearly no target. However, MIO can still cover nearly 80% of the 10 feasible testing targets. For very large numbers of infeasible targets like 100, still MIO can cover nearly 40% of the feasible ones. This much better performance is mainly due to the use of FDS (see the gap in Fig. 4 between MIO and MIO-noFDS). However, even without FDS, MIO still does achieve better results compared to the other algorithms.

> **RQ1**: *on all the considered problems, MIO is the algorithm that scaled best. Coverage improvements were even up to 80% in some cases.*

When using a search algorithm, some parameters need to be set, like the population size or crossover probability in a GA. Usually, common settings in the literature can already achieve good results on average [4]. Finding tuned settings that work better on average on a large number of different artefacts is not trivial.

Ideally, a user should just choose for how long a search algorithm should run, and not do long tuning phases by himself on his problem artefacts. Parameter tuning can also play a role in algorithm comparisons: what if a compared algorithm performed worse just because one of its chosen settings was sub-optimal?

Arguably, among the most important parameters for a search algorithm are the ones that most impact the tradeoff between the exploration and the exploitation of the search landscape. In the case of MIO, this is clearly controlled by the F parameter (low values put more emphasis on exploitation, whereas for high values a large number of tests are simply sampled at random). In the case of population-based algorithms, the population size can be considered as a parameter to control such tradeoff. Small populations would reward exploitation, whereas large populations would reward exploration.

To study these effects, we carried out a further series of experiments on the *Gradient*, *Plateau* and *Deceptive* problem types. For MIO, we studied six different values for F, in particular $\{0, 0.2, 0.4, 0.6, 0.8, 1\}$. For MOSA, we studied six different values for the population size, i.e. $\{4, 8, 16, 32, 64, 128\}$. Each experiment was repeated 100 times. Figure 5 shows the results of these experiments.

For MIO, the results in Fig. 5 do match expectation: for problems with clear gradient or with just some plateaus, a more focused search that rewards exploitation is better. The best setting is a low $F = 0.2$, although the lowest $F = 0$ is not particularly good. You still need some genetic diversity at the beginning of the search, and not rely on just one single individual. For deceptive landscapes, exploration can be better, especially for a low number of targets. For example, with $z = 1$ then $F = 1$ provides the best performance. However, for larger number of targets, too much exploration would not be so beneficial, as it would not have enough time to converge to cover the targets.

In the case of MOSA, Fig. 5 provides some interesting insight. For simple problems with clear gradient, one would expect that a focused search should provide better results. However, the small population size of 4 is actually the configuration that gave the worst results. The reason is that there is only little genetic material at the beginning of the search, and new one is only generated with the mutation operator. However, a too large population size would still be detrimental, as not focused enough. In that particular problem type, the best population size seems ranging from 16 to 32, i.e., not too large, but not too small either. In case of plateaus, still a too small population size (e.g., 4) gives the worst result. However, in case of plateaus, there is a need to have some more exploration in the search landscape, and this confirmed by the fact that the best results are obtained with large population sizes (e.g., 64 and 128). This effect is much more marked in the case of deceptive landscapes, where large population sizes lead to much better results.

The experiments reported in Fig. 5 clearly points out to a challenge in population-based algorithms when dealing with many-objective problems. A too small population size would reduce diversity in the initial genetic material. But a too large population size would hamper convergence speed. Finding a fixed, right population size that works on most problem sizes (e.g., $z = 10$ vs $z = 1m$) might

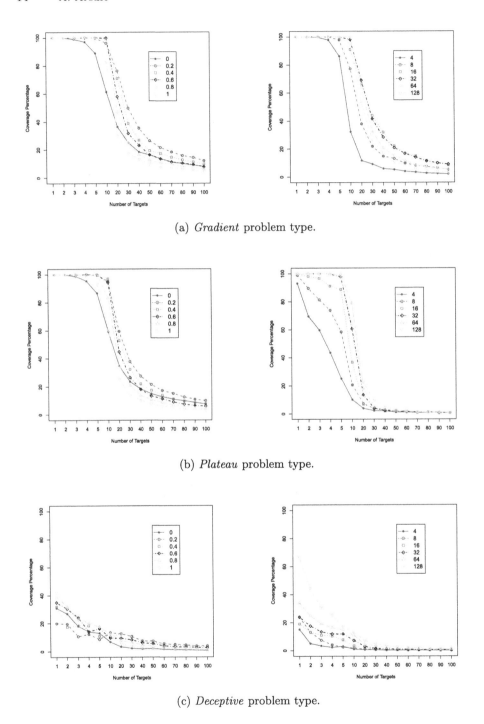

(a) *Gradient* problem type.

(b) *Plateau* problem type.

(c) *Deceptive* problem type.

Fig. 5. Tuning of F for MIO (left side) and population size for MOSA (right side).

not be feasible. To overcome this issue, MIO uses a dynamically sized population, whereas the tradeoff between exploration and exploitation is controlled by a dynamically decreasing probability P_r of creating new tests at random (instead of mutating the current ones stored in the archive).

RQ2: *On the analysed problems, the population size and the F parameter have clear effects on performance, which strongly depend on whether on the given problem one needs more or less exploitation/exploration.*

4.2   Numerical Functions

When designing algorithms to work on a large class of problems, it is common to evaluate them on artificial problems to try to abstract away and analyse in details the characteristics for which such algorithms perform best. For example, the very popular NSGA-II algorithm (on which MOSA is based on) was originally evaluated only on nine numerical functions [5]. However, using only artificial problems is risky, as those might abstract away some very important factors. A good example of this issue is Adaptive Random Testing, where artificial problems with artificially high fault rates were masking away its very prohibitive computational cost [2].

Table 1. Comparions of algorithms on three different numerical functions. Coverage is not a percentage, but rather the average raw sum of statements and branches that are covered. For each algorithm, we also specify if better than any of the others, i.e. $\hat{A}_{12} > 0.5$ (in parenthesis) and p-value less than 0.05.

SUT	Algorithm	Tests	Coverage	Better than
Expint	MIO	9.4	63.7	RAND(1.00) WTS(0.82)
	MOSA	14.0	63.2	RAND(1.00) WTS(0.80)
	RAND	5.4	38.7	
	WTS	9.3	62.5	RAND(1.00)
Gammq	MIO	9.2	69.1	MOSA(0.83) RAND(1.00) WTS(0.90)
	MOSA	8.0	65.9	RAND(1.00)
	RAND	1.0	32.0	
	WTS	6.8	67.2	MOSA(0.60) RAND(1.00)
Triangle	MIO	12.6	38.9	MOSA(0.71) RAND(1.00) WTS(0.98)
	MOSA	14.2	37.8	RAND(0.99) WTS(0.86)
	RAND	11.1	31.7	
	WTS	11.3	35.7	RAND(0.97)

To somehow mitigate this issue, as a safety-net we also carried out some experiments on actual software, where we aim at unit testing for line and branch coverage. We use the branch distance as heuristic for the fitness function. We considered three numerical functions previously used in the literature (e.g., [2]): *Expint* (88 LOC, including everything, also empty lines), *Gammq* (91 LOC), and *Triangle* (29 LOC). Each algorithm was run for up to 5000 fitness evaluations. Each experiment was repeated 100 times. Average values are reported in Table 1, where we also report the Vargha-Delaney effect sizes $\hat{A}_{12}$ and the results of Mann-Whitney-Wilcoxon U-tests at $\alpha = 0.05$ level [3]. In all these three numerical functions, the MIO algorithm is the one achieving the highest coverage of the targets. However, the three chosen numerical functions are not particularly difficult, and, as such, the performance difference between MIO, MOSA and WTS is not so large.

There is one thing to notice in these results: WTS is much better than Random, whereas in the previous experiments they were very similar. After an investigation, the reason for this behaviour is rather obvious. With a population size of 50, and up to 50 tests in the same test suite, on average the first population would have a size of $50 \times 50/2 = 1250$ tests, which is higher than the search budget $b = 1000$. In other words, in those experiments WTS was practically doing just a random search. However, this is not the case here, as we have $b = 5000$. In retrospective, on one hand those experiments could be considered unfair to WTS. On the other hand, this issue further stresses out the need for a dynamically sized population when dealing with many-objective problems.

> **RQ3**: *the experiments on actual software are consistent with the ones on artificial problems: the MIO algorithm still achieves the best results.*

5   Conclusion

In this paper, we have presented a novel search algorithm that is tailored for the problem of generating test suites. We call it the Many Independent Objective (MIO) algorithm. We have carried out an empirical study to compare MIO with the other main algorithms for test suite generation: the Whole Test Suite (WTS) approach and the Many-Objective Sorting Algorithm (MOSA). We also used random search as a baseline. On artificial problems with increasing complexity and on some numerical functions, MIO achieved better results than the other algorithms. In some cases, coverage improvements were even in the order of +80%.

Future work will focus on implementing the MIO algorithm in different test generation frameworks, especially in system-level testing, and empirically evaluate how it fares in those contexts. To help researchers integrate MIO in their frameworks, all the code used for the experiments in this paper is available online on a public repository, as part of the EVOMASTER tool at www.evomaster.org.

Acknowledgments. This work is supported by the National Research Fund, Luxembourg (FNR/P10/03).

References

1. Ali, S., Iqbal, M.Z., Arcuri, A., Briand, L.C.: Generating test data from OCL constraints with search techniques. IEEE Trans. Softw. Eng. (TSE) **39**(10), 1376–1402 (2013)
2. Arcuri, A., Briand, L.: Adaptive random testing: an illusion of effectiveness? In: ACM International Symposium on Software Testing and Analysis (ISSTA), pp. 265–275 (2011)
3. Arcuri, A., Briand, L.: A hitchhiker's guide to statistical tests for assessing randomized algorithms in software engineering. Softw. Test. Verification Reliab. (STVR) **24**(3), 219–250 (2014)
4. Arcuri, A., Fraser, G.: Parameter tuning or default values? an empirical investigation in search-based software engineering. Empirical Softw. Eng. (EMSE) **18**(3), 594–623 (2013)
5. Deb, K., Pratap, A., Agarwal, S., Meyarivan, T.: A fast and elitist multiobjective genetic algorithm: NSGA-II. IEEE Trans. Evol. Comput. (TEVC) **6**(2), 182–197 (2002)
6. Fraser, G., Arcuri, A.: Whole test suite generation. IEEE Trans. Softw. Eng. **39**(2), 276–291 (2013)
7. Fraser, G., Arcuri, A.: Achieving scalable mutation-based generation of whole test suites. Empirical Softw. Eng. (EMSE) **20**(3), 783–812 (2015)
8. Harman, M., McMinn., P.: A theoretical and empirical study of search based testing: local, global and hybrid search. IEEE Trans. Softw. Eng. (TSE) **36**(2), 226–247 (2010)
9. Harman, M., Mansouri, S.A., Zhang, Y.: Search-based software engineering: trends, techniques and applications. ACM Comput. Surv. (CSUR) **45**(1), 11 (2012)
10. Li, B., Li, J., Tang, K., Yao, X.: Many-objective evolutionary algorithms: a survey. ACM Comput. Surv. (CSUR) **48**(1), 13 (2015)
11. Panichella, A., Kifetew, F., Tonella, P.: Automated test case generation as a many-objective optimisation problem with dynamic selection of the targets. IEEE Trans. Softw. Eng. (TSE) **PP**(99), 1 (2017). http://ieeexplore.ieee.org/abstract/document/7840029/
12. Rojas, J.M., Vivanti, M., Arcuri, A., Fraser, G.: A detailed investigation of the effectiveness of whole test suite generation. Empirical Softw. Eng. (EMSE) **22**(2), 852–893 (2017). https://link.springer.com/article/10.1007/s10664-015-9424-2
13. Wolpert, D.H., Macready, W.G.: No free lunch theorems for optimization. IEEE Trans. Evol. Comput. **1**(1), 67–82 (1997)

Search Based Path and Input Data Generation for Web Application Testing

Matteo Biagiola[1,2]([✉]), Filippo Ricca[2], and Paolo Tonella[1]

[1] Fondazione Bruno Kessler, Trento, Italy
{biagiola,tonella}@fbk.eu
[2] University of Genova, Genoa, Italy
filippo.ricca@unige.it

Abstract. Test case generation for web applications aims at ensuring full coverage of the navigation structure. Existing approaches resort to crawling and manual/random input generation, with or without a preliminary construction of the navigation model. However, crawlers might be unable to reach some parts of the web application and random input generation might not receive enough guidance to produce the inputs needed to cover a given path. In this paper, we take advantage of the navigation structure implicitly specified by developers when they write the page objects used for web testing and we define a novel set of genetic operators that support the joint generation of test inputs and feasible navigation paths. On a case study, our tool SUBWEB was able to achieve higher coverage of the navigation model than crawling based approaches, thanks to its intrinsic ability of generating inputs for feasible paths and of discarding likely infeasible paths.

Keywords: Web testing · Test case generation

1 Introduction

The main goal of end-to-end test case generation when the program under test is a web application is to ensure that the functionalities of the web application are fully exercised by the generated test cases. Usually no explicit navigation graph is available to guide the creation of test cases and to measure the degree of navigation coverage achieved. Existing approaches resort to web crawling in order to build the missing navigation model [1]. However, crawling is severely limited in its ability to fully explore the navigation graph, which depends on the input generation strategy. Such strategy is usually manual input definition, random input generation, or a mixture of the two. Another limitation of crawling based approaches is that not all paths in the crawled model are feasible (i.e., admit a test input that traverses them upon execution). As a consequence not all test paths derived from the crawled model can be turned into test cases that traverse the desired paths upon execution. When they don't cover the test paths for which they are generated, we say the test case is *divergent* (e.g., a step in a

© Springer International Publishing AG 2017
T. Menzies and J. Petke (Eds.): SSBSE 2017, LNCS 10452, pp. 18–32, 2017.
DOI: 10.1007/978-3-319-66299-2_2

test case triggers an error, hence preventing the execution of the next steps; the app state does not allow the next action in the test path to be taken).

We address the problem of navigation graph construction by taking advantage of a design pattern commonly used in web testing: the Page Object (PO) design pattern. The purpose of POs is to encapsulate the details necessary to access the web elements in a web page (e.g., CSS or XPath locators, text extraction from HTML page, etc.) and to expose an abstract interface to developers, who can use it to perform high level operations against the web application under test. Such operations are exposed as methods of the PO class (e.g., a method to login; another to select an item and add it to a cart; etc.). The key benefit of this design pattern is the confinement of fragile web page access operations (e.g., implementation details concerning locators) within a single class, the PO, instead of spreading them across all test cases. This ensures higher maintainability of the test code when the web application evolves [2]. There is however another indirect benefit: when defining the POs for a web application, developers implicitly define also its navigation structure, since navigation methods in POs return the next PO encountered after triggering the navigation action. We resort to such property of POs to build the navigation graph to be covered by the automatically generated test cases.

We address the *problem of path feasibility* by means of a *novel search based test generation algorithm* (in particular, we use a genetic algorithm), which performs path selection and input generation at the same time. In our algorithm, a chromosome is a variable length sequence of navigation method invocations, each with the actual parameter values required for the invocations. Chromosomes are evolved by means of custom genetic operators that ensure compliance of the navigation sequences with the navigation graph and reachability of the remaining coverage targets. The fitness function that guides the generation of test cases is based on the distance between the executed sequence and the current set of coverage targets.

We have implemented our approach in the tool SUBWEB (Search based web test generator) and we have evaluated its effectiveness on the AddressBook case study, by comparing it with crawling based approaches. SUBWEB achieves higher coverage with smaller test suites than crawling based approaches. Moreover, the test cases generated by SUBWEB are feasible by construction, while on Address-Book the test cases derived from the crawled model are divergent test cases 17% of the times.

2   Related Work

Several (semi-)automated web testing techniques have been proposed in the literature in the last few years, to reduce the human effort and the amount of work required for test case creation [1,3,4]. Most approaches rely on web application crawling for the construction of a navigation model and on graph visit algorithms for the selection of navigation paths that ensure high coverage of the model (e.g., transition coverage). Input data generation to turn the selected paths into executable test cases is either manual or random [5]. The proposal by Mesbah et al. [1] belongs to this category. They use a crawler, *Crawljax*, to derive a state flow graph consisting of states and transitions that model the Ajax web application under test. Then, the tool *Atusa* uses the inferred model to generate test cases with predefined invariants as test oracles. Another approach for testing Ajax web applications has been proposed by Marchetto et al. [4]. A Finite State Machine (FSM) that models the Ajax web application is built using a combination of dynamic and static analysis. Differently from *Atusa*, the adopted coverage criterion, used also in GUI-testing, is based on the notion of semantically interacting events. An alternative to *Atusa* is *Artemis*, a framework for automated testing of JavaScript web applications proposed by Artzi et al. [3]. The distinctive feature of *Artemis* is the usage of feedback-directed random testing [6].

There are several remarkable differences between our tool, SUBWEB, and existing approaches. First, coverage of the navigation model and input data generation are handled jointly by SUBWEB. Existing approaches [1,4] first generate a navigation model and then extract paths from it, without considering the problem that the generation of inputs for such paths might be difficult, requiring manual intervention, or even impossible, if the selected paths are infeasible. Another key difference is that input generation is search-based in SUBWEB, while it is either manual or random in existing approaches [1,3,4]. Finally, the abstraction from HTML pages to equivalence classes of pages that deserve separate test generation resorts to heuristic in existing approaches [1,4], while SUBWEB takes advantage of the abstraction defined by the developers when writing the POs for the web application under test.

To the best of our knowledge, the only attempt to use POs for test case generation is the proposal contained in a workshop paper by Yu et al. [7]. Similarly to *Artemis*, the proposed tool, called *InwertGen*, performs iterative feedback directed random test generation using the tool *Randoop* [6]. The key difference from our tool is that SUBWEB makes explicit use of the navigation model defined by developers through POs and uses a search-based approach, instead of a random one, to generate inputs that ensure high coverage of the navigation model.

3   Navigation Model Specification via Page Objects

POs are widely used in web testing to decouple the implementation details that depend on the web page structure from the test logics. The PO design pattern was first proposed by Martin Fowler[1] as an abstraction of the page under test that can be reused across test cases [2]. In fact, different test cases can refer to the same page object for locating and activating the HTML elements of the page under test, without having to duplicate the HTML access instructions multiple times, in different test cases.

While the main purpose of POs is to improve the modularization of the test code, POs implicitly specify a navigation model for the web application under

---

[1] https://martinfowler.com/bliki/PageObject.html.

test. In fact, one of the best practices recommended for PO creation requires that PO navigation methods return the PO of the next page upon invocation [8]. This means that POs specify the navigation structure of the web application under test in terms of method invocations (i.e., operations executed within each abstract web page) and page objects returned by the invoked methods (i.e., next PO reached during navigation in the web application). We use such implicit navigation model for automated test case generation.

3.1 Page Objects

The API of a PO is application-specific and provides an abstraction of the concrete HTML page functionalities to the test case. Despite the term "page" object, these objects are not necessarily built for an entire page. In fact, a PO may wrap an entire HTML page or a cohesive fragment that performs a specific functionality. The rule of thumb is to group and model the functionalities offered by a page as they are perceived by the user of the application.

```
1  public class ProductsPage implements PageObject {
2      public WebDriver driver;
3      public ProductsPage(WebDriver driver) {...}
4      public int getActiveCategory() {...}
5
6      public ProductDetailPage selectProduct(int id, int category) {
7          if((id >= 1 && id <= 6) &&
8              (category >= 1 && category <= 3) &&
9              (this.getActiveCategory() == category)) {
10             this.driver.findElement(By.id("product-" + id + "-" +
                   category)).click();
11             return new ProductDetailPage(this.driver);
12         } else {
13             throw new IllegalArgumentException("Invalid parameter values");
14         }
15     }
16 }
```

Fig. 1. PO example

Let us consider an example of e-commerce single page web application, named *Shopping Cart*. Figure 1 shows the code of the PO ProductsPage.

Among others, this PO contains method selectProduct that models the user action consisting of the selection of a specific product from the product list displayed in the home page. The actual selection is performed at line 10 (if the precondition at lines 7–9 is satisfied), where Selenium WebDriver's APIs are used to locate and operate some web elements inside the concrete HTML page of the web application. Specifically, the web element of interest is located by its unique identifier, by means of the Selenium method findElement(By.id(...)). The action performed on the web element located by id is a click (Selenium method click, still at line 10). Since after the click navigation continues on the next page, which is modelled by the PO `ProductDetailPage`, method `selectProduct` returns a new instance of the PO reached after the click, of type `ProductDetailPage`.

In general, PO methods may return values of any type (*void, int, String,* etc.). However, a recommended best practice is that *navigational* PO methods return the next PO encountered in the navigation (`this` if navigation does not leave the current PO). We strictly require that the tester specifies the navigation among the pages of the application through the POs returned by navigation methods, since we rely on them for the construction of the PO navigation graph. In the following, we call a *navigational method* any PO method that returns a PO. The second assumption that our technique makes on the way POs are written is that navigational methods include preconditions, i.e., each navigational method should specify the condition under which it can be safely executed. Such condition may depend on the invocation parameter values, as well as the state of the application, which is determined by the actions performed on the application in the previous navigation steps. In Fig. 1, the precondition of method `selectProduct` deals with the proper selection of a product from the list of products shown in the home page. Each product is uniquely identified by the pair of parameters `id` and `category`. In the running example, the number of products shown in `ProductsPage` is known statically (it is always 6, for each category of products), while the category is the currently active category. So, the valid value for the `category` parameter must match the value returned by method `getActiveCategory`, while `id` can vary from 1 to 6. If the precondition is not respected, an exception is thrown.

We think the assumptions we make on how POs should be written to be processable by our technique are reasonable and do not impact to a significant extent the normal way in which developers write POs. In fact, the requirement that every navigational method returns the next PO is a best practice which is commonly followed, although it is not enforced by the PO pattern. The inclusion of preconditions is a bit more impactful, since in practice developers write test code that respect preconditions by construction, making them not strictly necessary. We think however that preconditions are a good programming practice, independently of the use of our technique. Moreover, in our experience (see Sect. 5), when they have to be written from scratch, such activity does not require much effort from the developers. In some cases it would be even possible to extract them automatically from the web application code (e.g., when parameter ranges can be obtained by static code analysis).

3.2   Navigation Graph

Intuitively, the navigation graph is obtained from the POs by associating nodes to page objects and edges to navigational methods. More specifically, given a navigational method that, starting from a PO node, leads either to the same PO or to another PO, such method induces either a self loop edge or an edge to another node (corresponding to the returned PO) in the graph. Formally, we can define the navigation graph and its relation with POs as follows:

Definition 1 (PO Navigation Graph). *Given a set of page objects P, the associated navigation graph $G = \langle N, E \rangle$ consists of a set of nodes N bijectively mapped to P by function $po : N \to P$ and of a set of edges E that connect pairs of nodes $\langle n, m \rangle$ such that the page object $po(n)$ contains a* return *statement whose returned type is $po(m)$.*

Algorithm 1. Navigation graph extraction

```
1  Procedure extractNavGraph(G, po)
       Input:
       G: navigation graph computed so far
       po: page object to be analyzed
       Output:
       G: updated navigation graph
2      begin
3          n := getNodeByPO(G, po)
4          l := getNextPOsByStaticAnalysis(po)
5          v = ∅
6          for po' ∈ l do
7              m := getNodeByPO(G, po')
8              if m = NULL then
9                  m := newNode(po')
10                 G.N := G.N ∪ {m}
11                 v := v ∪ {m}
12             G.E := G.E ∪ {⟨n, m⟩}
13         for m ∈ v do
14             extractNavGraph(G, mapNodeToPO(m))
```

Algorithm 1 shows the recursive navigation graph extraction procedure. The loop at lines 6–12 iterates over all POs that are possibly returned by the PO under analysis. The set of such POs is obtained by static code analysis (line 4). When the returned PO is not already mapped to a graph node, a new node is created (line 9) and added to the graph (line 10). An edge $\langle n, m \rangle$ from the node n associated with the PO under analysis to the returned PO node m is then added to the graph (line 12). Graph extraction continues recursively on all newly created PO nodes (stored in variable v), i.e., all PO nodes not already present in the initial graph G (lines 13–14).

4   Search Based Path and Input Data Generation

Given the navigation graph $G = \langle N, E \rangle$, we can extract or generate test paths that exercise significant parts of the application. For instance, according to the *transition coverage* adequacy criterion, all edges E must be traversed at least once by the test paths. Formally, we can define a test path in the navigation graph as $p = \langle ns, es, pr \rangle$, where $ns \in N^+$ is a sequence of one or more graph nodes; $es \in E^*$ is a sequence of zero or more edges, such that $\mid es \mid = \mid ns \mid -1$ and if $e_i = \langle n, m \rangle \in es$, then $n_i = n \in ns, n_{i+1} = m \in ns$; $pr \in V^*$ is a sequence of zero or more parameter names, equal to the parameter values required by the method invocations associated with es.

Let us take a simple path $p = \langle ns, es, pr \rangle$ from the *Shopping Cart* running example, with $ns = \langle$ProductsPage, ProductDetailPage$\rangle$, $es = \langle$selectProduct$\rangle$, $pr = \langle$id, category$\rangle$. The precondition of method selectProduct (see Fig. 1) constrains the valid ranges of parameters id and category. As a consequence, not any arbitrary pair of integer values assigned to id and category will execute the path of interest. More generally, given a path p and a parameter sequence pr, we say p is *feasible* if there exists a parameter-value assignment that executes path p; we say path p is *infeasible* if there does not exist any parameter-value assignment that executes it. In order for a path $p = \langle ns, es, pr \rangle$ to be feasible, the conjunction of the constraints in the method preconditions associated with the edge sequence es must be satisfiable. Since some of the values evaluated in the method preconditions may depend on the server/client side state (e.g., this.getActiveCategory() in Fig. 1), in general the problem of determining whether a path p is feasible or not is an *undecidable* problem. Moreover, since feasibility depends on the server/client state, which is computed by arbitrarily complex programs, SAT solvers are generally not a viable tool to address the path feasibility problem. For these reasons, we resort to a meta-heuristic algorithm. The *test generation problem* that we address (for the transition coverage adequacy criterion) is then to *generate a set of feasible paths, as well as the related parameter-value assignment, which, upon execution, ensure that all navigation graph edges are traversed at least once.*

4.1   Problem Reformulation

The problem of generating test cases that cover all navigation graph edges can be reformulated as a standard branch coverage problem on an *artificial class* generated from the navigation graph and the POs. In fact, a path $p = \langle ns, es, pr \rangle$ consists of a method sequence (namely, the sequence of method invocations associated with es), for which suitable parameter values must be found. Hence, we can solve the feasible path generation problem and the parameter input value generation problem by applying the search based approaches that have been proposed for object oriented testing [9], where method sequence and parameter values are generated at the same time. This requires the creation of an artificial class under test CUT whose methods are the methods associated with the navigation graph edges and whose state is the currently visited web page and more specifically, the currently instantiated PO for such web page.

Figure 2 shows the program transformation that creates class CUT. Its input is a set of POs and its output is class CUT, containing a private field to store the current page object, cp. Each PO method becomes a method of the new class, whose return type becomes void. The method can be called only if current PO cp is an instance of the PO where the method originally belonged to. When this condition is satisfied, current page object is cast to its concrete type and assigned to local variable p. This variable must replace any occurrence of this

```
class cid₁ implements PageObject {
    public cid₂ mid₁ (pms₁) {
        if (pre₁)
        .   stbl₁
            return new cid₂
        else thst₁
    }
}
class cid₂ implements PageObject { ... }
```

$\Rightarrow$

```
class CUT {
    private PageObject cp;
    public void mid₁ (
        <mapParamTypes>(pms₁)) {
        if (cp instanceof cid₁)
            cid₁ p =  (cid₁) cp
            if (<replParam>(<replThis>(pre₁)))
                <replParam>(<replThis>(stbl₁))
                cp = new cid₂
            else thst₁
        else thst₁
    }
    public void mid₂ (
        <mapParamTypes>(pms₂) { ... }
}
```

Fig. 2. Automated program transformation that generates class CUT from the POs

in the body of the original method, including its precondition pre_1. This is performed by function <replThis>. The instruction that returns a new PO in the original code is transformed into a statement that assigns such new PO to the class field cp (*current page*) of CUT.

To facilitate the job of the test generator, the original parameter types (e.g., Id:int) are mapped to a type with smaller range (e.g., Id $\in [1 : 6]$) by function <mapParamTypes>. Such a smaller range can be determined by static analysis, in simple cases as those in Fig. 1, or can be specified by the tester. As a consequence, any occurrence of the original parameter identifiers must be replaced with an accessor to the parameter value (e.g., x becomes x.value). This is performed by function <replParam>. Figure 3 shows the result of the transformation when it is applied to the PO in Fig. 1.

```
1  public class CUT {
2      private PageObject currentPage;
3      public void selectProduct(Id id, Category category) {
4          if (this.currentPage instanceof ProductsPage) {
5              ProductsPage page = (ProductsPage) this.currentPage;
6              if(page.getActiveCategory() == category.value){
7                  page.driver.findElement(By.id("product-" + id.value + "-" + category.value)).click();
8                  this.currentPage = new ProductDetailPage(page.driver);
9              } else { throw new IllegalArgumentException("Invalid parameter values"); }
10         } else { throw new IllegalArgumentException("You are not in the right page"); }
11     }
12 }
```

Fig. 3. Excerpt of CUT generated from the POs of the Shopping Cart example

We apply search based test case generation as instantiated for object oriented systems [9] in order to find the method sequences and parameter values that cover the last statements of the transformed method bodies, which correspond to the statements returning a new PO in the original methods (i.e., this.currentPage = new ProductDetailPage(page.driver) for selectProduct). In fact, coverage of all the statements that return the next PO in the navigation is equivalent to covering all the edges in the navigation graph, i.e., to transition coverage. In particular, we use a Genetic Algorithm (GA) and the evolved chromosomes are test cases, i.e., sequences of method calls. The fitness function is the sum of the branch distances of the yet uncovered branches [9]. On the other hand, the standard genetic operators for object oriented test generation do not work properly in our case, because they do not take the structure of the navigation graph into account. Hence, we have defined new crossover and mutation operators, described in the next section. The initial population is obtained by performing multiple random walks on the navigation graph.

4.2   Genetic Operators

We defined new genetic operators with the aim of modifying the chromosomes during evolution, taking into account the constraints imposed by the navigation graph.

Crossover: We have defined a crossover operator that works at test case level, in addition to the usual test suite crossover operator [9]. Our new crossover operator is shown in Fig. 4a, where the notation $P_i \rightarrow P_j$ above the method name $m_k()$ indicates that method $m_k()$ has PO P_i as starting node and PO P_j as target node. Crossover is straightforward to apply if the cut point selected on the two chromosomes is between method calls that refer to the same PO (in Fig. 4a, the cut point between $m_1()$ and $m_2()$ in both chromosomes refer to the same PO, P_1, which is the target of $m_1()$ and the source of $m_2()$). When this does not happen, the two different POs are connected by performing a random walk in the hammock subgraph between them. To ensure reachability during the random walk, head and tail of the new chromosome are possibly shortened, until reachability holds between the two POs.

Mutation: We have maintained the test suite mutation operator [9], but we have modified the delete and insert method call operators, which work at the test case level. An example of how they manipulate the chromosome is provided in Fig. 4b. The *change* method call operator is applicable only if the alternative method has the same source and target POs as the original method call.

The *delete operator* randomly selects a starting method from the test case and, given the target PO of the selected method (in Fig. 4b, method $m_2()$ and target node P_2), it removes all the following method calls until it finds one with a source node that is equal to the target node of the starting method. If it does not find it, it deletes all the methods from the selected point until the end of the chromosome (as in Fig. 4b). This operation cannot remove all the statements (at least one, the first method call, is always left), to avoid the generation of an empty test case.

The *insert operator* always starts at the end of the test case (in Fig. 4b, method $m_2()$, which has become the last method call after application of the *delete* operator) and it selects a method corresponding to a yet uncovered branch (e.g., $m_6()$). Then it performs a random walk on the hammock subgraph between the target node and the source node of the two selected methods (i.e., the hammock subgraph between P_2 and P_5). The path obtained in such random walk is appended to the chromosome (in Fig. 4b, methods $m_8()$, $m_4()$, $m_7()$, plus the target method $m_6()$). If the source node of the uncovered method is unreachable from the end of the chromosome, the insert operator fails and does not change the chromosome.

Insert and delete operations balance each other, by extending and shrinking the chromosomes, hence providing a mechanism for bloat control (*bloat* occurs when negligible improvements in the fitness value are obtained by extremely large solutions).

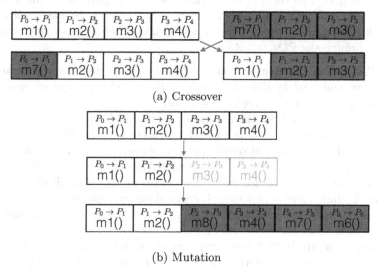

(a) Crossover

(b) Mutation

Fig. 4. Crossover and mutation (with *delete* followed by *insert*)

5 Empirical Validation

The *goal* of the case study is to assess pros and cons of the proposed approach. The baseline for comparison is the navigation graph produced by a state of the art crawler, Crawljax [10], and the test cases derived from such graph. We have formulated the following research questions:

RQ1 (Cost): *What is the size of the page objects to be written manually and what is the size and complexity of the Page Object method pre-conditions, required by our approach?*

To analyze the manual cost that a tester incurs when using our approach, we measure the lines of code (LOC^2) of all POs needed to model the subject application. In particular, we are interested in the manual cost for writing the preconditions, since they represent a requirement specific of our approach. We

---

[2] Non-commenting lines of code, calculated by *cloc* (https://github.com/AlDanial/cloc).

measure the total number of preconditions, the total number of logical operators in such preconditions and the lines of code of methods used exclusively by preconditions.

RQ2 (Navigation graph): *How does the navigation graph specified through POs differ from the navigation graph obtained through crawling?*

Since the navigation graph extracted from the POs is specified directly by the testers, we assume it as the reference and we measure the difference between the crawled graph and such a reference, in terms of graph size, states/transitions missing in the crawled graph and split/merged states/transitions in the crawled graph as compared to the PO navigation graph. The purpose of this research question is to understand whether crawling alone, with no human involvement for PO definition, is able to produce a navigation graph close to the ideal one, specified through the POs.

RQ3 (Test suite features): *What is the size of the test suite generated by* SUBWEB *as compared to that derived from the crawled navigation graph and what is the proportion of divergent test cases?*

Test case derivation from the navigation graph produced by *Crawljax* is supported by the tool *Atusa* [1], which is unfortunately unavailable. Hence, we have reimplemented the test derivation algorithm of *Atusa* by following its description in the reference paper [1]. We call our reimplementation *Ext-Crawljax*. We are interested in comparing the size of the test suites produced by SUBWEB vs *Ext-Crawljax*. A smaller size is preferable because it makes manual oracle creation or validation easier for testers. Moreover, we measure the proportion of divergent test cases (i.e., those that upon execution do not cover the test path for which they were generated). In fact, the occurrence of divergences is detrimental to the actually achieved coverage, with respect to the theoretical coverage guaranteed by the test case derivation algorithm.

RQ4 (Coverage): *What is the level of coverage reached by the test cases generated by* SUBWEB *in comparison with the coverage reached by the test cases derived from the crawled navigation graph?*

Regarding coverage, which represents the core objective of test generation, we consider the transition coverage adequacy criterion, measured in the navigation graph specified by testers through POs. This required to manually map states and transitions in the crawled navigation graph to states and transitions in the PO navigation graph.

5.1   Tool

We have implemented SUBWEB on top of *EvoSuite* [9]. In particular, we have enabled the *Whole Test Suite* strategy, because we have multiple targets to satisfy. We have modified *EvoSuite* in order to take the navigation graph into account, both when generating the initial random population of individuals and in the genetic operators, which must generate method sequences compliant with the navigation graph.

We use *Selenium WebDriver* to instantiate the driver needed to launch and send commands to the browser, when test cases have to be executed in order to measure their fitness. The constructor of the class under test contains a method that instantiates the Selenium driver and resets the state of the application (e.g., ensuring the database is initially empty).

5.2 Case Study

AddressBook[3] is a web-based address and phone book, contact manager and organizer. It is written in *PHP* and it uses *JavaScript* for handling and modifying *HTML* elements at runtime; moreover it is backed by a *MySQL* database. The size of the application, shown in Table 1a, is non trivial. Moreover, this application has been used as a case study in previous works [11].

We have removed a few features from the application, regarding uploads and downloads of files (photos and text files for instance), as well as address locations in a map, since they increase the navigation/testing time while being straightforward to test.

5.3 Experimental Procedure

For the sake of fairness, we granted both tools, SUBWEB and Crawljax, an overall execution budget of 2 hours and we ran both tools on the same subject 10 times, because both tools have non deterministic behaviour. In SUBWEB we have disabled the minimization step of *EvoSuite*, because it requires multiple, costly test case executions on the browser, which makes it too inefficient for our purposes. In Crawljax, we use the default configuration with the default parameter values. We only provide Crawljax with custom values for those form inputs in the application that require very specific values.

To measure test case divergences, we transform each path obtained from the crawled navigation graph into a JUnit test case. The JUnit test case fires a sequence of events that should bring the application from the initial to the end state of the path. If an event is a form submission, we insert all the needed input values (either random or custom values, when necessary). The execution of such test case is deemed divergent when a *Selenium* exception is thrown during the execution. In fact, divergences happen if an element existing at crawling time is no longer found at test time, when the application state is different, so that the desired path cannot be followed. The missing element triggers a *Selenium* exception.

5.4 Results

The data in Table 1a show that the 13 POs written manually account for 764 LOC in total. This is a small fraction of the overall application size (around 2%). Preconditions, that are required exclusively by our approach, represent an even

---

[3] https://sourceforge.net/projects/php-addressbook/.

smaller portion of the application size: precondition method LOC account for 0.2% of the application size, while the 16 preconditions use on average 3 logical operator each. Moreover, the first author wrote the 13 POs in, approximately, one day; however this metric clearly depends on many factors, the main one is the level of confidence the developer has with the Page Object pattern.

Table 1. Size of application, POs and PO preconditions (a); size of PO vs crawled graph, with missing/split states/transitions (b); number of test cases and divergent test cases (c)

App	PHP LOC	30223
	JavaScript LOC	1288
POs	LOC	764
	Total number	13
	Navig. methods	73
Preconds	Method LOC	75
	Total number	16
	Logic operators	54

PO graph	States	12
	Transitions	73
Crawled graph	States	329
	Transitions	927
	Missing states	0
	Missing trans	5
	Split state ratio	27
	Split trans ratio	13

(a) RQ1   (b) RQ2

SUBWEB	Test cases	54
Ext-Crawljax	Test cases	598
	Divergent test cases	104 (17%)

(c) RQ3

> **RQ1**: *Based on the size data collected on our case study, the manual cost for writing POs and PO preconditions seems relatively low.*

As shown in Table 1b, the crawled navigation graph is huge if compared to the PO navigation graph (approximately ×27 states; ×13 transitions). While it does not miss any state, despite its size it misses on average 5 transitions, which are specified by testers, but are not covered during some executions of crawling (5 is the average computed over 10 runs of Crawljax). No single case of state/transition merge was observed, while, as expected from the larger graph size, several states and transitions are split in the crawled graph.

> **RQ2**: *The crawled graph deviates from the ideal, manually specified, PO graph to a major extent, because of its larger size, missing transitions and split states/transitions.*

Table 1c shows that SUBWEB generates much smaller test suites than Ext-Crawljax. This is a consequence of the different navigation graph size. Moreover, while SUBWEB generates non divergent test cases by construction, the crawling based approach generates as many as 17% divergent test cases.

> **RQ3**: *The test suites produced by SUBWEB are approximately 11 times smaller than the test suites produced by Ext-Crawljax. The latter include a relatively large proportion of divergent test cases.*

Figure 5 shows the box plots of the transition coverage reached by SUBWEB and Ext-Crawljax. The mean coverage of SUBWEB is on average 13pp (percentage points) above the mean coverage of Ext-Crawljax and such a difference is statistically significant according to the Mann-Whitney U test (at 5% significance level), that we applied since we didn't have a priori knowledge about the distribution of the data.

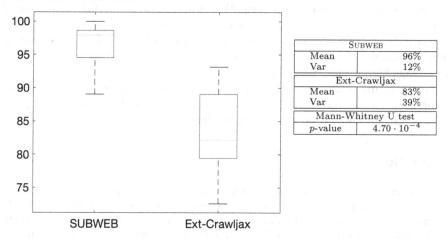

	SUBWEB	
Mean		96%
Var		12%
	Ext-Crawljax	
Mean		83%
Var		39%
	Mann-Whitney U test	
p-value		$4.70 \cdot 10^{-4}$

Fig. 5. Transition coverage (percentage) reached by SUBWEB and Ext-Crawljax in 10 runs; the two distributions differ in a statistically significant way according to the Mann-Whitney U test.

RQ4: *The test cases generated by* SUBWEB *achieve higher transition coverage than those generated by Ext-Crawljax.*

5.5   Threats to Validity

Threats to the *internal validity* might come from how the empirical study was carried out. Each test case was run starting from an empty database, under the assumption that the tester is interested in the behaviour of the application when no record has been persisted yet. If, on the contrary, a non empty database is created at each test case start up, the traversal of paths for which populating the database is a prerequisite becomes easier for both approaches.

Moreover, we didn't use a case study with existing POs and measured the effort needed to modify them in order to enable our technique; indeed it is difficult to find open source projects with existing selenium tests using the PO design pattern.

Threats to the *external validity* mainly regard the use of only one case study, which prevents us from generalizing our findings to substantially different cases. On the other hand, AddressBook is a non trivial application that has been used in several previous works on web testing.

6   Conclusions and Future Work

We have presented SUBWEB, a web testing tool for the joint generation of test inputs and feasible navigation paths. Although SUBWEB requires a manual step for POs writing, whereas a crawling-based approach is completely automatic, the effort of such manual step is quite limited while, on the other hand, the achieved advantages are major ones: the navigation graph is much smaller; correspondingly, the test suites derived from the navigation graph have substantially smaller size; by construction, test cases are never divergent, while this is not the case of crawling-based test cases; finally, the transition coverage reached by SUBWEB is on average higher (96% vs 83%).

In our future work, we will investigate techniques to support the automatic generation of assertions starting from the generated test suite. Moreover, we plan to evaluate SUBWEB on other web applications, in addition to *AddressBook*.

References

1. Mesbah, A., van Deursen, A.: Invariant-based automatic testing of AJAX user interfaces. In: Proceedings of the 31st International Conference on Software Engineering, ICSE 2009, pp. 210–220. IEEE Computer Society, Washington, DC (2009)
2. Leotta, M., Clerissi, D., Ricca, F., Tonella, P.: Approaches and tools for automated end-to-end web testing. Adv. Comput. **101**, 193–237 (2016)
3. Artzi, S., Dolby, J., Jensen, S.H., Møller, A., Tip, F.: A framework for automated testing of Javascript web applications. In: Proceedings of the 33rd International Conference on Software Engineering, ICSE 2011, pp. 571–580. ACM, New York (2011)
4. Marchetto, A., Tonella, P., Ricca, F.: State-based testing of ajax web applications. In: Proceedings of the 2008 International Conference on Software Testing, Verification, and Validation, ICST 2008, pp. 121–130. IEEE Computer Society, Washington, DC (2008)
5. Tonella, P., Ricca, F., Marchetto, A.: Recent advances in web testing. Adv. Comput. **93**, 1–51 (2014)
6. Pacheco, C., Lahiri, S.K., Ernst, M.D., Ball, T.: Feedback-directed random test generation. In: Proceedings of the 29th International Conference on Software Engineering, ICSE 2007, pp. 75–84. IEEE Computer Society, Washington, DC (2007)
7. Yu, B., Ma, L., Zhang, C.: Incremental web application testing using page object. In: Proceedings of the 2015 Third IEEE Workshop on Hot Topics in Web Systems and Technologies (HotWeb), HOTWEB 2015, pp. 1–6. IEEE Computer Society, Washington, DC (2015)
8. van Deursen, A.: Testing web applications with state objects. Commun. ACM **58**(8), 36–43 (2015)
9. Fraser, G., Arcuri, A.: Whole test suite generation. IEEE Trans. Softw. Eng. **39**(2), 276–291 (2013)
10. Mesbah, A., van Deursen, A., Lenselink, S.: Crawling ajax-based web applications through dynamic analysis of user interface state changes. ACM Trans. Web (TWEB) **6**(1), 3:1–3:30 (2012)
11. Leotta, M., Stocco, A., Ricca, F., Tonella, P.: Robula+: an algorithm for generating robust xpath locators for web testing. J. Softw. Evol. Process **28**(3), 177–204 (2016)

An Empirical Evaluation of Evolutionary Algorithms for Test Suite Generation

José Campos[1], Yan Ge[1], Gordon Fraser[1(✉)], Marcelo Eler[2],
and Andrea Arcuri[3,4]

[1] Department of Computer Science, The University of Sheffield, Sheffield, UK
{jose.campos,yge5,gordon.fraser}@sheffield.ac.uk
[2] University of São Paulo, São Paulo, Brazil
marceloeler@usp.br
[3] Westerdals Oslo ACT, Oslo, Norway
[4] University of Luxembourg, Luxembourg, Luxembourg
arcand@westerdals.no

Abstract. Evolutionary algorithms have been shown to be effective at
generating unit test suites optimised for code coverage. While many
aspects of these algorithms have been evaluated in detail (e.g., test length
and different kinds of techniques aimed at improving performance, like
seeding), the influence of the specific algorithms has to date seen less
attention in the literature. As it is theoretically impossible to design an
algorithm that is best on all possible problems, a common approach in
software engineering problems is to first try a Genetic Algorithm, and
only afterwards try to refine it or compare it with other algorithms to
see if any of them is more suited for the addressed problem. This is particularly important in test generation, since recent work suggests that
random search may in practice be equally effective, whereas the refor-
mulation as a many-objective problem seems to be more effective. To
shed light on the influence of the search algorithms, we empirically evaluate six different algorithms on a selection of non-trivial open source
classes. Our study shows that the use of a test archive makes evolutionary algorithms clearly better than random testing, and it confirms that
the many-objective search is the most effective.

1 Introduction

Search-based testing has been successfully applied to generating unit test suites
optimised for code coverage on object-oriented classes. A popular approach is to
use evolutionary algorithms where the individuals of the search population are
whole test suites, and the optimisation goal is to find a test suite that achieves
maximum code coverage [8]. Tools like EvoSuite [6] have been shown to be
effective in achieving code coverage on different types of software [9].

Since the original introduction of whole test suite generation, many different
techniques have been introduced to improve performance even further and to get
a better understanding of the current limitations. For example, the insufficient

T. Menzies and J. Petke (Eds.): SSBSE 2017, LNCS 10452, pp. 33–48, 2017.
DOI: 10.1007/978-3-319-66299-2_3

guidance provided by basic coverage-based fitness functions has been shown to cause random search to often be equally effective as evolutionary algorithms [23]. Optimisation now no longer focuses on individual coverage criteria, but combinations of criteria [10,20]. To cope with the resulting larger number of coverage goals, evolutionary search can be supported with archives [21] that keep track of useful solutions encountered throughout the search. To improve effectiveness, whole test suite optimisation has been re-formulated as a many-objective optimisation problem [18]. In the context of these developments, one aspect of whole test suite generation remains largely unexplored: What is the influence of the specific flavour of evolutionary algorithms applied to evolve test suites?

In this paper, we aim to shed light on the influence of the different evolutionary algorithms in whole test suite generation, to find out whether the choice of algorithm is important, and which one should be used. By using a large set of complex Java classes as case study, and the EVOSUITE [6] search-based test generation tool, we specifically investigate:

RQ1: Which evolutionary algorithm works best when using a test archive for partial solutions?

RQ2: How does evolutionary search compare to random search and random testing?

RQ3: How does evolution of whole test suites compare to many-objective optimisation of test cases?

We investigate each of these questions in the light of individual and multiple coverage criteria as optimisation objectives, and we study the influence of the search budget. Our results show that in most cases a simple $\mu + \lambda$ Evolutionary Algorithm (EA) is better than other, more complex algorithms. In most cases, the variants of EAs and GAs are also clearly better than random search and random testing, when a test archive is used. Finally, we confirm that many-objective search achieves higher branch coverage, even in the case of optimisation for multiple criteria.

2 Evolutionary Algorithms for Test Suite Generation

Evolutionary Algorithms (EAs) are inspired by natural evolution, and have been successfully used to address many kinds of optimisation problems. In the context of EAs, a solution is encoded "genetically" as an individual ("chromosome"), and a set of individuals is called a population. The population is gradually optimised using genetic-inspired operations such as crossover, which merges genetic material from at least two individuals to yield new offspring, and mutation, which independently changes the elements of an individual with a low probability. While it is impossible to comprehensively cover all existing algorithms, in the following we discuss common variants of EAs for test suite optimisation. Expansion of the evaluation to less common algorithms will be future work.

2.1   Representation

For test suite generation, the individuals of a population are sets of test cases (test suites); each test case is a sequence of calls. Crossover on test suites is based on exchanging test cases [8]; mutation adds/modifies tests to suites, and adds/removes/changes statements within tests. While standard selection techniques are largely used, the variable size representation (number of statements in a test and number of test cases in a suite can vary) requires modification to avoid bloat [7]; this is typically achieved by ranking individuals with identical fitness based on their length, and then using rank selection.

2.2   Optimisation Goals and Archives

The selection of individuals is guided by fitness functions, such that individuals with good fitness values are more likely to survive and be involved in reproduction. In the context of test suite generation, the fitness functions are based on code coverage criteria such as statement or branch coverage. More recently, there is a trend to optimise for multiple coverage criteria at the same time. Since coverage criteria usually do not represent conflicting goals, it is possible to combine fitness functions with a weighted linear combination [20]. However, the increased number of coverage goals may affect the performance of the EA. To counter these effects, it is possible to store tests for covered goals in an archive [21], and then to dynamically adapt the fitness function to optimise only for the remaining uncovered goals. This, however, may again have effects on the underlying EA. Furthermore, search operators can be adapted to make use of the test archive; for example, new tests may be created by mutating tests in the archive rather than randomly generating completely new tests.

2.3   Random Search

Random search is a baseline search strategy which does not use crossover, mutation, or selection, but a simple replacement strategy [14]. Random search consists of repeatedly sampling candidates from the search space; the previous candidate is replaced if the fitness of the new sampled individual is better. Random search can make use of a test archive by changing the sampling procedure as indicated above. *Random testing* is a variant of random search in test generation which builds test suites incrementally. Test cases (rather than test suites) are sampled individually, and if a test improves coverage, it is retained in the test suite, otherwise it is discarded. It has been shown that in unit test generation, due to the flat fitness landscapes and often simple search problems, random search is often as effective as EAs, and sometimes even better [23].

2.4   Genetic Algorithms

The Genetic Algorithm (GA) is one of the most widely-used EAs in many domains because it can be easily implemented and obtains good results on average. Algorithm 1 illustrates a Standard GA. It starts by creating an initial random population of size p_n (Line 1). Then, a pair of individuals is selected from

---

Algorithm 1. Standard genetic algorithm

Input: Stopping condition C, Fitness function δ, Population size p_s, Selection function s_f, Crossover function c_f, Crossover probability c_p, Mutation function m_f, Mutation probability m_p

Output: Population of optimised individuals P

1: $P \leftarrow$ GENERATERANDOMPOPULATION(p_s)
2: PERFORMFITNESSEVALUATION(δ, P)
3: **while** $\neg C$ **do**
4:     $N_P \leftarrow \{\}$
5:     **while** $|N_P| < p_s$ **do**
6:         $p_1, p_2 \leftarrow$ SELECTION(s_f, P)
7:         $o_1, o_2 \leftarrow$ CROSSOVER(c_f, c_p, p_1, p_2)
8:         MUTATION(m_f, m_p, o_1)
9:         MUTATION(m_f, m_p, o_2)
10:        $N_P \leftarrow N_P \cup \{o_1, o_2\}$
11:     **end while**
12:     $P \leftarrow N_P$
13:     PERFORMFITNESSEVALUATION(δ, P)
14: **end while**
15: **return** P

---

the population using a strategy s_f, such as rank-based, elitism or tournament selection (Line 6). Next, both selected individuals are recombined using crossover c_f (e.g., single point, multiple-point) with a probability of c_p to produce two new offspring o_1, o_2 (Line 7). Afterwards, mutation is applied on both offspring (Lines 8–9), independently changing the genes with a probability of m_p, which usually is equal to $\frac{1}{n}$, where n is the number of genes in a chromosome. The two mutated offspring are then included in the next population (Line 10). At the end of each iteration the fitness value of all individuals is computed (Line 13).

Many variants of the Standard GA have been proposed to improve effectiveness. Specifically, we consider a *monotonic* version of the Standard GA which, after mutating and evaluating each offspring, only includes either the best offspring or the best parent in the next population (whereas the Standard GA includes both offspring in the next population regardless of their fitness value). Another variation of the Standard GA is a *Steady State* GA, which uses the same replacement strategy as the Monotonic GA, but instead of creating a new population of offspring, the offspring replace the parents from the current population immediately after the mutation phase.

The $1 + (\lambda, \lambda)$ GA, introduced by Doerr et al. [5], starts by generating a random population of size 1. Then, mutation is used to create λ different mutated versions of the current individual. Mutation is applied with a high mutation probability, defined as $m_p = \frac{k}{n}$, where k is typically greater than one, which allows, on average, more than one gene to be mutated per chromosome. Then, uniform crossover is applied to the parent and best generated mutant to create λ offspring. While a high mutation probability is intended to support faster exploration of the search space, a uniform crossover between the best individual among the λ mutants and the parent was suggested to repair the defects caused by the aggressive mutation. Then all offspring are evaluated and the best one is selected. If the best offspring is better than the parent, the population of size one is replaced by the best offspring. $1 + (\lambda, \lambda)$ GA could be very expensive for large values of λ, as fitness has to be evaluated after mutation and after crossover.

2.5 $\mu + \lambda$ Evolutionary Algorithm

The $\mu + \lambda$ Evolutionary Algorithm (EA) is a mutation-based algorithm [24]. As its name suggests, the number of parents and offspring are restricted to μ and λ, respectively. Each gene is mutated independently with probability $\frac{1}{n}$. After mutation, the generated offspring are compared with each parent, aiming to preserve so-far best individual including parents; that is, parents are replaced once a better offspring is found. Among the different $(\mu + \lambda)$ EA versions, two common settings are $(1 + \lambda)$ EA and $(1 + 1)$ EA, where the population size is 1, and the number of offspring is also limited to 1 for the $(1 + 1)$ EA.

2.6   Many-Objective Sorting Algorithm

Unlike the single-objective optimisation on the test suite level described above, the Many-Objective Sorting Algorithm (MOSA) [18] regards each coverage goal as an independent optimisation objective. MOSA is a variant of NSGA-II [4], and uses a preference sorting criterion to reward the best tests for each non-covered target, regardless of their dominance relation with other tests in the population. MOSA also uses an archive to store the tests that cover new targets, which aiming to keep record on current best cases after each iteration.

Algorithm 2 illustrates how MOSA works. It starts with a random population of test cases. Then, and similar to typical EAs, the offspring are created by applying crossover and mutation (Line 6). Selection is based on the combined set of parents and offspring. This set is sorted (Line 9) based on a non-dominance relation and preference criterion. MOSA selects non-dominated individuals based on the resulting rank, starting from the lowest rank (F_0), until the population size is reached (Lines 11–14). In fewer than p_s individuals are selected, the individuals of the current rank (F_r) are sorted by crowding distance (Line 16–17), and the individuals with the largest distance are added. Finally, the archive that stores previously uncovered branches is updated in order to yield the final test suite (Line 18). In order to cope with the large numbers of goals resulting from the combination of multiple coverage criteria, the DynaMOSA [17] extension dynamically selects targets based on the dependencies between the uncovered targets and the newly covered targets. Both, MOSA and DynaMOSA, have been shown to result in higher coverage of some selected criteria than traditional GAs for whole test suite optimisation.

Algorithm 2. Many-Objective Sorting Algorithm (MOSA)

Input: Stopping condition C, Fitness function δ, Population size p_s, Crossover function c_f, Crossover probability c_p, Mutation probability m_p
Output: Archive of optimised individuals A

1: $p \leftarrow 0$
2: $N_p \leftarrow$ GENERATERANDOMPOPULATION(p_s)
3: PERFORMFITNESSEVALUATION(δ, N_p)
4: $A \leftarrow \{\}$
5: **while** $\neg C$ **do**
6:     $N_o \leftarrow$ GENERATEOFFSPRING(c_f, c_p, m_p, N_p)
7:     $R_t \leftarrow P \cup N_o$
8:     $r \leftarrow 0$
9:     $F_r \leftarrow$ PREFERENCESORTING(R_t)
10:     $N_{p+1} \leftarrow \{\}$
11:     **while** $|N_{p+1}| + |F_r| \leq p_s$ **do**
12:         CALCULATECROWDINGDISTANCE(F_r)
13:         $N_{p+1} \leftarrow N_{p+1} \cup F_r$
14:         $r \leftarrow r + 1$
15:     **end while**
16:     DISTANCECROWDINGSORT(F_r)
17:     $N_{p+1} \leftarrow N_{p+1} \cup F_r$ with size $p_s - |N_{p+1}|$
18:     UPDATEARCHIVE(A, N_{p+1})
19:     $p \leftarrow p + 1$
20: **end while**
21: **return** A

---

3   Empirical Study

In order to evaluate the influence of the evolutionary algorithm on test suite generation, we conducted an empirical study. In this section, we describe the experimental setup as well as results.

3.1   Experimental Setup

Selection of Classes Under Test: A key factor of studying evolutionary algorithms on automatic test generation is the selection of classes under test. As many open source classes, for example contained in the SF110 [9] corpus, are trivially simple [23] and would not reveal differences between algorithms, we used the selection of non-trivial classes from the DynaMOSA study [17]. This is a corpus of 117 open-source Java projects and 346 classes, selected from four different benchmarks. The complexity of classes ranges from 14 statements and 2 branches to 16,624 statements and 7,938 branches. The average number of statements is 1,109, and the average number of branches is 259.

Unit Test Generation Tool: We used EVOSUITE [6], which provides search algorithms to evolve coverage-optimised test suites. By default, EVOSUITE uses a Monotonic GA described in Sect. 2.4. It also provides a Standard and Steady

State GA, Random search, Random testing and, more recently, MOSA and DynaMOSA. For this study, we added the $1 + (\lambda, \lambda)$ GA and the $\mu + \lambda$ EA. All evolutionary algorithms use a test archive.

Experiment Procedure: We performed two experiments to assess the performance of six evolutionary algorithms (described in Sect. 2). First, we conducted a tuning study to select the best population size (μ) of four algorithms, number of mutations (λ) of $1 + (\lambda, \lambda)$ GA, and population size (μ) and number of mutations (λ) of $\mu + \lambda$ EA, since the performance of each EA can be influenced by the parameters used [1]. Random-based approaches do not require any tuning. Then, we conducted a larger study to perform the comparison.

For both experiments we have four configurations: two search budgets, EvoSuite's default search budget (i.e., a small search budget) of 1 min, and a larger search budget of 10 min to study the effect of the search budget on the coverage of resulting test suites; single-criterion optimisation (branch coverage) and multiple-criteria optimisation[1] (i.e., line, branch, exception, weak-mutation, output, method, method-no-exception, and cbranch) [20]. Due to the randomness of EAs, we repeated the one minute experiments 30 times, and the 10 min experiments 10 times.

For the tuning study, we randomly selected 10% (i.e., 34) of DynaMOSA's study classes [17][2] (with 15 to 1,707 branches, 227 on average) from 30 Java projects. This resulted in a total of 79,200 (59,400 one minute configurations, and 19,800 ten minutes configurations) calls to EvoSuite and more than 175 days of CPU-time overall. For the second experiment, we used the remaining 312 classes[3] (346 total - 34 used to tune each EA) from the DynaMOSA study [17]. Besides the tuned μ and λ parameters, we used EvoSuite's default parameters [1].

Experiment Analysis: For any test suite generated by EvoSuite on any experimental configuration we measure the coverage achieved on eight criteria, alongside other metrics, such as the number of generated test cases, the length of generated test suites, number of iterations of each EA, number of fitness evaluations. As described by Arcuri et al. [1] "easy" branches are always covered independently of the parameter settings used, and several others are just infeasible. Therefore, rather than using raw coverage values, we use relative coverage [1]: Given the coverage of a class c in a run r, $c(r)$, the best and worst coverage of c in any run, $max(c)$ and $min(c)$ respectively, a *relative coverage* (r_c) can be defined as $\frac{c(r) - min(c)}{max(c) - min(c)}$. If the best and worst coverage of c is equal, i.e., $max(c) == min(c)$, then r_c is 1 (if range of $c(r)$ is between 0 and 1) or 100 (if range of $c(r)$ is between 0 and 100). In order to statistically compare the performance of each EA we use the Vargha-Delaney $\hat{A}_{12}$ effect size,

---

[1] At the time of writing this paper, DynaMOSA did not support all the criteria used by EvoSuite.

[2] Class `com.yahoo.platform.yui.compressor.YUICompressor` was excluded from tuning experiments due to a bug in EvoSuite.

[3] Nine classes were discarded from the second experiment due to crashes of EvoSuite.

and the Wilcoxon-Mann-Whitney U-test with a 95% confidence level. Besides the Vargha-Delaney effect size we also consider a *relative average improvement*. Given two sets of coverage values, configuration A and configuration B, a *relative average improvement* is defined as $\frac{mean(A) - mean(B)}{mean(B)}$.

Threats to Validity: The results reported in this paper are limited to the number and type of EAs used in the experiments. However, we believe these are representative of state-of-art algorithms. Although we used a large number of different subjects (346 complex classes from 117 open-source Java projects), also used by a previous study [17] on test generation, our results may not generalise to other subjects. The range of parameters used in the tuning experiments was limited to only 4 values per EA. Although common or reported as best values, different values might influence the performance of each EA. The two search budgets used in the tuning experiments and in the empirical study are based on EVOSUITE's defaults (1 min), and used by previous studies to assess the performance of EAs with a larger search budget (10 min) [20].

3.2 Parameter Tuning

The execution of an EA requires a number of parameters to be set. As there is not a single best configuration setting to solve all problems [27] in which an EA could be applied, a possible alternative is to tune EA's parameters for a specific problem at hand to find the "best" ones. We largely rely on a previous tuning study [1] in which default values were determined for most parameters of EVOSUITE. However, the main distinguishing factor between the algorithms we are considering in this study are μ (i.e., the population size) and λ (i.e., the number of mutations). In particular, we selected common values used in previous studies and reported to be the best for each EA:

- Population size of 10, 25, 50, and 100 for Standard GA, Monotonic GA, SteadyState GA, MOSA, and DynaMOSA.
- λ size of 1, 8 [5], 25, and 50 for $1 + (\lambda, \lambda)$ GA.
- μ size of 1, 7 [13], 25, and 50, and λ size of 1, 7, 25, and 50 for $\mu + \lambda$ EA.

Thus, for Standard GA, Monotonic GA, SteadyState GA, MOSA, DynaMOSA, and $1 + (\lambda, \lambda)$ GA there are 4 different configurations; for $\mu + \lambda$, and as λ must be divisible by μ, there are 8 different configurations (i.e., $1 + 1$, $1 + 7$, $1 + 25$, $1 + 50$, $7 + 7$, $25 + 25$, $25 + 50$, $50 + 50$); i.e., a total of 32 different configurations.

To identify the best population size of each EA, we performed a pairwise comparison of the coverage achieved by using any population size. The population size that achieved a significantly higher coverage more often was selected as the best. Table 1 shows that, for a search budget of 60 s and single-criteria, the best population size is different for almost all EAs (e.g., Standard GA works best with a population size of 10, and MOSA with a population size of 100). For a search budget of 600 s and multiple-criteria several EAs share the same population size, for example, the best value for Standard GA, Monotonic GA

Table 1. Best population/λ size of each EA per search budget, and single and multiple criteria optimisation. "Br. Cov." column reports the branch coverage per EA, and column "Over. Cov.", the overall coverage of a multiple-criteria optimisation.

Algorithm	Single-criteria					Multiple-criteria					
	$\mid P \mid$	Br. Cov.	Avg. $\hat{A}_{12}$	Better $\hat{A}_{12}$	Worse $\hat{A}_{12}$	$\mid P \mid$	Br. Cov.	Over. Cov.	Avg. $\hat{A}_{12}$	Better $\hat{A}_{12}$	Worse $\hat{A}_{12}$
Search budget of 60 seconds											
Standard GA	10	0.83	0.52	0.75	0.24	100	0.78	0.88	0.52	0.75	0.23
Monotonic GA	25	0.83	0.52	0.76	0.32	100	0.78	0.88	0.52	0.77	0.21
Steady-State GA	100	0.81	0.50	0.72	0.32	100	0.74	0.86	0.53	0.75	0.27
$1 + (\lambda, \lambda)$ GA	50	0.57	0.58	0.70	N/A	50	0.65	0.81	0.53	0.69	0.33
$\mu + \lambda$ EA	1+7	0.84	0.55	0.74	0.21	1+7	0.79	0.89	0.56	0.76	0.28
MOSA	100	0.84	0.51	0.79	0.32	25	0.81	0.62	0.54	0.70	0.21
DynaMOSA	25	0.84	0.51	0.68	0.28	—	—	—	—	—	—
Search budget of 600 seconds											
Standard GA	100	0.86	0.50	0.84	0.21	25	0.84	0.93	0.51	0.76	0.23
Monotonic GA	100	0.87	0.53	0.83	0.22	25	0.84	0.92	0.52	0.80	0.24
Steady-State GA	10	0.85	0.51	0.80	0.23	25	0.79	0.90	0.51	0.79	0.26
$1 + (\lambda,\ )$ GA	50	0.57	0.57	0.83	N/A	8	0.75	0.81	0.53	0.85	0.19
$\mu + \lambda$ EA	50+50	0.85	0.49	0.84	0.12	1+1	0.85	0.92	0.53	0.86	0.22
MOSA	50	0.86	0.53	0.88	0.18	10	0.87	0.68	0.54	0.86	0.12
DynaMOSA	25	0.85	0.50	0.83	0.19	—	—	—	—	—	—

A *N/A* worse effect size means there is no other configuration that achieved a significantly higher coverage than the best configuration.

and Steady-State GA on multiple-criteria is 25. Table 1 also reports the average effect size of the best parameter value when compared to all possible parameter values; and the effect size of pairwise comparisons in which the best parameter was significantly better/worse.

3.3   RQ1 – Which Evolutionary Algorithm Works Best When Using a Test Archive for Partial Solutions?

Table 2 summarises the results of a pairwise tournament of all EAs. An EA X is considered to be better than an EA Y if it performs significantly better on a higher number of comparisons. For example, for a search budget of 60 s and single-criteria, $1 + (\lambda, \lambda)$ was statistically significantly better than on 53 comparisons, while it was statistically significantly worse on 432 comparisons out of 1,212 – which make it the worst EA. On the other hand, $\mu + \lambda$ was the one with more positive comparisons (387) and the least negative comparisons (just 35) – thus, being the best EA for a search budget of 60 s and single-criteria, and for a search budget of 600 s on single and multiple-criteria. While it is ranked only third for 60 s search budget and multiple-criteria, the coverage is only slightly lower compared to the higher ranked algorithms (0.79 vs. 0.80), with an $\hat{A}_{12}$ effect size of 0.59 averaged over all comparisons.

Table 2. Pairwise comparison of all evolutionary algorithms. "Better than" and "Worse than" give the number of comparisons for which the best EA is statistically significantly (i.e., $p\text{-value} < 0.05$) better and worse, respectively. Columns $\hat{A}_{12}$ give the average effect size.

Algorithm	Tourn. Position	Branch Cov.	Overall Cov.	$\hat{A}_{12}$	Better than	$\hat{A}_{12}$	Worse than	$\hat{A}_{12}$
Search budget of 60 seconds – Single-criteria								
Standard GA	3	0.80	—	0.52	223 / 1212	0.79	149/ 1212	0.25
Monotonic GA	2	0.82	—	0.56	299 / 1212	0.78	57 / 1212	0.27
Steady-State GA	4	0.77	—	0.42	112 / 1212	0.76	401 / 1212	0.19
$1+(\lambda,\lambda)$ GA	5	0.74	—	0.40	53 / 1212	0.73	432 / 1212	0.22
$\mu+\lambda$ EA	1	0.83	—	0.60	387 / 1212	0.79	35 / 1212	0.26
Search budget of 600 seconds – Single-criteria								
Standard GA	3	0.87	—	0.52	129 / 1212	0.87	96/ 1212	0.16
Monotonic GA	2	0.89	—	0.57	192 / 1212	0.89	20 / 1212	0.16
Steady-State GA	4	0.86	—	0.44	50 / 1212	0.80	217 / 1212	0.10
$1+(\lambda,\lambda)$ GA	5	0.77	—	0.39	14 / 1212	0.82	258 / 1212	0.13
$\mu+\lambda$ EA	1	0.90	—	0.59	224 / 1212	0.88	18 / 1212	0.19
Search budget of 60 seconds – Multiple-criteria								
Standard GA	2	0.77	0.79	0.62	473/ 1212	0.85	98 / 1212	0.20
Monotonic GA	1	0.78	0.80	0.62	470/ 1212	0.85	95 / 1212	0.21
Steady-State GA	4	0.72	0.76	0.43	233 / 1212	0.88	503 / 1212	0.19
$1+(\lambda,\lambda)$ GA	5	0.53	0.70	0.25	140 / 1212	0.86	896 / 1212	0.10
$\mu+\lambda$ EA	3	0.77	0.79	0.59	493 / 1212	0.84	217/ 1212	0.19
Search budget of 600 seconds – Multiple-criteria								
Standard GA	2	0.84	0.85	0.59	357/ 1212	0.93	112 / 1212	0.11
Monotonic GA	3	0.85	0.85	0.58	345/ 1212	0.93	125 / 1212	0.13
Steady-State GA	5	0.72	0.79	0.33	118 / 1212	0.94	566 / 1212	0.08
$1+(\lambda,\lambda)$ GA	4	0.62	0.75	0.35	254 / 1212	0.91	623 / 1212	0.05
$\mu+\lambda$ EA	1	0.87	0.86	0.64	437 / 1212	0.93	85/ 1212	0.09

> *RQ1: In 3 out of 4 configurations, $\mu+\lambda$ EA is better than the other considered evolutionary algorithms.*

3.4   RQ2 – How Does Evolutionary Search Compare to Random Search and Random Testing?

Table 3 compares the results of each EA with the two random-based techniques, Random search and Random testing. On one hand, Random search performs better than Random testing on single-criteria. However, the overall coverage in the multiple-criteria case is higher for Random testing than Random search. Our conjecture is that, in the multiple-criteria scenario, there are many more trivial coverage goals where the fitness function provides no guidance (thus benefiting Random testing); in contrast, branch coverage goals seem to benefit from the test archive when generating new individuals (thus benefiting Random search).

Table 3. Comparison of evolutionary algorithms and two random-based approaches: Random search and Random testing.

Algorithm	Branch Cov.	Overall Cov.	EA vs. Random search $\hat{A}_{12}$	p	Rel. Impr.	EA vs. Random testing $\hat{A}_{12}$	p	Rel. Impr.
Search budget of 60 seconds – Single-criteria								
Random search	0.78	—	—	—	—	—	—	—
Random testing	0.72	—	—	—	—	—	—	—
Standard GA	0.80	—	0.62	0.26	+15.9%	0.68	0.22	+62.4%
Monotonic GA	0.82	—	0.66	0.23	+21.9%	0.71	0.20	+68.9%
Steady-State GA	0.77	—	0.51	0.27	+2.9%	0.60	0.28	+37.8%
$1 + (\lambda, \lambda)$ GA	0.74	—	0.50	0.32	+1.5%	0.58	0.34	+36.1%
$\mu + \lambda$ EA	0.83	—	0.69	0.22	+23.5%	0.73	0.19	+71.8%
Search budget of 600 seconds – Single-criteria								
Random search	0.80	—	—	—	—	—	—	—
Random testing	0.73	—	—	—	—	—	—	—
Standard GA	0.87	—	0.69	0.19	+29.0%	0.73	0.16	+116.0%
Monotonic GA	0.89	—	0.73	0.16	+35.2%	0.76	0.14	+122.0%
Steady-State GA	0.86	—	0.63	0.22	+20.9%	0.71	0.19	+97.3%
$1 + (\lambda, \lambda)$ GA	0.77	—	0.57	0.39	+8.4%	0.63	0.38	+63.6%
$\mu + \lambda$ EA	0.90	—	0.74	0.16	+36.5%	0.76	0.12	+128.7%
Search budget of 60 seconds – Multiple-criteria								
Random search	0.76	0.65	—	—	—	—	—	—
Random testing	0.71	0.67	—	—	—	—	—	—
Standard GA	0.77	0.79	0.79	0.20	+36.2%	0.84	0.19	+26.7%
Monotonic GA	0.78	0.80	0.80	0.21	+37.6%	0.84	0.18	+28.5%
Steady-State GA	0.72	0.76	0.72	0.23	+29.6%	0.78	0.24	+18.8%
$1 + (\lambda, \lambda)$ GA	0.53	0.70	0.62	0.26	+20.1%	0.62	0.39	+9.7%
$\mu + \lambda$ EA	0.77	0.79	0.76	0.21	+35.9%	0.83	0.20	+25.8%
Search budget of 600 seconds – Multiple-criteria								
Random search	0.70	0.65	—	—	—	—	—	—
Random testing	0.72	0.74	—	—	—	—	—	—
Standard GA	0.84	0.85	0.88	0.17	+64.0%	0.83	0.20	+28.0%
Monotonic GA	0.85	0.85	0.88	0.18	+64.8%	0.83	0.20	+28.7%
Steady-State GA	0.72	0.79	0.79	0.23	+51.4%	0.71	0.29	+17.6%
$1 + (\lambda, \lambda)$ GA	0.62	0.75	0.79	0.30	+49.1%	0.72	0.40	+14.0%
$\mu + \lambda$ EA	0.87	0.86	0.88	0.15	+66.1%	0.84	0.18	+30.6%

On average, EAs achieve higher coverage (either branch-coverage on single-criteria or overall coverage on multiple-criteria) than Random search and Random testing. For instance, for a search budget of 600 s and single-criteria, Random search covers 80% of all branches on average and $\mu + \lambda$ EA covers 90% (a relative improvement of +36.5%). This result is different to the earlier study by Shamshiri et al. [23], where random testing achieved similar, and sometimes higher coverage. Our conjecture is that the better performance of the EAs in our evaluation is due to (1) the use of the test archive, and (2) the use of more complex classes in the experiment.

> *RQ2: Evolutionary algorithms (in particular $\mu + \lambda$ EA) perform better than random search and random testing.*

3.5   RQ3 – How Does Evolution of Whole Test Suites Compare to Many-Objective Optimisation of Test Cases?

Table 4 compares each EA with the many-objective optimisation techniques MOSA and DynaMOSA. Our results confirm and enhance previous studies [17,18] by evaluating four different EAs (i.e., Standard GA, Steady-State GA, $1 + (\lambda, \lambda)$ GA, and $\mu + \lambda$ EA) in addition to Monotonic GA, and show that

Table 4. Comparison of evolutionary algorithms on whole test suites optimisation and many-objective optimisation algorithms of test cases.

Algorithm	Branch Cov.	Overall Cov.	EA vs. MOSA			EA vs. DynaMOSA		
			$\hat{A}_{12}$	p	Rel. Impr.	$\hat{A}_{12}$	p	Rel. Impr.
Search budget of 60 seconds – Single-criteria								
MOSA	0.84	—	—	—	—	—	—	—
DynaMOSA	0.85	—	—	—	—	—	—	—
Standard GA	0.80	—	0.39	0.27	-3.6%	0.37	0.28	-6.0%
Monotonic GA	0.82	—	0.43	0.26	-0.4%	0.41	0.28	-2.3%
Steady-State GA	0.77	—	0.30	0.19	-9.7%	0.28	0.19	-10.7%
$1 + (\lambda, \lambda)$ GA	0.74	—	0.31	0.26	-12.5%	0.29	0.25	-14.3%
$\mu + \lambda$ EA	0.83	—	0.46	0.28	+0.8%	0.44	0.29	-1.5%
Search budget of 600 seconds – Single-criteria								
MOSA	0.90	—	—	—	—	—	—	—
DynaMOSA	0.91	—	—	—	—	—	—	—
Standard GA	0.87	—	0.42	0.24	-3.2%	0.40	0.23	-4.6%
Monotonic GA	0.89	—	0.47	0.24	+0.2%	0.44	0.23	-1.4%
Steady-State GA	0.86	—	0.38	0.22	-3.5%	0.36	0.21	-5.1%
$1 + (\lambda, \lambda)$ GA	0.77	—	0.34	0.37	-14.3%	0.33	0.35	-15.6%
$\mu + \lambda$ EA	0.90	—	0.49	0.22	+1.6%	0.47	0.23	-0.7%
Search budget of 60 seconds – Multiple-criteria								
MOSA	0.80	0.58	—	—	—	—	—	—
DynaMOSA	—	—	—	—	—	—	—	—
Standard GA	0.77	0.79	0.71	0.18	+8737.7%	—	—	—
Monotonic GA	0.78	0.80	0.71	0.17	+9069.9%	—	—	—
Steady-State GA	0.72	0.76	0.63	0.17	+9058.6%	—	—	—
$1 + (\lambda, \lambda)$ GA	0.53	0.70	0.59	0.21	+7941.9%	—	—	—
$\mu + \lambda$ EA	0.77	0.79	0.70	0.17	+9071.2%	—	—	—
Search budget of 600 seconds – Multiple-criteria								
MOSA	0.87	0.71	—	—	—	—	—	—
DynaMOSA	—	—	—	—	—	—	—	—
Standard GA	0.84	0.85	0.64	0.19	+772.4%	—	—	—
Monotonic GA	0.85	0.85	0.64	0.20	+773.4%	—	—	—
Steady-State GA	0.72	0.79	0.52	0.19	+694.6%	—	—	—
$1 + (\lambda, \lambda)$ GA	0.62	0.75	0.56	0.27	+632.7%	—	—	—
$\mu + \lambda$ EA	0.87	0.86	0.67	0.18	+769.5%	—	—	—

MOSA and DynaMOSA perform better at optimising test cases than any EA at optimising test suites for single criteria. Although $\mu + \lambda$ achieves a marginally higher average coverage on single criteria (600 s) with a relative improvement of +1.6%, it is still slightly worse than MOSA with an average effect size of 0.49.

In the multiple-criteria scenario (in which we can only compare to MOSA), MOSA performs better than any other EA at optimising branch coverage, but the overall coverage is substantially lower compared to all other EAs. On the one hand, the lower overall coverage is expected since MOSA is not efficient for very large sets of coverage goals (this is what DynaMOSA addresses). However, the fact that branch coverage is nevertheless higher is interesting. A possible conjecture is that this is due to MOSA's slightly different fitness function for branch coverage [18], which includes the approach level (whereas whole test suite optimisation considers only branch distances).

> RQ3: MOSA improves over EAs for individual criteria; for multiple-criteria it achieves higher branch coverage even though overall coverage is lower.

4   Related Work

Although a common approach in search-based testing is to use genetic algorithms, numerous other algorithms have been proposed in the domain of nature-inspired algorithms, as no algorithm can be best on all domains [27]. Many researchers compared evolutionary algorithms to solve problems in domains outside software engineering [2,26,28]. Within search-based software engineering, comparative studies have been conducted in several domains such as discovery of software architectures [19], pairwise testing of software product lines [15], or finding subtle higher order mutants [16].

In the context of test data generation, Harman and McMinn [12] empirically compared GA, Random testing and Hill Climbing for structural test data generation. While their results indicate that sophisticated evolutionary algorithms can often be outperformed by simpler search techniques, there are more complex scenarios, for which evolutionary algorithms are better suited. Ghani et al. [11] compared Simulated Annealing (SA) and GA for the test data generation for Matlab Simulink models, and their results show that GA performed slightly better than SA. Sahin and Akay [22] evaluated Particle Swarm Optimisation (PSO), Differential Evolution (DE), Artificial Bee Colony, Firefly Algorithm and Random search algorithms on software test data generation benchmark problems, and concluded that some algorithms performs better than others depending on the characteristics of the problem. Varshney and Mehrotra [25] proposed a DE-based approach to generate test data that cover data-flow coverage criteria, and compared the proposed approach to Random search, GA and PSO with respect to number of generations and average percentage coverage. Their results show that the proposed DE-based approach is comparable to PSO and has better performance than Random search and GA. In contrast to these studies, we consider unit test generation, which arguably is a more complex scenario than test data generation, and in particular local search algorithms are rarely applied.

Although often newly proposed algorithms are compared to random search as a baseline (usually showing clear improvements), there are some studies that show that random search can actually be very efficient for test generation. In particular, Shamshiri et al. [23] compared GA against Random search for generating test suites, and found almost no difference between the coverage achieved by evolutionary search compared to random search. They observed that GAs covers more branches when standard fitness functions provide guidance, but most branches of the analyzed projects provided no such guidance. Similarly, Sahin and Akay [22] showed that Random search is effective on simple problems.

To the best of our knowledge, no study has been conducted to evaluate several different evolutionary algorithms in a whole test suite generation context and considering a large number of complex classes. As can be seen from this overview of comparative studies, it is far from obvious what the best algorithm is, since there are large variations between different search problems.

5   Conclusions

Although evolutionary algorithms are commonly applied for whole test suite generation, there is a lack of evidence on the influence of different algorithms. Our study yielded the following key results:

– The choice of algorithm can have a substantial influence on the performance of whole test suite optimisation, hence tuning is important. While EVOSUITE provides tuned default values, these values may not be optimal for different flavours of evolutionary algorithms.
– EVOSUITE's default algorithm, a Monotonic GA, is an appropriate choice for EVOSUITE's default configuration (60 s search budget, multiple criteria). However, for other search budgets and optimisation goals, other algorithms such as a $\mu + \lambda$ EA may be a better choice.
– Although previous studies showed little benefit of using a GA over random testing, our study shows that on complex classes and with a test archive, evolutionary algorithms are superior to random testing and random search.
– The Many Objective Sorting Algorithm (MOSA) is superior to whole test suite optimisation; it would be desirable to extend EVOSUITE so that DynaMOSA supports all coverage criteria.

It would be of interest to extend our experiments to further search algorithms. In particular, the use of other non-functional attributes such as readability [3] suggests the exploration of multi-objective algorithms. Considering the variation of results with respect to different configurations and classes under test, it would also be of interest to use these insights to develop hyper-heuristics that select and adapt the optimal algorithm to the specific problem at hand.

Acknowledgments. This work is supported by EPSRC project EP/N023978/1, São Paulo Research Foundation (FAPESP) grant 2015/26044-0, and the National Research Fund, Luxembourg (FNR/P10/03).

References

1. Arcuri, A., Fraser, G.: Parameter tuning or default values? An empirical investigation in search-based software engineering. Empir. Softw. Eng. **18**(3), 594–623 (2013)
2. Basak, A., Lohn, J.: A comparison of evolutionary algorithms on a set of antenna design benchmarks. In: de la Fraga, L.G. (ed.) 2013 IEEE Conference on Evolutionary Computation, Cancun, vol. 1, pp. 598–604, 20–23 June 2013
3. Daka, E., Campos, J., Fraser, G., Dorn, J., Weimer, W.: Modeling readability to improve unit tests. In: Proceedings of the Joint Meeting on Foundations of Software Engineering (ESEC/FSE 2015), pp. 107–118. ACM, New York (2015)
4. Deb, K., Agrawal, S., Pratap, A., Meyarivan, T.: A fast elitist non-dominated sorting genetic algorithm for multi-objective optimization: NSGA-II. In: Schoenauer, M., Deb, K., Rudolph, G., Yao, X., Lutton, E., Merelo, J.J., Schwefel, H.-P. (eds.) PPSN 2000. LNCS, vol. 1917, pp. 849–858. Springer, Heidelberg (2000). doi:10. 1007/3-540-45356-3_83
5. Doerr, B., Doerr, C., Ebel, F.: From black-box complexity to designing new genetic algorithms. Theor. Comput. Sci. **567**, 87–104 (2015)
6. Fraser, G., Arcuri, A.: EvoSuite: automatic test suite generation for object-oriented software. In: Proceedings of ESEC/FSE, pp. 416–419. ACM (2011)
7. Fraser, G., Arcuri, A.: Handling test length bloat. Softw. Test. Verif. Reliab. **23**(7), 553–582 (2013)
8. Fraser, G., Arcuri, A.: Whole test suite generation. IEEE Trans. Softw. Eng. **39**(2), 276–291 (2013)
9. Fraser, G., Arcuri, A.: A large-scale evaluation of automated unit test generation using evosuite. ACM Trans. Softw. Eng. Methodol. (TOSEM) **24**(2), 8:1–8:42 (2014)
10. Gay, G.: The fitness function for the job: search-based generation of test suites that detect real faults. In: 2017 IEEE 10th International Conference on Software Testing, Verification and Validation (ICST). IEEE (2017)
11. Ghani, K., Clark, J.A., Zhan, Y.: Comparing algorithms for search-based test data generation of matlab simulink models. In: 2009 IEEE Congress on Evolutionary Computation, pp. 2940–2947, May 2009
12. Harman, M., McMinn, P.: A theoretical & empirical analysis of evolutionary testing and hill climbing for structural test data generation. In: Proceedings of the International Symposium on Software Testing and Analysis, pp. 73–83. ACM (2007)
13. Jansen, T., De Jong, K.A., Wegener, I.: On the choice of the offspring population size in evolutionary algorithms. Evol. Comput. **13**(4), 413–440 (2005)
14. Karnopp, D.C.: Random search techniques for optimization problems. Automatica **1**(2–3), 111–121 (1963)
15. Lopez-Herrejon, R.E., Ferrer, J., Chicano, F., Egyed, A., Alba, E.: Comparative analysis of classical multi-objective evolutionary algorithms and seeding strategies for pairwise testing of software product lines. In: Proceedings of the IEEE Congress on Evolutionary Computation (CEC), pp. 387–396 (2014)

16. Omar, E., Ghosh, S., Whitley, D.: Comparing search techniques for finding subtle higher order mutants. In: Proceedings of the Conference on Genetic and Evolutionary Computation (GECCO 2014), pp. 1271–1278. ACM (2014)
17. Panichella, A., Kifetew, F., Tonella, P.: Automated test case generation as a many-objective optimisation problem with dynamic selection of the targets. IEEE Trans. Softw. Eng. **PP**(99), 1 (2017)
18. Panichella, A., Kifetew, F.M., Tonella, P.: Reformulating branch coverage as a many-objective optimization problem. In: 2015 IEEE 8th International Conference on Software Testing, Verification and Validation (ICST), pp. 1–10. IEEE (2015)
19. Ramírez, A., Romero, J.R., Ventura, S.: A comparative study of many-objective evolutionary algorithms for the discovery of software architectures. Empir. Softw. Engg. **21**(6), 2546–2600 (2016)
20. Rojas, J.M., Campos, J., Vivanti, M., Fraser, G., Arcuri, A.: Combining multiple coverage criteria in search-based unit test generation. In: Barros, M., Labiche, Y. (eds.) SSBSE 2015. LNCS, vol. 9275, pp. 93–108. Springer, Cham (2015). doi:10.1007/978-3-319-22183-0_7
21. Rojas, J.M., Vivanti, M., Arcuri, A., Fraser, G.: A detailed investigation of the effectiveness of whole test suite generation. Empir. Softw. Eng. **22**, 852–893 (2016)
22. Sahin, O., Akay, B.: Comparisons of metaheuristic algorithms and fitness functions on software test data generation. Appl. Soft Comput. **49**, 1202–1214 (2016)
23. Shamshiri, S., Rojas, J.M., Fraser, G., McMinn, P.: Random or genetic algorithm search for object-oriented test suite generation? In: Proceedings of the Conference on Genetic and Evolutionary Computation, pp. 1367–1374. ACM (2015)
24. Ter-Sarkisov, A., Marsland, S.R.: Convergence properties of $(\mu + \lambda)$ evolutionary algorithms. In: AAAI (2011)
25. Varshney, S., Mehrotra, M.: A differential evolution based approach to generate test data for data-flow coverage. In: 2016 International Conference on Computing, Communication and Automation (ICCCA), pp. 796–801, April 2016
26. Wolfram, M., Marten, A.K., Westermann, D.: A comparative study of evolutionary algorithms for phase shifting transformer setting optimization. In: 2016 IEEE International Energy Conference (ENERGYCON), pp. 1–6, April 2016
27. Wolpert, D.H., Macready, W.G.: No free lunch theorems for optimization. IEEE Trans. Evol. Comput. **1**(1), 67–82 (1997)
28. Zitzler, E., Deb, K., Thiele, L.: Comparison of multiobjective evolutionary algorithms: empirical results. Evol. Comput. **8**(2), 173–195 (2000)

Automatic Detection of Incomplete Requirements Using Symbolic Analysis and Evolutionary Computation

Byron DeVries[✉] and Betty H.C. Cheng

Department of Computer Science and Engineering,
Michigan State University, East Lansing, MI 48823, USA
devri117@cse.msu.edu

Abstract. The usefulness of a system specification depends on the completeness of the requirements specified. Unfortunately it is difficult to ensure a requirements specification includes all necessary requirements, especially when the system interacts with an unpredictable and often idealized environment. Worse yet, a single completeness counterexample may not clearly indicate the extent that incomplete requirements impacts the system or what range of environmental scenarios are affected. This paper introduces *Ares-EC*, a design-time approach for detecting incomplete requirements decomposition using a combination of evolutionary computation and symbolic analysis of hierarchical requirements models to detect a set of representative incompleteness counterexamples. We illustrate our approach by applying *Ares-EC* to a requirements model of an industry-based automotive adaptive cruise control system. *Ares-EC* is able to apply symbolic analysis and evolutionary computation to automatically detect diverse and representative sets of requirements incompleteness counterexamples at design time.

1 Introduction

Developing complete requirements is often a challenge. Exhaustively enumerating all cases sufficient to satisfy expected functionality can be prohibitively difficult, especially when unexpected environmental scenarios arise. Even when requirements incompleteness is automatically identified, a single counterexample is not sufficient. Just as it is not sufficient for a system designer to correct a single environmental scenario impacted by incompleteness, neither is it sufficient to simply indicate that requirements are incomplete. Instead, the range of environmental scenarios impacted by incomplete requirements decomposition should be identified in order to facilitate the task of revising the requirements. This paper presents *Ares-EC*,[1] an approach that combines symbolic analysis and evolutionary computation to automatically identify diverse and representative sets of counterexamples that represent requirements incompleteness in hierarchical requirements models.

---

[1] *Ares* is the Greek god of war, especially the untamed aspects of war.

© Springer International Publishing AG 2017
T. Menzies and J. Petke (Eds.): SSBSE 2017, LNCS 10452, pp. 49–64, 2017.
DOI: 10.1007/978-3-319-66299-2_4

While methods exist to create requirements that are complete with respect to specific decomposition rules [5], creating complete requirements and detecting incomplete requirements is still an area of active research [1,2,10,13,19,27]. For example, a requirement for a vehicle may be to stop. In an idealized system, applying brake force (e.g., from hydraulic brakes) would be sufficient. Applying the brakes may be insufficient if the throttle can overwhelm the braking force, thus indicating that the decomposition is incomplete. However, that single counterexample is not representative of the range of operational scenarios that are impacted by incompleteness. For example, in inclement weather, brake force may not be sufficient without anti-lock brakes. Not only is enumerating all necessary decomposed requirements difficult, it is also challenging to identify the range of impacted scenarios to assess necessary additional requirements. Currently, formal methods exist that define formal decomposition rules with guaranteed completeness [5], though system designers are limited to those specific formal decomposition rules. Multiple counterexamples can be identified [1], but require manual review for relevance and applicability. Currently, a single method, that we previously developed, exists that automatically detects incomplete requirements decomposition without imposing restrictions on how requirements are decomposed or described, but it only returns a single counterexample for each incomplete decomposition [10].

This paper describes *Ares-EC*, an approach that combines symbolic analysis and evolutionary computation to automatically identify sets of representative environmental configurations where completeness properties are violated in a hierarchical requirements model. Hierarchical requirements satisfaction can be assessed in two ways: its individual satisfaction or the satisfaction of a requirement's aggregate decomposed requirements (i.e., children or sub-requirements). Given complete decomposition, a requirement should be satisfied whenever its aggregate decomposed requirements are satisfied [10]. *Ares-EC* uses symbolic analysis to identify individual counterexamples and uses evolutionary computation to search for sets of diverse representations of counterexamples based on the previously identified counterexamples. By employing symbolic analysis, *Ares-EC* can guarantee that a single counterexample will be found, if one exists. Evolutionary computation, on the other hand, can identify multiple diverse counterexamples in parallel. *Ares-EC* identifies incomplete decompositions in the form of sets of representative environmental scenarios, or counterexamples, within a valid range of values for the variables in the system in which the incompleteness is expressed. Counterexamples are then summarized for the system designer to revise the requirements accordingly.

Ares-EC applies utility functions [20] to assess individual requirements for completeness within a hierarchical requirements model. Expressions representing completeness counterexamples used in both symbolic and evolutionary computation are defined in terms of these utility functions. While utility functions have been used to measure run-time satisfaction of requirements [15,20], *Ares-EC* analyzes the utility functions (via expressions representing incompleteness) at design-time. For each requirement's decomposition, *Ares-EC* identifies a representative set of counterexamples from the range of possible requirement variables' values. Counterexamples are identified as environmental conditions that cause a requirement to be unsatisfied while its aggregate decomposed requirements are satisfied. Sets of counterexamples are identified for an industry-based requirements model for an automotive application, and the incomplete requirements decompositions along with their representative set of counterexamples are summarized for the system designer.

The contributions of this paper are as follows:

– We introduce a design-time, symbolic analysis and evolutionary computation approach to automatically detect diverse and representative sets of completeness counterexamples in hierarchical requirements models.
– We present a prototype implementation of the *Ares-EC* approach.
– We demonstrate the applicability of *Ares-EC* on an industry-based automotive example, an adaptive cruise control system.

The remainder of this paper is organized into the following sections. Section 2 overviews background information. Section 3 details the *Ares-EC* approach. Section 4 describes the results of a case study, and Sect. 5 details related work. Finally, Sect. 6 discusses the conclusions and avenues of future work.

2   Background

This section covers background information on hierarchical requirements modeling, utility functions, and the Adaptive Cruise Control (ACC) system used in this paper.

2.1   Hierarchical Requirements Modeling

Hierarchical requirements modeling frameworks, including i^* [26], KAOS goal modeling [22], or simply hierarchical requirements modeling [21], all decompose requirements into hierarchical requirements that are sufficient to satisfy their parent requirement. Each decomposed requirement is also subsequently decomposed until some termination criteria is met. *Ares-EC* is generally applicable to any hierarchical goal and requirements model, therefore we refer to goals and requirements interchangeably.

KAOS goal modeling implements Goal-Oriented Requirements Engineering (GORE) via a graph-based AND and OR decomposition that terminates in requirements and expectations at the leaf level. Requirements are satisfied by the system-to-be, while expectations are satisfied by agents of the environment [22]. AND decomposition requires all decomposed requirements to be satisfied to satisfy the parent, while OR decomposition only requires one requirement to be satisfied [22].

A requirement decomposition is complete when the satisfaction of the set of decomposed requirements imply the satisfaction of the parent requirement. That is, if the decomposed requirements are satisfied then the parent must be satisfied *if* the decomposition is complete. Often requirements incompleteness is due to unexpected scenarios that were unanticipated by the system designer [1]. In the remainder of this paper, requirement labels are in **bold courier** font. Variable names, requirement text, and emphasis are indicated by *italics*

2.2   Utility Functions

Utility functions [23] are typically used as run-time monitors [12,14] to assess the satisfaction or satisficement of requirements. While satisfaction is generally represented as either satisfied or unsatisfied, satisficement represents a degree of satisfaction [24]. We use Athena [20], an existing method of generating utility functions from environmental properties (**ENV, MON, REL**).

- **ENV** represents properties that are not directly observable and must be viewed indirectly through other environmental properties (e.g., future speed of a vehicle may be estimated using acceleration, time, and current speed),
- **MON** represents properties that are directly observable via agents and sensors (e.g., current vehicle speed as measured by the GPS), and
- **REL** represents relationships between the **MON** properties and requirement satisfaction (e.g., a relationship that measures the satisficement of a requirement to increase speed).

The environmental properties (**ENV, MON, REL**) are specified manually by the system designer [3] and are used by Athena to automatically generate the utility functions [20].

2.3   Adaptive Cruise Control Systems

An Adaptive Cruise Control (ACC) system uses radar to adjust vehicle speed ensuring a safe following distance from the car ahead while maintaining as close to the desired speed as possible. An ACC can be viewed in four parts: cruise control modes, increasing speed, lowering speed, and maintaining speed. Speed is increased or lowered to match the desired speed, however speed may also be lowered if there is not a safe distance to the target car (i.e., car immediately in front). Similarly, the speed will not continue to increase if the safe distance is violated. The speed is maintained if both the desired speed is met and the target car is a safe distance.

Figure 1 represents a partial goal model of an ACC where portions not explicitly included due to relevance are replaced with ellipses. This goal model includes two requirements that have been previously shown to have incomplete decompositions, goals **D.1** and **B.3** [10]. Goal **D.1** is a portion of the specification to maintain speed and ensures the throttle is maintained at its current position (via Goal **D.3**) by reading the current throttle position (via Goal **D.5** when the speed is as desired and the distance from any leading car is adequate (via Goal **D.2**). Goal **D.1** can be shown to be incomplete when the speed is not maintained even though the throttle is maintained due to a change in the amount of braking.

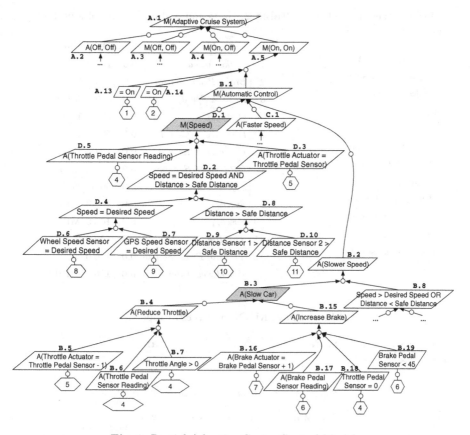

Fig. 1. Partial Adaptive Cruise Control Model

Goal **B.3** is a portion of the specification to perform the task of slowing the car, and decomposes to reducing the throttle (Goal **B.4**) or increasing the amount of braking (Goal **B.15**). Goal **B.3** can also be shown to be incomplete by increasing the speed of the vehicle by increasing the brake slightly while also increasing the throttle significantly, since Goal **B.3** is OR decomposed and requires only one decomposed goal to satisfy the top level goal.

Keywords *Maintain* and *Achieve* are abbreviated to M and A, respectively. The numbered agents (i.e., leaf nodes) referenced in the model are given in Table 1. Ellipses are used to indicate the continuation of the goal model outside of the partially displayed goal model.

Utility functions are defined based on the **ENV, MON**, and **REL** properties for the goal model in Fig. 1, as shown in Table 3. The values in Table 3 are defined and provided by the system designer. Due to space constraints, only values related to requirements **D.1** and **B.3** are shown in detail, as they were previously shown to be incomplete [10]. The variables defined in Table 3 each have ranges of values and units as defined in Table 2. For example, the utility

Table 1. Agents used in Goal Model

#	Agent (Sensor/Actuator)
1	Cruise Switch Sensor
2	Cruise Active Sensor
3	Cruise Active Switch
4	Throttle Pedal Sensor
5	Throttle Actuator
6	Brake Pedal Sensor
7	Brake Actuator
8	Wheel Speed Sensor
9	GPS Speed Sensor
10	Distance Sensor 1
11	Distance Sensor 2

Table 2. Units and scaling for variables in Table 3

ID	Variable	Min	Max	Unit
1	*Brake Actuator*	0.0	100.0	%
2	*Brake Pedal Sensor*	0.0	100.0	%
3	*Desired Speed*	0.0	100.0	MPH
4	*Distance*	0.0	50.0	Feet
5	*Distance Sensor 1*	0.0	50.0	Feet
6	*Distance Sensor 2*	0.0	50.0	Feet
7	*GPS Speed Sensor*	0.0	100.0	MPH
8	*Safe Distance*	0.0	50.0	Feet
9	$Speed_t$	0.0	100.0	MPH
10	$Speed_{t+1}$	0.0	100.0	MPH
11	*Throttle Actuator*	0.0	100.0	%
12	*Throttle Pedal Sensor*	0.0	100.0	%
13	*Wheel Speed Sensor*	0.0	100.0	MPH

Table 3. ENV, MON, and **REL** Properties

	ENV	MON	REL
B.3	$Speed_t$, $Speed_{t+1}$		$Speed_t > Speed_{t+1} \vee (Speed_t == MIN \wedge Speed_{t+1} == MIN)$
B.4		*Throttle Actuator, Throttle Pedal Sensor*	*Throttle Actuator* < *Throttle Pedal Sensor*
B.15		*Brake Actuator, Brake Pedal Sensor*	*Brake Actuator* > *Brake Pedal Sensor*
D.1	$Speed_t$, $Speed_{t+1}$		$Speed_t == Speed_{t+1}$
D.2	$Speed_t$, *Distance*	*Desired Speed, Safe Distance*	$Speed_t == $ *Desired Speed* $\wedge$ *Distance* > *Safe Distance*
D.3		*Throttle Actuator, Throttle Pedal Sensor*	*Throttle Actuator* == *Throttle Pedal Sensor*
D.5			*true*
$Speed_t$		*Wheel Speed Sensor, GPS Speed Sensor*	*Wheel Speed Sensor* $\vee$ *GPS Speed Sensor*
$Speed_t$		*Throttle Pedal Sensor, Brake Pedal Sensor*	**max**(*MIN*, *Throttle Pedal Sensor*− *Brake Pedal Sensor*)
$Speed_{t+1}$		*Throttle Actuator, Brake Actuator*	**max**(*MIN*, *Throttle Actuator*− *Brake Actuator*)
Distance		*Distance Sensor 1, Distance Sensor 2*	*Distance Sensor 1* $\vee$ *Distance Sensor 2*

function for requirement **D.1** is given in Expression 1 indicating that goal **D.1** (*'Maintain Speed'*) is satisfied if the value of the current speed ($Speed_t$) is equal to the speed in the future ($Speed_{t+1}$).

$$\text{Satisficement}(\textbf{D.1}) = Speed_t == Speed_{t+1} \qquad (1)$$

3   Approach

Ares-EC is an automated method for identifying sets of completeness counterexamples in a hierarchical requirements model. A requirement is considered to be incompletely decomposed if there exists a case such that a parent requirement is unsatisfied while the set of its decomposed requirements are satisfied [10]. The *Ares-EC* process generates detection logic using utility functions and the decompositions in a hierarchical goal model. These logical expressions are then processed by one of four methods to identify dispersed solutions that represent completeness counterexamples. Next, we detail the *Ares-EC* approach and then provide a comparison of the search methods applied to our running example.

3.1   Step 1: Generate Detection Logic

Ares-EC makes use of utility functions generated by Athena [20] to measure the satisfaction of individual goals within a requirements model. We have two types of utility functions. If assessing a Boolean property then the possible values are 0.0 or 1.0, indicating false or true, respectively. If assessing a property that can have degrees of satisfaction, termed *satisficement* [24], then the value ranges from 0.0 to 1.0. The utility functions representing the satisfaction of parent and decomposed requirements are combined to form expressions that, when equal to 1.0, represents a completeness counterexample comprised of concrete instantiations of the variables referenced. Specifically a completeness counterexample is an unsatisfied parent requirement with a set of satisfied decomposed requirements [10] indicating there are additional child requirements necessary to satisfy the parent requirement. For example, **D.1** is incompletely decomposed if it is not satisfied according to its utility function value, but the set of its decomposed requirements (i.e., **D.2**, **D.5**, and **D.3**) is satisfied (i.e., the minimum of an AND-decomposition) as shown in Eq. 2. The 'Satisficement' function represents the utility function for the requirement passed as a parameter, where the return value is in the range of 0.0 to 1.0 (for unsatisfied and satisfied, respectively). If both the parent requirement and the decomposed children requirements are satisfied, then the counterexample equation is 0.0 indicating no completeness counterexample.

$$
\begin{aligned}
\text{Counterexample}_{\mathbf{D.1}} = \min(&\text{Satisficement}(\mathbf{D.2}), \\
&\text{Satisficement}(\mathbf{D.5}), \\
&\text{Satisficement}(\mathbf{D.3})) - \text{Satisficement}(\mathbf{D.1}).
\end{aligned}
\tag{2}
$$

Each of the requirements referenced in Eq. 2 may either be satisfied (i.e., 1.0) or unsatisfied (i.e., 0.0) based on their utility function. By instantiating the satisficement expressions in Eq. 2 with their respective utility values (from Table 3), we obtain the expression in Eq. 3.

$$\text{Counterexample}_{\textbf{D.1}} = \min(Speed_t == Desired\ Speed \wedge \qquad (3)$$
$$Distance > Safe\ Distance,$$
$$true,$$
$$Throttle\ Actuator == Throttle\ Pedal\ Sensor) -$$
$$Speed_t == Speed_{t+1}$$

Similarly, OR-decomposed requirements such as **B.3** use the maximum of the decomposed requirements, as shown in Eq. 4.

$$\text{Counterexample}_{\textbf{B.3}} = \max(\text{Satisficement}(\textbf{B.4}), \qquad (4)$$
$$\text{Satisficement}(\textbf{B.15})) - \text{Satisficement}(\textbf{B.3}).$$

A similar expression is generated for every requirement that is decomposed. Identifying an optimum (i.e., a return value of 1.0) for a completeness counterexample expression indicates a counterexample exists.

3.2   Step 2: Search for Counterexamples and Summarize

Ares-EC applies one of the following methods, as chosen by the system designer, to identify counterexamples from the completeness counterexample expressions from Step 1 (e.g., Eqs. 2 and 4). In this work, we compare the four methods to provide a basis for the selection. Previously, symbolic analysis has been used to identify single counterexamples of incomplete requirements decomposition [10]. In contrast, here we apply evolutionary computation to search for a range of distributed counterexamples. Since we know that evolutionary computation is not guaranteed to find a solution, especially in 'needle in a haystack' cases, we supplement our evolutionary approach with initial optimal results from our symbolic approach. Finally, we periodically use our symbolic approach to reseed the evolutionary population as a means to overcome additional 'needle in a haystack' cases.

For simplicity, we configure the parameters for evolutionary computation based on empirical feedback with an emphasis on optimal results and execution time. All instances of evolutionary computation used in this work make use of 200 individuals in the population, a tournament size of 8 is used for mating selection, a tournament of size 4 is used for survival selection, and a mutation rate of 5%. Executions have been limited to 2000 generations and execution is on the order of seconds. Mating selection is performed by an eight-way tournament based on the novelty of individuals within a set of randomly-selected individuals. Crossover for mating is performed by the SBX crossover operator [8] for each real-value (i.e., variable in the completeness counterexample expressions) in the individuals selected. Mutation is performed on five percent of the individuals by randomly modifying a single real-value representing a variable in the genome. Survival via a four-way tournament is used to maintain population size and is based on fitness as measured by the satisfaction of the completeness counterexample expression and is elite preserving as no member of the population will be replaced with a less optimal member. Tournaments of this size were selected in an effort to increase the likelihood that an optimal value takes part in the tournament.

The genetic algorithm emphasizes search diversity via the mating selection and mutation operators (5% chance of mutation), while survival selection optimizes the results of the diverse search. The optimal is a population where each individual is at an optimum *and* each individual is as far as possible from the other individuals based on the Manhattan distance [4] of the genotype. The genetic evolution described here differs from other genetic algorithms that search for a single optimal individual, since we are looking for a collection of diverse solutions.

Symbolic Analysis Only: For each requirement, a utility function is used to represent the satisfaction of the requirement based on a set of environmental and system variables that make up the utility function. The parent requirement is symbolically compared to the combined derived requirements, via the completeness counterexample expressions. Detecting a single completeness counterexample is identified via symbolic analysis of the completeness counterexample expressions (e.g., Eq. 2 or 4) using existing techniques [10]. We include this technique here as a means to establish existence of at least one counterexample and for comparison to the other search-based techniques. Specifically, symbolic analysis, via Microsoft's SMT solver Z3 [6], is used to evaluate the entire range of applicable environmental configurations and system variables used in the completeness counterexample expressions for each decomposed requirement.

In cases where the completeness counterexample expression cannot be satisfied, then no counterexample exists and the requirement is thus complete, thereby alleviating the need to perform additional analysis.

Evolutionary Computation Only: *Ares-EC* employs evolutionary computation in the form of a genetic algorithm to search for *both* novel and optimal results. Instead of searching for a single optimal solution to a counterexample expression, *Ares-EC* searches for multiple solutions with optimal phenotype responses (e.g., requirements with utility function values that indicate an incomplete decomposition) and maximized genotype novelty (e.g., a large difference in the environmental scenario the requirements are applied on). The expected results are a population of optimal individuals dispersed across the range of the genotype. The genome is an array of real-valued variables, one for each variable that exists in the completeness counterexample expression.

Symbolic Analysis, then Evolutionary Computation: While evolutionary computation alone can provide a method of searching with an emphasis on diversity, two issues can occur:

- First, the so called 'needle in a haystack' problem may make finding the optimum solution significantly unlikely to be found.
- Second, expressions without a gradient between satisfied and unsatisfied are likely to take more time to find the optimum, and perhaps degenerate to

random search, since the requirements satisfaction is used to calculate the fitness function.

Ares-EC alleviates these two problems by utilizing symbolic analysis to identify a single optimum, which is used to seed a portion (10%, or 20 of the 200 individuals) of the initial population. Given an initial optimum, the diverse search is intended to identify a dispersed set of optimum values.

Evolutionary Computation with Symbolic Analysis: Symbolic analysis may provide a starting point for evolutionary computation, yet despite the guarantee of optimal individuals in the initial population, two issues can still occur:

– First, while the 'needle in a haystack' problem is alleviated for a *single* optimum, additional optima may also be similarly unlikely to be found.
– Second, a change in one variable may require a change in another variable in a single individual to identify another optimum, resulting in additional search time.

Ares-EC overcomes these problems by periodically re-analyzing the completeness counterexample expression symbolically, with an added constraint to maximize the distance from a selection of existing individuals in the population. If another optimum is found then that individual is added to the population. In this paper, we allow *Ares-EC* to select up to 10 random individuals in the population to create a distance constraint from each of them during the first half of the generations. If a new and diverse counterexample is found, then 20 random individuals are replaced with the new counterexample.

3.3   Scalability and Limitations

Ares-EC is not guaranteed to identify all completeness counterexamples, even when using evolutionary computation with periodic symbolic analysis. For example, given a set of 'needles in a haystack,' two 'needles' that are close in genotype distance (e.g., when the throttle is at 72% and 74%, but not at 73%) may cause one to be ignored in favor of counterexamples that are further afield. While no guarantees can be made about identifying all completeness counterexamples, the larger the set of counterexamples and greater the diversity found, the more representative the solution set is of the incompleteness. Ultimately, detecting completeness counterexamples is limited to the quality and fidelity of the hierarchical requirements model and utility functions.

4   Results

This section describes and compares the results of applying the four different methods of identifying counterexamples that satisfy the generated requirement completeness counterexample expressions. These methods are symbolic analysis only (SA), evolutionary computation only (EC), SA-Initialized EC (SAIEC), and

Periodic-SA with EC (PSAEC). Each of these methods were executed 50 times. For the SA results, there is no difference between executions, but for the results that include EC, the results vary across executions. Results are compared for two incomplete requirements (Goals **D.1** and **B.3**, to 'Maintain Speed' and 'Slow Car', respectively) that were previously shown to be incomplete using SA [10]. However in contrast to previous solutions [10], *Ares-EC* identifies multiple representative counterexamples. Methods are compared based on their ability to return disperse counterexamples. Next, we describe in detail the results from applying each of these four techniques and analyze the results.

4.1 Symbolic Analysis

SA identified a single counterexample for both goals **D.1** and **B.3**. Intrinsically, there is no range or diversity in a solution set of one result. SA has been previously used to identify completeness counterexamples [10] and is included here for comparison with the other search-based methods.

4.2 Evolutionary Computation

EC attempts to address the fundamental shortcoming with the results from only SA by identifying a population of results, rather than a single result. However, even after 50 executions, no counterexamples could be identified. Unlike the single SA result, EC attempts to identify a range of solutions that are more representative of the scope in which the requirement incompleteness exists. In this case, the lack of variation in fitness (i.e., fitness values are either 0.0 or 1.0) reduces the EC to random search. Significantly larger populations (5000) and generations (20000) were also used with no success.

4.3 SA Initialization Then EC

While the EC-based method alone was unable to provide counterexamples to a single requirement incompleteness, it is possible to start with a known optimum and search for similar counterexamples. The SAIEC method results in 200 counterexamples within a population of 200. This result does not mean that there are 200 missing or incomplete requirements, only that this method identified 200 representative counterexamples for each single incomplete requirement. For example, if incomplete requirements decompositions were only found when the brake is depressed more than 50%, then the 200 counterexamples should be in a distribution ranging from being pressed 50% to being pressed 100%. Unlike the EC-only method, providing the EC algorithm with a sample optimum has made it possible to find additional optima resulting in the identification of usable counterexamples from the population.

The SAIEC method is able to find a counterexample for every member of the population for each of the known incomplete requirements (Goals **D.1** and **B.3**). SAIEC is clearly superior to EC alone, as EC alone is unable to identify any counterexamples. SAIEC is also clearly superior to SA, as SA is unable to provide any range or diversity within its counterexamples as SA only identifies a single counterexample.

4.4 Periodic SA with EC Results

The additional number of optimal results provided by initializing the EC-based method with a counterexample found from SA still may leave an intrinsic bias to the original optimal set in the results. When multiple variables must change in order to maintain an optimum, it is more difficult to identify additional optima due to the likelihood of a crossover or mutation maintaining the relationship between those variables. In an effort to identify the largest range of counterexamples, it may be that periodically adding an optimal solution outside of the known solutions would improve the overall range of solutions by overcoming the dependencies between variables. Similar to the SAIEC method, the PSAEC identifies 200 diverse counterexamples within a population of 200.

Similar to SAIEC, the PSAEC method is clearly superior to EC alone for the same reason that PSAEC is able to identify counterexamples while using EC only is not. PSAEC is also superior to SA only, as SA only identifies a single counterexample.

4.5 Comparison

While SA can only be used to identify the existence of a requirement completeness counterexample, additional counterexamples provide more information on the range and scope of the incompleteness. EC-based methods can identify additional counterexamples in parallel, but encounter difficulties satisfying expressions with fitness cliffs or 'needle in a haystack' solutions (i.e., in an EC-only method) or difficulties with identifying additional novel solutions due to correlated variables (i.e., in a SAIEC search method). In fact, in this specific case, the EC-only method was unable to identify results due to the lack of a fitness gradient. In the general case, the greatest range of optimal genotype values is provided by the PSAEC that escapes limitations of the SAIEC search methods. Evidence of this finding can be seen in Figs. 2 and 3 for requirements incompleteness for goals **D.1** and **B.3**, respectively, where the mean range of genotype values in each individual can be seen in box plots.

It is necessary to statistically compare the two methods that identified a range of solutions (i.e., SAIEC and PSAEC), since they are both able to identify the same number of counterexamples. We define the null hypothesis H_0 to state that there is no difference between the range of optimal solutions for the SAIEC and PSAEC methods. We also define an alternative hypothesis, H_1, that states that there is a difference between the range of optimal solutions for SAIEC and PSAEC methods. In both cases, in goals **B.3** and **D.1**, PSAEC achieves statistically significant larger mean range values over 50 executions as measured using the Mann-Whitney U-test ($p < 0.05$ where $p = 2.2 * 10^{-16}$). Therefore we

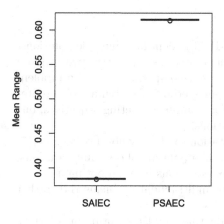
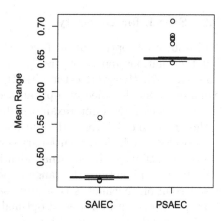

Fig. 2. Requirement **D.1**   **Fig. 3.** Requirement **B.3**

can reject the null hypothesis, H_0, in favor of the alternate hypothesis H_1 due to the statistically significant difference.

5 Related Work

This section covers related work for both requirements completeness and search methods that maintain diversity. While there is a broad collection of research into leveraging search-based techniques for requirements-related tasks, many of which are described in surveys [16,28], to the best of the authors' knowledge, none have explicitly tackled the problem of requirements decomposition incompleteness.

5.1 Requirements Completeness

Outside of process rigor [27], formal guarantees of requirements completeness exist in the form of decomposition strategies that are proven to define complete decomposed requirements [5]. Completeness criteria may be added to formal specification languages, though incomplete requirements may still exist due to criteria that cannot be enforced by language semantics [18]. A method exists to detect incomplete decompositions using symbolic analysis, however only a single counterexample for each incomplete requirement is produced [10].

Ares-EC is unique as it applies symbolic analysis and evolutionary computation to automatically-generated utility functions to detect *sets* of representative completeness counterexamples without restricting decompositions to a finite set of formal patterns.

5.2   Search for Diversity

Multi-objective optimization (e.g., NSGA-II [9]) identifies multiple solutions, but the solutions represent the Pareto front of a tradeoff between two or more objectives [7]. However, if the objectives are not competing, then the problem collapses to single-objective optimization. Our method of searching for requirement completeness counterexamples does not contain competing objectives, but rather a single objective with multiple solutions.

Novelty search uses evolutionary computation to identify novel behaviors [17] across the genotype. Rather than identifying a population of optimum solutions, novelty search identifies the range of possible solutions from an optimum to the worst solution. Niching is typically used for multi-modal problems [11], rather than problems with an area of optimal results.

The search method used by *Ares-EC* identifies multiple optimum solutions in parallel while maximizing diversity of the solutions.

6   Conclusions

In this paper, we have presented *Ares-EC*, a design-time approach for detecting incomplete requirements decomposition using symbolic analysis and evolutionary computation to analyze hierarchical requirements models. Unlike previous incomplete requirements detection methods, *Ares-EC* detects representative sets of incomplete requirements decompositions while not limiting the allowable decomposition strategies.

We demonstrate *Ares-EC* on an adaptive cruise control system developed in collaboration with our automotive industrial collaborators. We show that *Ares-EC* is able to automatically detect incomplete requirements decompositions and provide sets of completeness counterexamples in seconds. Further, by combining symbolic analysis with evolutionary computation we achieve the benefits of both techniques.

Future research directions will further expand the scope of *Ares-EC* analysis, including additional case studies. For example, we will explore the use of RELAXed goals [25] whose utility functions are evaluated according to fuzzy logic expressions or applying other transformations to introduce a gradient to requirements satisfaction in support of search. In addition, we will investigate applying *Ares-EC* to other hierarchical requirement frameworks (e.g., i^*) to further demonstrate *Ares-EC*'s applicability to generalized hierarchical requirement model analysis.

References

1. Alrajeh, D., Kramer, J., van Lamsweerde, A., Russo, A., Uchitel, S.: Generating obstacle conditions for requirements completeness. In: Proceedings of the 34th International Conference on Software Engineering, pp. 705–715 (2012)
2. Cheng, B.H.C., Atlee, J.M.: Research directions in requirements engineering. In: ICSE 2007 Future of Software Engineering, pp. 285–303 (2007)

3. Cheng, B.H.C., Sawyer, P., Bencomo, N., Whittle, J.: A goal-based modeling approach to develop requirements of an adaptive system with environmental uncertainty. In: Schürr, A., Selic, B. (eds.) MODELS 2009. LNCS, vol. 5795, pp. 468–483. Springer, Heidelberg (2009). doi:10.1007/978-3-642-04425-0_36

4. Cormen, T.H.: Introduction to Algorithms. MIT press, Cambridge (2009)

5. Darimont, R., Van Lamsweerde, A.: Formal refinement patterns for goal-driven requirements elaboration. ACM SIGSOFT Softw. Eng. Notes 21, 179–190 (1996)

6. de Moura, L., Bjørner, N.: Z3: an efficient SMT solver. In: Ramakrishnan, C.R., Rehof, J. (eds.) TACAS 2008. LNCS, vol. 4963, pp. 337–340. Springer, Heidelberg (2008). doi:10.1007/978-3-540-78800-3_24

7. Deb, K.: Multi-objective Optimization Using Evolutionary Algorithms. Wiley, New York (2005)

8. Deb, K., Agrawal, R.B.: Simulated binary crossover for continuous search space. Complex Syst. 9(3), 1–15 (1994)

9. Deb, K., Pratap, A., Agarwal, S., Meyarivan, T.: A fast and elitist multiobjective genetic algorithm: NSGA-II. IEEE Trans. Evol. Comput. 6(2), 182–197 (2002)

10. DeVries, B., Cheng, B.H.C.: Automatic detection of incomplete requirements via symbolic analysis. In: 19th International Conference on Model Driven Engineering Languages and Systems (MODELS 2016), Proceedings, Saint-Malo, France, October 2–7, pp. 385–395 (2016)

11. Eiben, A.E., Smith, J.E., et al.: Introduction to Evolutionary Computing, vol. 53. Springer, Heidelberg (2003). doi:10.1007/978-3-662-05094-1

12. Feather, M.S., Fickas, S., Van Lamsweerde, A., Ponsard, C.: Reconciling system requirements and runtime behavior. In: Proceedings of the 9th International Workshop on Software Specification and Design, p. 50 (1998)

13. Ferrari, A., dell'Orletta, F., Spagnolo, G.O., Gnesi, S.: Measuring and improving the completeness of natural language requirements. In: Salinesi, C., Weerd, I. (eds.) REFSQ 2014. LNCS, vol. 8396, pp. 23–38. Springer, Cham (2014). doi:10.1007/978-3-319-05843-6_3

14. Fickas, S., Feather, M.S.: Requirements monitoring in dynamic environments. In: Proceedings of the Second IEEE International Symposium on Requirements Engineering, pp. 140–147 (1995)

15. Garlan, D., Cheng, S.W., Huang, A.C., Schmerl, B., Steenkiste, P.: Rainbow: architecture-based self-adaptation with reusable infrastructure. Computer 37(10), 46–54 (2004)

16. Harman, M., Mansouri, S.A., Zhang, Y.: Search-based software engineering: trends, techniques and applications. ACM Comput. Surv. (CSUR) 45(1), 11 (2012)

17. Lehman, J., Stanley, K.O.: Abandoning objectives: evolution through the search for novelty alone. Evol. Comput. 19(2), 189–223 (2011)

18. Leveson, N.: Completeness in formal specification language design for process-control systems. In: Proceedings of the Third Workshop on Formal Methods in Software Practice, pp. 75–87 (2000)

19. Menzel, I., Mueller, M., Gross, A., Doerr, J.: An experimental comparison regarding the completeness of functional requirements specifications. In: 2010 18th IEEE International Requirements Engineering Conference (RE), pp. 15–24 (2010)

20. Ramirez, A.J., Cheng, B.H.C.: Automatic derivation of utility functions for monitoring software requirements. In: Whittle, J., Clark, T., Kühne, T. (eds.) MODELS 2011. LNCS, vol. 6981, pp. 501–516. Springer, Heidelberg (2011). doi:10.1007/978-3-642-24485-8_37

21. Souyris, J., Wiels, V., Delmas, D., Delseny, H.: Formal verification of avionics software products. In: Cavalcanti, A., Dams, D.R. (eds.) FM 2009. LNCS, vol. 5850, pp. 532–546. Springer, Heidelberg (2009). doi:10.1007/978-3-642-05089-3_34
22. Van Lamsweerde, A., et al.: Requirements Engineering: From System Goals to UML Models to Software Specifications. Wiley, Chichester (2009)
23. Walsh, W.E., Tesauro, G., Kephart, J.O., Das, R.: Utility functions in autonomic systems. In: International Conference on Autonomic Computing, Proceedings, pp. 70–77 (2004)
24. Whittle, J., Sawyer, P., Bencomo, N., Cheng, B.H.C.: A language for self-adaptive system requirements. In: International Workshop on Service-Oriented Computing: Consequences for Engineering Requirements (SOCCER 2008), pp. 24–29 (2008)
25. Whittle, J., Sawyer, P., Bencomo, N., Cheng, B.H.C, Bruel, J.M.: Relax: incorporating uncertainty into the specification of self-adaptive systems. In: 17th IEEE International Requirements Engineering Conference (RE 2009), pp. 79–88 (2009)
26. Yu, E.S.: Towards modelling and reasoning support for early-phase requirements engineering. In: Proceedings of the Third IEEE International Symposium on Requirements Engineering, pp. 226–235 (1997)
27. Zenun, M.M., Loureiro, G.: A framework for dependability and completeness in requirements engineering. In: Latin American Symposium on Dependable Computing, pp. 1–4 (2013)
28. Zhang, Y., Finkelstein, A., Harman, M.: Search based requirements optimisation: existing work and challenges. In: International Working Conference on Requirements Engineering: Foundation for Software Quality, pp. 88–94 (2008)

Generating Effective Test Suites
by Combining Coverage Criteria

Gregory Gay[✉]

University of South Carolina, Columbia, SC, USA
greg@greggay.com

Abstract. A number of criteria have been proposed to judge test suite adequacy. While search-based test generation has improved greatly at criteria coverage, the produced suites are still often ineffective at detecting faults. Efficacy may be limited by the single-minded application of one criterion at a time when generating suites—a sharp contrast to human testers, who simultaneously explore multiple testing strategies. We hypothesize that automated generation can be improved by selecting and simultaneously exploring multiple criteria.

To address this hypothesis, we have generated multi-criteria test suites, measuring efficacy against the Defects4J fault database. We have found that multi-criteria suites can be up to 31.15% more effective at detecting complex, real-world faults than suites generated to satisfy a single criterion and 70.17% more effective than the default combination of all eight criteria. Given a fixed search budget, we recommend pairing a criterion focused on structural exploration—such as Branch Coverage—with targeted supplemental strategies aimed at the type of faults expected from the system under test. Our findings offer lessons to consider when selecting such combinations.

Keywords: Search-based test generation · Automated test generation · Adequacy criteria · Search-based software engineering

1 Introduction

With the exponential growth in the complexity of software, the cost of testing has risen accordingly. One way to lower costs without sacrificing quality may lie in automating the generation of test input [1]. Consider search-based generation—given a testing goal, and a scoring function denoting *closeness to attainment of that goal*, optimization algorithms can search for input that achieves that goal [12].

As we cannot know what faults exist a priori, dozens of criteria—ranging from the measurement of structural coverage to the detection of synthetic faults [14]—have been proposed to judge testing *adequacy*. In theory, if such criteria are fulfilled, tests should be *adequate* at detecting faults. Adequacy criteria are important for search-based generation, as they can guide the search [12].

© Springer International Publishing AG 2017
T. Menzies and J. Petke (Eds.): SSBSE 2017, LNCS 10452, pp. 65–82, 2017.
DOI: 10.1007/978-3-319-66299-2_5

Search techniques have improved greatly in terms of achieved coverage [2]. However, the primary goal of testing is not coverage, but fault detection. In this regard, automated generation often does not produce human competitive results [2,3,5,15]. If automation is to impact testing practice, it must match—or, ideally, outperform—manual testing in terms of fault-detection efficacy.

The current use of adequacy criteria in automated generation sharply contrasts how such criteria are used by humans. For a human, coverage typically serves an advisory role—as a way to point out gaps in existing efforts. Human testers build suites in which adequacy criteria contribute to a *multifaceted* combination of testing strategies. Previous research has found that effectiveness of a criterion can depend on factors such as how expressions are written [4] and the types of faults that appear in the system [6]. Humans understand such concepts. They build and vary their testing strategy based on the needs of their current target. Yet, in automated generation, coverage is typically *the* goal, and a single criterion is applied at a time.

However, search-based techniques need not be restricted to one criterion at a time. The test obligations of multiple criteria can be combined into a single score or simultaneously satisfied by multi-objective optimization algorithms. We hypothesize that the efficacy of automated generation can be improved by applying a targeted, multifaceted approach—where multiple testing strategies are selected and simultaneously explored.

In order to examine the efficacy of suites generated by combining criteria, we have used EvoSuite and eight coverage criteria to generate multi-criteria test suites—as suggested by three selection strategies—with efficacy judged against the Defects4J fault database [10]. Based on experimental observations, we added additional configurations centered around the use of two criteria, Exception and Method Coverage, that performed poorly on their own, but were effective in combination with other criteria.

By examining the proportion of suites that detect each fault for each configuration, we can examine the effect of combining coverage criteria on the efficacy of search-based test generation, identify the configurations that are more effective than single-criterion generation, and explore situations where particular adequacy criteria can effectively cooperate to detect faults. To summarize our findings:

- For all systems, at least one combination is more effective than a single criterion, offering efficacy improvements of 14.84–31.15% over the best single criterion.
- The most effective combinations pair a structure-focused criterion—such as Branch Coverage—with supplemental strategies targeted at the class under test.
  - Across the board, effective combinations include Exception Coverage. As it can be added to a configuration with minimal effect on generation complexity, we recommend it as part of any generation strategy.
  - Method Coverage can offer an additional low-cost efficacy boost.

- Additional targeted criteria—such as Output Coverage for code that manipulates numeric values or Weak Mutation Coverage for code with complex logical expressions—offer further efficacy improvements.

Our findings offer lessons to consider when selecting such combinations, and a starting point in discovering the best combination for a given system.

2 Background

As we cannot know what faults exist without verification, and as testing cannot—except in simple cases—conclusively prove the absence of faults, a suitable approximation must be used to measure the adequacy of testing efforts. Common methods of measuring adequacy involve coverage of structural elements of the software, such as individual statements, points where control can branch, and complex boolean expressions [7].

The idea of measuring adequacy through coverage is simple, but compelling: unless code is executed, many faults are unlikely to be found. If tests execute elements in the manner prescribed by the criterion, than testing is deemed "adequate" with respect to faults that manifest through such structures. Adequacy criteria have seen widespread use in software development, as they offer clear checklists of testing goals that can be objectively evaluated and automatically measured [7]. Importantly, they offer *stopping criteria*, advising on when testing can conclude. These very same qualities make adequacy criteria ideal for use as automated test generation targets.

Of the thousands of test cases that could be generated for any SUT, we want to select—systematically and at a reasonable cost—those that meet our goals [12]. Given scoring functions denoting *closeness to the attainment of those goals*—called *fitness functions*—optimization algorithms can sample from a large and complex set of options as guided by a chosen strategy (the *metaheuristic*). Metaheuristics are often inspired by natural phenomena. For example, genetic algorithms evolve a group of candidate solutions by filtering out bad "genes" and promoting fit solutions [2].

Due to the non-linear nature of software, resulting from branching control structures, the search space of a real-world program is large and complex. Metaheuristic search—by strategically sampling from that space—can scale effectively to large problems. Such approaches have been applied to a wide variety of testing scenarios [1].

While adequacy has been used in almost all generation methods, it is particularly relevant to metaheuristic search-based generation. In search-based generation, the fitness function must capture the testing objective and provide feedback to guide the search. Through this guidance, the fitness function has a major impact on the quality of the solutions generated. Adequacy criteria are common optimization targets for automated test case generation, as they can be straightforwardly transformed into distance functions that lead to the search to better solutions [12].

3   Study

We hypothesize that the efficacy of automated generation can be improved by selecting and simultaneously exploring a combination of testing strategies. In particular—in this project—we are focused on combinations of common adequacy criteria.

Rojas et al. previously found that multiple fitness functions could be combined with minimal loss in coverage of any single criterion and with a reasonable increase in test suite size [14]. Indeed, recent versions of the EvoSuite framework[1] now, by default, combine eight coverage criteria when generating tests. However, their work did not assess the effect of combining criteria on the fault-detection efficacy of the generated suites. We intend to focus on the performance of suites generated using a combination of criteria. In particular, we wish to address the following research questions:

1. Do test suites generated using a combination of two or more coverage criteria have a higher likelihood of fault detection than suites generated using a single criterion?
2. For each system, and across all systems, which combinations are most effective?
3. What effect does an increased search budget have on the studied combinations?
4. Which criteria best pair together to increase the likelihood of fault detection?

The first two questions establish a basic understanding of the effectiveness of criteria combinations—given fixed search budgets, are *any* of the combinations more effective at fault detection than suites generated to satisfy a single criterion? Further, we hypothesize that the most effective combination will vary across systems. We wish to understand the degree to which results differ across the studied systems, and whether the search budget plays a strong role in determining the resulting efficacy of a combination. In each of these cases, we would also like to better understand *why* and *when* particular combinations are effective.

In order to examine the efficacy of suites generated using such combinations, we have first applied EvoSuite and eight coverage criteria to generate test suites for the systems in the Defects4J fault database [10]. We have performed the following:

1. **Collected Case Examples:** We have used 353 real faults, from five Java projects, as test generation targets (Sect. 3.1).
2. **Generated Test Cases:** For each fault, we generated 10 suites per criterion using the fixed version of each class-under-test (CUT). We use both a two-minute and a ten-minute search budget per CUT (Sect. 3.2).
3. **Removed Non-Compiling and Flaky Tests:** Any tests that do not compile, or that return inconsistent results, are automatically removed (Sect. 3.2).
4. **Assessed Fault-finding Effectiveness:** For each fault, we measure the proportion of test suites that detect the fault to the number generated.

---

[1] Available from http://evosuite.org.

Following single-criterion generation, we applied three different selection strategies to build sets of multi-criteria configurations for each system (described in Sect. 3.3). We generated suites, following the steps above, using each of the configurations suggested by these strategies, as well as EvoSuite's default eight-criteria configuration. Based on our initial observations, we added additional configurations centered around two criteria—Exception and Method Coverage—that performed poorly on their own, but were effective in combination with other criteria (See Sect. 4).

3.1   Case Examples

Defects4J is an extensible database of real faults extracted from Java projects [10][2]. Currently, it consists of 357 faults from five projects: JFreeChart (26 faults), Closure compiler (133 faults), Apache Commons Lang (65 faults), Apache Commons Math (106 faults), and JodaTime (27 faults). Four faults from the Math project were omitted due to complications encountered during suite generation, leaving 353.

3.2   Test Suite Generation

EvoSuite uses a genetic algorithm to evolve test suites over a series of generations, forming a new population by retaining, mutating, and combining the strongest solutions. It is actively maintained and has been successfully applied to a variety of projects [15]. We used the following fitness functions, corresponding to common coverage criteria[3]:

Branch Coverage (BC): A test suite satisfies BC if all control-flow branches are taken by at least one test case—the test suite contains at least one test whose execution evaluates the branch predicate to `true`, and at least one whose execution evaluates to `false`. To guide the search, the fitness function calculates the *branch distance* from the point where the execution path diverged from the targeted branch. If an undesired branch is taken, the function describes how "close" the targeted predicate is to being true, using a cost function based on the predicate formula [14].

Direct Branch Coverage (DBC): Branch Coverage may be attained by calling a method *directly*, or *indirectly*—calling a method within another method. DBC requires each branch to be covered through a direct call.

Line Coverage (LC): A test suite satisfies LC if it executes each non-comment line of code at least once. To cover each line, EvoSuite tries to ensure that each basic code block is reached. The branch distance is computed for each branch that is a control dependency of any of the statements in the CUT. For

---

[2] Available from http://defects4j.org.
[3] Rojas et al. provide a primer on each fitness function [14].

each conditional statement that is a control dependency for some other line, EvoSuite requires that the branch of the statement leading to the dependent code is executed.

Exception Coverage (EC): EC rewards test suites that force the CUT to throw more exceptions—either declared or undeclared. As the number of possible exceptions that a class can throw cannot be known ahead of time, the fitness function rewards suites that throw the largest observed number of exceptions.

Method Coverage (MC): MC simply requires that all methods in the CUT be executed at least once, either directly or indirectly.

Method Coverage (Top-Level, No Exception) (MNEC): Test suites sometimes achieve MC while calling methods in an invalid state or with invalid parameters. MNEC requires that all methods be called directly and terminate without throwing an exception.

Output Coverage (OC): OC rewards diversity in method output by mapping return types to abstract values. A test suite satisfies OC if, for each public method, at least one test yields a concrete value characterized by each abstract value. For numeric data types, distance functions guide the search by comparing concrete and abstract values.

Weak Mutation Coverage (WMC): Suites that detect more mutants may be effective at detecting real faults as well. A test suite satisfies WMC if, for each mutated statement, at least one test detects the mutation. The search is guided by the *infection distance*, a variant of branch distance tuned towards detecting mutated statements.

To generate for multiple criteria, EvoSuite calculates the fitness score as a linear combination of the objectives for all of the criteria [14]. No ordering is imposed on the criteria when generating—combinations such as BC-LC and LC-BC are equivalent.

Test suites are generated for each class reported as faulty, using the fixed version of the CUT. They are applied to the faulty version in order to eliminate the oracle problem. This translates to a regression testing scenario, where tests guard against future issues.

Two search budgets were used—two minutes and ten minutes per class–allowing us to examine the effect of increasing the search budget. To control experiment cost, we deactivated assertion filtering—all possible regression assertions are included. All other settings were kept at their default values. As results may vary, we performed 10 trials for each fault and search budget, generating an initial pool of 56,480 test suites.

Generation tools may generate flaky (unstable) tests [15]. For example, a test case that makes assertions about the system time will only pass during generation. We automatically remove flaky tests. First, non-compiling test cases are removed. Then, each test is executed on the fixed CUT five times. If results are inconsistent, the test case is removed. On average, less than one percent of the tests are removed from each suite.

3.3   Selecting Criteria Combinations

Overall, suites generated to satisfy a single criterion detect 180 (50.99%) of the 353 studied faults. The average likelihood of fault detection is listed for each single criterion, by system and budget, in Table 1.

Table 1. Average likelihood of fault detection for single-criterion generation, divided by budget and system.

	Budget	Chart	Closure	Lang	Math	Time	Overall
BC	120	45.00%	4.66%	34.00%	27.94%	34.82%	22.07%
	600	48.46%	5.79%	40.15%	32.75%	39.26%	25.61%
DBC	120	34.23%	5.11%	30.00%	24.51%	31.11%	19.43%
	600	40.77%	6.09%	38.77%	28.63%	40.37%	23.80%
EC	120	22.31%	1.35%	7.54%	6.37%	9.26%	6.09%
	600	21.54%	0.98%	9.23%	7.06%	9.63%	6.43%
LC	120	38.85%	4.14%	31.23%	25.78%	30.00%	19.92%
	600	46.15%	4.81%	34.31%	29.22%	36.67%	22.78%
MC	120	30.77%	1.58%	7.54%	10.98%	8.15%	8.05%
	600	30.77%	2.26%	7.69%	10.88%	8.15%	8.30%
MNEC	120	23.46%	2.18%	6.62%	12.16%	6.67%	7.79%
	600	30.77%	1.88%	7.54%	12.06%	5.19%	8.24%
OC	120	21.15%	2.03%	7.85%	16.57%	9.63%	9.29%
	600	23.85%	2.56%	10.92%	16.76%	12.22%	10.51%
WMC	120	38.08%	4.44%	24.15%	23.04%	25.19%	17.51%
	600	46.15%	5.56%	32.15%	27.45%	27.04%	21.42%

BC is the most effective single criterion, detecting 158 of the 353 faults. BC suites have an average likelihood of fault detection of 22.07% given a two-minute search budget and 25.61% given a ten-minute budget. Line and Direct Branch Coverage follow with a 19.92–22.78% and 19.43–23.80% likelihood of detection. DBC and WMC benefit the most from an increased search budget, with average improvements of 22.45% and 22.33%. Criteria with distance-driven fitness functions—BC, DBC, LC, WMC, and, partially, OC—improve the most given more time.

We seek to identify whether combinations of criteria can outperform the top single criterion for each system—either BC or DBC. Studying all possible combinations is infeasible—even restricting to combinations of four criteria would result in 1,680 configurations. To control experiment cost, we have employed three strategies to suggest combinations. We have also used Evosuite's default configuration of all eight criteria. We perform selection using each strategy for each system and search budget, then build combinations using the entire pool of faults in order to suggest general combinations. The suggested combinations are then used to generate suites. All combinations are applied ten times per search budget. To converse space, we do not list all combinations. However, the top combinations are named and discussed in Sect. 4. The three selection strategies include:

"Top-Ranked" Strategy: This simple strategy build combinations by selecting the top two to four coverage criteria, as seen in Table 1, and combining them.

"Boost" Strategy: This strategy aims to select secondary criteria that "back up" a central criterion—the criterion that performed best on its own—in situations where that central criterion performs poorly. To select the additional criteria, the pool of faults is filtered for examples where that central criterion had <=30% likelihood of fault detection. Then, two to four top-ranked criteria from that filtered pool are selected for the combination. Criteria are only selected if they are more effective than the central criterion post-filtering.

"Unique Faults" Strategy: This greedy strategy favors the criteria that detect the highest number of unique faults. Combinations of criteria are selected by choosing the criterion that produced suites that detected the most faults, removing those faults from consideration, and choosing from the remaining faults and criteria. Ties are broken at random. Selection stops once four criteria are chosen, or if no faults remain.

Together, these three strategies (and EvoSuite's default) yielded 12 combinations for Chart, 12 for Closure, 17 for Lang, 14 for Math, and 11 for Time—resulting in the generation of 94,760 test suites.

4   Results and Discussion

Tables 2 and 3 show—for each system, and across all systems—the combinations that are more effective than the top single criterion for the two-minute and ten-minute search budgets. We also list the performance of EvoSuite's default combination of eight criteria. Combinations outperformed by the top criterion, except for the default, are omitted. For the overall results, only combinations generated for all systems are considered. The abbreviations for each criterion are listed in Sect. 3.2. For each combination, we note the strategies that suggested the combination and the average efficacy. In Table 3, we also note the improvement from the increased budget.

For all systems and both budgets, at least one combination outperforms the top single criterion. This validates our core hypothesis—the likelihood of fault detection can be increased by combining criteria. As can be seen in Tables 2 and 3, EvoSuite's default combination of all eight criteria rarely manages to outperform the top single criterion. As the number of criteria expands, the difficulty of the search process also grows. While criteria can work together to produce more effective suites, there is a point where the generation task becomes too difficult to achieve within the selected budget. Our observations, instead, point towards the wisdom of choosing a *targeted* set of criteria for the CUT.

We proposed three strategies to suggest combinations—the Top-Ranked, Boosting, and Unique Faults strategies. Examining the results of this experiment, the Unique Faults strategy seems to produce the best overall results, suggesting nine of the top strategies for the two-minute budget and 24 for the ten-minute budget. The Boosting strategy suggests only three for the two-minute budget and 17 for the ten-minute budget, and the Top Ranked strategy suggests seven for the two-minute budget and 14 for the ten-minute budget.

However, while these strategies have yielded effective combinations, we cannot recommend any of them as a general-purpose strategy for testing new systems. Each also suggested a large number of ineffective combinations. With a two-minute budget, only 28% of the Top Ranked strategy combinations were effective. For the Boosting strategy, the total was only 8%, and for the Unique Faults strategy, the total was only 19%. With a ten-minute budget, 56% of the combinations for the Top Ranked strategy were effective. For the Boosting strategy, this was 45%, and for the Unique Faults strategy, the total was 50%.

Table 2. Efficacy (average likelihood of fault detection) for the initial set of combinations, when generated with a two-minute search budget. TR = Top-Ranked Strategy, BS = Boosting Strategy, UF = Unique Faults Strategy.

System	Combination	Strategy	Efficacy
Chart	Default	–	47.30%
	BC	–	45.00%
Closure	BC-LC	TR, UF	6.00%
	DBC	–	5.10%
	Default	–	4.50%
Lang	BC-EC-LC-MC	UF	40.00%
	BC-EC	UF	39.40%
	BC-LC	TR, BS, UF	36.50%
	BC-EC-LC	UF	35.70%
	BC-DBC	TR, BS, UF	35.50%
	BC-LC-DBC	TR, BS	34.00%
	BC	–	34.00%
	Default	–	23.80%
Math	BC-LC-OC-EC	UF	32.40%
	BC-LC	TR, UF	31.90%
	BC	–	27.90%
	Default	–	25.80%
Time	DBC-BC-LC	TR, BS	35.20%
	BC	–	34.80%
	Default	–	25.90%
Overall	BC-LC	TR, UF	24.00%
	BC	–	22.10%
	Default	–	19.00%

Table 3. Efficacy for the initial set of combinations (ten-minute search budget).

System	Combination	Strategy	Efficacy	Improvement From Budget
Chart	BC-LC-WMC-EC	UF	57.30%	35.46%
	BC-EC-DBC	BS	55.80%	28.28%
	BC-EC	BS	54.60%	23.53%
	BC-DBC-WMC-OC	UF	49.20%	54.23%
	BC-LC-WMC	TR, UF	48.90%	49.71%
	BC-WMC-MC	BS	48.90%	27.01%
	BC-WMC	BS, UF	48.80%	39.43%
	BC	–	48.50%	7.78%
	Default	–	48.10%	1.69%
Closure	BC-LC	TR, UF	7.6%	26.67%
	BC-LC-DBC	TR	7.30%	48.98%
	BC-LC-WMC-EC	UF	7.20%	94.59%
	BC-DBC	TR, BS, UF	7.10%	51.05%
	Default	–	7.10%	57.78%
	BC-WMC-DBC-LC	TR, BS	7.00%	42.86%
	DBC-WMC	BS, UF	6.80%	61.90%
	BC-WMC	BS	6.50%	54.76%
	DBC-WMC-BC	TR, BS, UF	6.40%	60.00%
	DBC	–	6.10%	19.61%
Lang	BC-EC	UF	47.50%	20.56%
	BC-EC-LC-MC	UF	45.70%	14.25%
	BC-EC-LC	UF	45.70%	28.00%
	BC-LC-DBC	TR, BS	42.30%	24.41%
	BC-LC-WMC-EC	UF	41.70%	44.79%
	BC-DBC	TR, BS, UF	41.10%	12.60%
	BC-LC	TR, BS, UF	40.90%	12.05%
	BC	–	40.20%	18.24%
	Default	–	32.60%	36.97%
Math	BC-LC-OC-EC	UF	38.00%	17.28%
	BC-OC-LC	BS, UF	35.80%	31.62%
	BC-OC	BS	34.70%	24.82%
	BC-OC-LC-WMC	BS, UF	33.70%	22.99%
	BC-LC	TR, UF	31.90%	3.76%
	BC-LC-WMC-EC	UF	33.00%	21.32%
	BC	–	32.80%	17.56%
	Default	–	32.80%	27.13%
Time	DBC-BC	TR, BS, UF	43.30%	39.22%
	DBC-BC-LC	TR, BS	41.50%	17.90%
	DBC	–	40.40%	29.90%
	Default	–	33.33%	28.68%
Overall	BC-LC-WMC-EC	UF	26.90%	33.83%
	BC-LC	TR, UF	26.40%	10.00%
	BC-DBC	TR, BS, UF	25.80%	20.00%
	BC-LC-DBC	TR	25.60%	28.00%
	BC	–	25.60%	15.84%
	Default	–	24.20%	27.39%

Therefore, while the basic hypothesis—that combinations *can* outperform a single criterion—seems to be valid, more research is needed in how to determine the best combination.

Table 4. Efficacy of Exception Coverage-based combinations (two-minute budget). The top combination from Table 2, top single criterion, and EvoSuite's default combination are shown for context. A * means that the combination was also suggested by a previous strategy.

System	Combination	Efficacy
Chart	*Default*	47.30%
	BC	45.00%
Closure	BC-LC	6.00%
	BC-LC-EC	5.70%
	DBC-EC	5.10%
	DBC	5.10%
	Default	4.50%
Lang	BC-EC-LC-MC	40.00%
	BC-EC*	39.40%
	BC-LC-EC*	35.70%
	BC	34.00%
	Default	23.80%
Math	BC-LC-OC-EC	32.40%
	BC-EC	31.70%
	BC	27.90%
	Default	25.80%
Time	BC-EC	39.60%
	DBC-BC-LC-EC	39.30%
	DBC-EC	37.80%
	DBC-BC-LC	35.20%
	BC	34.80%
	Default	25.90%
Overall	BC-EC	24.50%
	BC-LC	24.00%
	BC-LC-EC	22.40%
	BC	22.10%
	Default	19.00%

Table 5. Efficacy of EC-based combinations (ten-minute budget). The top combination from Table 3, top single criterion, and EvoSuite's default combination are shown for context.

System	Combination	Efficacy	Improvement From Budget
Chart	*BC-LC-WMC-EC*	57.30%	35.46%
	BC-EC*	54.60%	23.53%
	BC-LC-EC	50.40%	14.81%
	BC	48.50%	7.78%
	Default	48.10%	1.69%
Closure	*BC-LC*	7.6%	26.67%
	BC-LC-EC	7.40%	29.82%
	BC-EC	7.10%	47.92%
	Default	7.10%	57.78%
	DBC	6.10%	19.61%
Lang	BC-EC*	47.50%	20.56%
	BC-LC-EC*	45.70%	28.00%
	BC	40.20%	18.24%
	Default	32.60%	36.97%
Math	*BC-LC-OC-EC*	38.00%	17.28%
	BC-EC	34.00%	7.25%
	BC	32.80%	17.56%
	Default	32.80%	27.13%
Time	BC-EC	44.80%	13.13%
	DBC-BC-EC	44.10%	38.25%
	DBC-BC	43.30%	39.22%
	DBC-BC-LC-EC	42.60%	8.40%
	BC-LC-EC	41.10%	18.10%
	DBC-EC	41.10%	8.73%
	DBC	40.40%	29.90%
	Default	33.33%	28.68%
Overall	BC-EC	28.70%	17.14%
	BC-LC-EC	27.50%	22.77%
	BC-LC-WMC-EC	26.90%	33.83%
	BC	25.60%	15.84%
	Default	24.20%	27.39%

4.1 Additional Configurations

Following test generation, we noticed that (a) Exception Coverage was frequently selected as part of combinations, despite performing poorly on its own, and (2), that these combinations are often highly effective. For example, the top combinations for Chart, Lang, and Math in Tables 2 and 3 all contain EC. Of the studied criteria, EC is unique in that it does not prescribe static test obligations. Rather, it simply rewards suites that cause more exceptions to be thrown. This means that it can be added to a combination with little increase in search complexity.

To further study the potential of EC as a "low-cost" addition to combinations, we added a set of additional combinations to our study. Specifically, we generated tests for all systems using the BC-EC and BC-LC-EC combinations—the combination of EC with the overall best single criterion, and the combination of

EC with the best overall combination seen to this point. As DBC outperformed BC for the Closure and Time systems, we also generated tests for the DBC-EC combination in those two cases. Finally, as the top-ranked combination Time lacked EC, we added the DBC-BC-LC-EC and DBC-BC-EC combinations for that system. In total, this adds one new configuration for Chart, three for Closure, zero for Lang, two for Math, and five for Time—resulting in the generation of an additional 15,280 test suites.

Results can be seen in Tables 4 and 5 for the two budgets. From these results, we can see that—almost universally—the best observed combination of criteria includes Exception Coverage. In fact, the best overall configuration—up to this point—is a simple combination of BC and EC. The simplicity of EC explains its poor performance as the *primary* criterion. It lacks a feedback mechanism to drive generation towards exceptions. However, EC appears to be effective *when paired with criteria that effectively explore the structure of the CUT*, such as Branch or Line Coverage. Exception Coverage adds little cost in terms of generation difficulty, and almost universally outperforms the use of Branch Coverage alone.

An example of effective combination can be seen in fault 60 for Lang[4]—a case where two methods can look beyond the end of a string. No single criterion is effective, with a maximum of 10% chance of detection given a two-minute budget and 20% with a ten-minute budget. However, combining BC and EC boosts the likelihood of detection to 40% and 90% for the two budgets. In this case, if the fault is triggered, the incorrect string access will cause an exception to be thrown. However, this only occurs under particular circumstances. Therefore, EC alone never detects the fault. BC provides the necessary means to drive program execution to the correct location. However, two suites with an equal coverage score are considered equal. BC alone may prioritize suites with slightly higher (or different) coverage, missing the fault. By combining the two, exception-throwing tests are prioritized and retained, succeeding where either criterion would fail alone.

Given that EC can boost the likelihood of fault detection without a substantial cost increase, it seems reasonable to look for other "low-cost" criteria that could provide a similar effect. The two forms of Method Coverage used in this project are ideal candidates. In general, a class will not have a large number of methods, and methods are either covered or not covered. Additionally, MC also appears in some of the top combinations—such as those for Lang—despite poor performance on its own.

Therefore, we have also generated tests for the BC-EC-MC, BC-LC-MC, and BC-EC-LC-MC combinations for all systems. We have also added MC to the top combination for any system that did not already have one of the above as the resulting combination, adding BC-LC-WMC-EC-MC for Chart and BC-LC-OC-EC-MC for Math. In total, this adds four new combinations for Chart, three for Closure, two for Lang, four for Math, and three for Time—yielding 22,400 additional test suites.

---

[4] https://github.com/apache/commons-lang/commit/
a8203b65261110c4a30ff69fe0da7a2390d82757.

Table 6. Efficacy of Method Coverage-based combinations (two-minute budget). The top combinations from Tables 2 and 4, top single criterion, and EvoSuite's default combination are are shown for context. A * means that the combination was also suggested by a previous strategy.

System	Combination	Efficacy
Chart	*Default*	47.30%
	BC	45.00%
Closure	*BC-LC*	6.00%
	BC-LC-EC	5.70%
	BC-EC-MC	5.60%
	BC-LC-MC	5.30%
	DBC	5.10%
	Default	4.50%
Lang	BC-EC-MC	40.50%
	BC-EC-LC-MC*	40.00%
	BC-EC	39.40%
	BC-LC-MC	38.00%
	BC	34.00%
	Default	23.80%
Math	BC-LC-OC-EC-MC	32.90%
	BC-LC-OC-EC	32.40%
	BC-EC	31.70%
	BC-EC-MC	30.40%
	BC-EC-LC-MC	30.20%
	BC	27.90%
	Default	25.80%
Time	*BC-EC*	39.60%
	BC-EC-MC	35.90%
	DBC-BC-LC	35.20%
	BC	34.80%
	Default	25.90%
Overall	*BC-EC*	24.50%
	BC-EC-MC	24.30%
	BC-LC	24.00%
	BC-EC-LC-MC	23.60%
	BC-LC-MC	22.20%
	BC	22.10%
	Default	19.00%

Table 7. Efficacy of MC-based combinations (ten-minute budget). Top combinations from Tables 3 and 5, top single criterion, and EvoSuite's default combination are shown for context.

System	Combination	Efficacy	Improvement From Budget
Chart	*BC-LC-WMC-EC*	57.30%	35.46%
	BC-EC	54.60%	23.53%
	BC-EC-MC	53.90%	25.06%
	BC-LC-EMC-EC-MC	53.50%	19.96%
	BC	48.50%	7.78%
	Default	48.10%	1.69%
Closure	BC-EC-MC	8.00%	42.86%
	BC-EC-LC-MC	7.70%	54.00%
	BC-LC	7.6%	26.67%
	BC-LC-EC	7.40%	29.82%
	Default	7.10%	57.78%
	DBC	6.10%	19.61%
Lang	BC-EC-MC	48.20%	19.01%
	BC-EC	47.50%	20.56%
	BC-EC-LC-MC*	45.70%	14.25%
	BC-LC-MC	43.70%	15.00%
	BC	40.20%	18.24%
	Default	32.60%	36.97%
Math	BC-LC-OC-EC-MC	39.00%	18.54%
	BC-LC-OC-EC	38.00%	17.28%
	BC-EC-MC	34.30%	12.83%
	BC-EC-LC-MC	34.10%	12.91%
	BC-EC	34.00%	7.25%
	BC	32.80%	17.56%
	Default	32.80%	27.13%
Time	BC-EC-MC	47.00%	30.92%
	BC-EC	44.80%	13.13%
	DBC-BC	43.30%	39.22%
	BC-EC-LC-MC	41.10%	18.10%
	DBC	40.40%	29.90%
	Default	33.33%	28.68%
Overall	BC-EC-MC	29.40%	20.99%
	BC-EC	28.70%	17.14%
	BC-EC-LC-MC	27.80%	17.80%
	BC-LC-WMC-EC	26.90%	33.83%
	BC-LC-MC	25.60%	15.31%
	BC	25.60%	15.84%
	Default	24.20%	27.39%

The results of these combinations can be seen in Tables 6 and 7. With a two-minute budget, the addition of Method Coverage can improve results—as seen in Lang, where BC-EC-MC outperforms BC-EC, and Math, where BC-LC-OC-EC-MC outperforms BC-LC-OC-EC. However, in other cases—such as with Closure and Time—the addition of MC decreases efficacy. Results improve across the board with a ten-minute budget, where the top combinations for Closure, Lang, Math, and Time all contain MC. Overall, with a ten-minute budget, the combination of BC-EC-MC outperforms any other blanket policy. It seems that MC can improve a combination, but does not have the same impact as EC.

Given a high enough search budget, we do recommend its inclusion. An example where the addition of MC could boost efficacy can be seen in Lang fault 34[5]. This fault resides in two small (1–2 line) methods. Calling either method will reveal the fault, but BC can easily overlook them.

4.2   Observations and Recommendations

We can address each research question in turn. First:

> For all systems and search budgets, at least one combination of criteria is more effective than a single criterion, with the top combination offering a 5.11–31.15% improvement in the likelihood of fault detection over the best single criterion and up to 70.17% improvement over the default combination of all eight criteria.

For each budget B, combination C, and individual criterion I, we formulate hypothesis H and null hypothesis $H0$:

- H: With budget B, test suites generated using X will have a higher likelihood of fault detection than suites generated using I.
- $H0$: Observations of efficacy for C and I are drawn from the same distribution.

Due to the limited number of faults for Chart and Time, we have focused on overall results. Our observations are drawn from an unknown distribution; therefore, we cannot fit our data to a theoretical probability distribution. To evaluate $H0$ without any assumptions on distribution, we use a one-sided (strictly greater) Mann-Whitney-Wilcoxon rank-sum test, a non-parametric hypothesis test for determining if one set of observations is drawn from a different distribution than another set of observations. We apply the test for each pairing of fitness function and search budget with $\alpha = 0.05$.

To save space, we focus on the top combinations—BC-EC for the two-minute budget and BC-EC-MC for the ten-minute budget. At the two-minute search budget, we can reject the null hypothesis for MC, MNEC, EC, OC (all < 0.001), and WMC (0.030). We cannot reject the null hypothesis for DBC (0.055), LC (0.057), or BC (0.304). At the ten-minute level, we can reject the null hypothesis for MC, MNEC, EC, OC, WMC, LC (all < 0.001), DBC (0.017), and BC (0.040). Therefore, the BC-EC-MC combination significantly outperforms all individual criteria, given sufficient search budget.

From Tables 3, 5, and 7, we can see that the search budget affects the efficacy of combinations. At a higher budget, more combinations outperform individual criteria, and the performance gap between combinations and individual criteria widens. While combinations *can* outperform individual criteria at the two-minute budget, a larger budget clearly benefits combinations.

---

[5] https://github.com/apache/commons-lang/commit/
496525b0d626dd5049528cdef61d71681154b660.

As more criteria are added, the generation task becomes more complex. There is a trade-off to be made in terms of the required search budget and the efficacy of the results. The default eight-way combination of criteria, even with a ten-minute budget, is ineffective in the majority of cases. While an even higher budget may help, we have seen that simple, *targeted* combinations can perform very well, even with a tight budget.

This leads, naturally, to the next question—which combinations are effective, in practice? At the two minute budget, a combination of all eight criteria is the most effective for Chart. BC-LC is best for Closure. For Lang, it is CB-EC-MC. For Math, it is BC-LC-OC-EC-MC. Finally, for Time, it is BC-EC. The best general policy, at that budget, is the BC-EC combination. More consensus is seen at the ten-minute budget level, where the BC-EC-MC combination is the best observed for Closure, Lang, and Time (and is the best general policy). For Chart, the top combination is BC-LC-WMC-EC. For Math, is BC-LC-OC-EC-MC.

We do not wish to advocate these as the best *possible* combinations. Even for the studied systems, we did not exhaustively try all possibilities. Further, while performance gains are reasonably significant, better performance is likely possible. Rather, we wish to use this study to derive a starting point for those who wish to generate effective tests.

Either Branch or DBC was found to be the most effective single criterion. Tests that fail to execute faulty lines of code are highly unlikely to reveal a fault, so a criterion intended to achieve code coverage should form the core of a combination. However, code coverage is not sufficient on its own. Merely executing code does not ensure a failure—*how* that code is executed is important. From our results, we can observe that the most effective combinations pair a structure-focused criterion with a small number of supplemental strategies that can guide the structure-based criterion towards the *correct* input for the CUT.

Across the board, effective combinations include Exception Coverage. As EC can be added to a combination with minimal effect on generation complexity, we recommend it as part of any generation strategy. Although Method Coverage does not have the clear symbiotic relationship with BC that EC has, it offers a slight boost to efficacy at a low cost. We recommend its inclusion in combinations with a longer search budget.

We recommend a combination of Branch or Direct Branch Coverage with Exception and Method Coverage as a *base* approach to test generation. Additional criteria, targeted towards the CUT, may further improve efficacy.

We observed several situations where the central structure-based criterion is boosted by secondary criteria. First, Output Coverage often assists in revealing faults for Math. OC divides the data type of the method output into a series of abstract values, then rewards suites that cover each of those classes. In particular, OC offers the search feedback for numeric data types [14], explaining its utility for Math. For example, consider Fault 53[6]. The patch removes a misbehaving check for *NaN*. As the fixed version *removes* code, BC does not reveal the fault. However, Output Coverage ensures that method calls return a variety of values—raising the likelihood of fault detection.

Weak Mutation Coverage can also boost BC. Consider Lang fault 28[7]. BC alone fails to detect the fault, while WMC alone has a 40% chance of detection. A BC-WMC combination has a 90% chance of detection. The patched code includes an if-condition that can be mutated in several ways. BC assists in mutation detection by driving execution to, and into, the if-block. This combination is effective for other similar faults.

Combining structure-focused criteria seems potentially redundant. However, BC-LC and BC-DBC combinations can be effective (see Table 7). Consider Closure fault 94[8]. No single criterion detects the fault. However, at the ten-minute budget, the BC-LC combination has a 30% detection likelihood. The BC-LC combination is not only more effective, but also achieves higher levels of coverage. BC suites attain an average of 54.91% LC and 37.46% BC. LC-based suites attain 58.94% LC and 33.99% BC. Suites generated using the combination achieve 59.09% LC and 42.45% BC. By attaining higher coverage, the combination is more likely to execute the faulty code.

While more research is needed to identify situations where criteria work well together, developers should be able to produce more effective test cases using automated generation by considering the CUT and choosing criteria accordingly.

5   Related Work

Advocates of adequacy criteria hypothesize that there should exist a correlation between higher attainment of a criterion and fault detection efficacy [7]. Researchers have attempted to address whether such a correlation exists for almost as long as such criteria have existed [5,8,13]. Inozemtseva et al. provide a good overview [8].

Shamshiri et al. applied EvoSuite (Branch Coverage only), Randoop, and Agitar to each fault in Defects4J to assess the fault-detection capabilities of automated generation [15]. They found that the combination of tools could detect 55.70% of the faults. Their work identifies several reasons why faults were not detected, including low levels of coverage, heavy use of private methods and variables, and issues with simulation of the execution environment. Our recent experiments expand on this work, comparing fitness functions from EvoSuite in terms of fault detection efficacy [3].

---

[6] https://github.com/rjust/defects4j/blob/master/framework/projects/Math/patches/53.src.patch.

[7] https://github.com/apache/commons-lang/commit/3e1afecc200d7e3be9537c95b7cf52a7c5031300.

[8] https://github.com/rjust/defects4j/blob/master/framework/projects/Closure/patches/94.src.patch.

Rojas et al. previously found that, given a fixed generation budget, multiple fitness functions could be combined with minimal loss in coverage of any single criterion and with a reasonable increase in test suite size [14]. Others have explored combinations of coverage criteria with non-functional criteria, such as memory consumption [11] or execution time [16]. Few have studied the effect of such combinations on fault detection. Jeffrey et al. found that combinations are effective following suite reduction [9].

6   Threats to Validity

External Validity: We have focused on five systems. We believe such systems are representative of small to medium-sized open-source Java systems, and that we have examined a sufficient number of faults to offer generalizable results.

We have used only one test generation framework. While other techniques may yield different results, no other framework offers the same variety of coverage criteria. Therefore, a more thorough comparison of tool performance cannot be made. While exact results may differ, we believe that general trends will remain the same, as the underlying criteria follow the same philosophy.

To control costs, we have only performed ten trials per combination of fault, budget, and configuration. Additional trials may yield different results. However, we believe that 134,300 suites is a sufficient number to draw conclusions.

Conclusion Validity: When using statistical analysis, we ensure base assumptions are met. We use non-parametric methods, as distribution characteristics are not known.

7   Conclusions

In this work, we have examined the effect of combining coverage criteria on the efficacy of search-based test generation, identified effective combinations, and explored situations where criteria can cooperate to detect faults. For all systems, we have found that at least one combination is more effective than individual criteria, with the top combinations offering up to a 31.15% improvements in efficacy over top individual criteria. The most effective combinations pair a criterion focused on structure exploration—such as Branch Coverage—with a small number of targeted supplemental strategies suited to the CUT. Our findings offer lessons to consider when selecting such combinations.

Although we recommend the combination of Branch, Exception, and Method Coverage as a starting point, further research is needed to determine how to select the best combination for a system. In future work, we plan to focus on automated means of selecting combinations, perhaps using hyperheuristic search.

Acknowledgements. This work is supported by National Science Foundation grant CCF-1657299.

References

1. Anand, S., Burke, E., Chen, T.Y., Clark, J., Cohen, M.B., Grieskamp, W., Harman, M., Harrold, M.J., McMinn, P.: An orchestrated survey on automated software test case generation. J. Syst. Softw. **86**(8), 1978–2001 (2013)
2. Fraser, G., Staats, M., McMinn, P., Arcuri, A., Padberg, F.: Does automated white-box test generation really help software testers? In: Proceedings of the 2013 International Symposium on Software Testing and Analysis (ISSTA 2013), pp. 291–301, New York, NY, USA. ACM (2013)
3. Gay, G.: The fitness function for the job: search-based generation of test suites that detect real faults. In: Proceedings of the 2017 International Conference on Software Testing (ICST 2017). IEEE (2017)
4. Gay, G., Rajan, A., Staats, M., Whalen, M., Heimdahl, M.P.E.: The effect of program and model structure on the effectiveness of MC/DC test adequacy coverage. ACM Trans. Softw. Eng. Methodol. **25**(3), 25:1–25:34 (2016)
5. Gay, G., Staats, M., Whalen, M., Heimdahl, M.: The risks of coverage-directed test case generation. IEEE Trans. Softw. Eng. **41**(8), 803–819 (2015)
6. Gopinath, R., Jensen, C., Groce, A.: Mutations: how close are they to real faults? In: 25th International Symposium on Software Reliability Engineering, pp. 189–200, November 2014
7. Groce, A., Alipour, M.A., Gopinath, R.: Coverage and its discontents. In: Proceedings of the 2014 ACM International Symposium on New Ideas, New Paradigms, and Reflections on Programming & Software (Onward! 2014), New York, NY, USA, pp. 255–268. ACM (2014)
8. Inozemtseva, L., Holmes, R.: Coverage is not strongly correlated with test suite effectiveness. In: Proceedings of the 36th International Conference on Software Engineering (ICSE 2014), New York, NY, USA, pp. 435–445. ACM (2014)
9. Jeffrey, D., Gupta, N.: Improving fault detection capability by selectively retaining test cases during test suite reduction. IEEE Trans. Softw. Eng. **33**(2), 108–123 (2007)
10. Just, R., Jalali, D., Ernst, M.D.: Defects4J: a database of existing faults to enable controlled testing studies for Java programs. In: Proceedings of the 2014 International Symposium on Software Testing and Analysis (ISSTA 2014), New York, NY, USA, pp. 437–440. ACM (2014)
11. Lakhotia, K., Harman, M., McMinn, P.: A multi-objective approach to search-based test data generation. In: Proceedings of the 9th Annual Conference on Genetic and Evolutionary Computation (GECCO 2007), New York, NY, USA, pp. 1098–1105. ACM (2007)
12. McMinn, P.: Search-based software test data generation: a survey. Softw. Testing Verification Reliabil. **14**, 105–156 (2004)
13. Mockus, A., Nagappan, N., Dinh-Trong, T.: Test coverage and post-verification defects: a multiple case study. In: 3rd International Symposium on Empirical Software Engineering and Measurement (ESEM 2009), pp. 291–301, October 2009
14. Rojas, J.M., Campos, J., Vivanti, M., Fraser, G., Arcuri, A.: Combining multiple coverage criteria in search-based unit test generation. In: Barros, M., Labiche, Y. (eds.) SSBSE 2015. LNCS, vol. 9275, pp. 93–108. Springer, Cham (2015). doi:10. 1007/978-3-319-22183-0_7

15. Shamshiri, S., Just, R., Rojas, J.M., Fraser, G., McMinn, P., Arcuri, A.: Do automatically generated unit tests find real faults? An empirical study of effectiveness and challenges. In: Proceedings of the 30th IEEE/ACM International Conference on Automated Software Engineering (ASE 2015), New York, NY, USA. ACM (2015)
16. Yoo, S., Harman, M.: Using hybrid algorithm for pareto efficient multi-objective test suite minimisation. J. Syst. Softw. **83**(4), 689–701 (2010)

LIPS vs MOSA: A Replicated Empirical Study on Automated Test Case Generation

Annibale Panichella[1](✉), Fitsum Meshesha Kifetew[2], and Paolo Tonella[2]

[1] University of Luxembourg, Luxembourg, Luxembourg
annibale.panichella@uni.lu
[2] Fondazione Bruno Kessler, Trento, Italy
{kifetew,tonella}@fbk.eu

Abstract. Replication is a fundamental pillar in the construction of scientific knowledge. Test data generation for procedural programs can be tackled using a single-target or a many-objective approach. The proponents of LIPS, a novel single-target test generator, conducted a preliminary empirical study to compare their approach with MOSA, an alternative many-objective test generator. However, their empirical investigation suffers from several external and internal validity threats, does not consider complex programs with many branches and does not include any qualitative analysis to interpret the results. In this paper, we report the results of a replication of the original study designed to address its major limitations and threats to validity. The new findings draw a completely different picture on the pros and cons of single-target vs many-objective approaches to test case generation.

1 Introduction

Replications are one of the key scientific practices that allow researchers to confirm, refute or adjust the validity of previous findings. In recent years, the software engineering community has seen an increasing awareness about the importance of replications and several authors view replications as a fundamental step toward the construction of solid empirical evidence in the field [7,12,13].

Search based test case generation aims at automatically generating a set of input vectors that reach the desired level of adequacy (e.g., branch coverage) once they are turned into test cases and executed. While the first proposals of test generators addressed one coverage target at a time [8,14], recent approaches consider all coverage targets at the same time and either compute an aggregate fitness function for all yet uncovered targets [5] or apply a truly many-objective search to the test generation problem [10]. A novel single-target approach has been proposed in a recent paper by Scalabrino et al. [11]. The paper includes a comparison between their test generator LIPS (Linearly Independent Path based Search) and MOSA (Many-Objective Sorting Algorithm) [10]. We find the empirical investigation very interesting, since it tries to shed some light on the pros and cons of adopting a single-target vs many-objective test generation approach. However, the core contribution of the paper is not empirical. In

© Springer International Publishing AG 2017
T. Menzies and J. Petke (Eds.): SSBSE 2017, LNCS 10452, pp. 83–98, 2017.
DOI: 10.1007/978-3-319-66299-2_6

fact, the paper is mostly focused on the novel ideas implemented in LIPS and the empirical study is a very preliminary study, conducted on a few, small C functions. Since the research question (single-target vs many-objective test generation) behind the empirical part of the LIPS paper is a key research question in search based testing, we decided to replicate and extend the empirical study reported in the LIPS paper [11].

The replicated empirical study described in this paper addresses the main threats to validity and limitations of the original study – namely, the threats to the external validity of the results, due to the size and complexity of the sample of C functions considered in the study, the threats to the internal validity, due to the way efficiency was measured and the way the parameters of the algorithms were set, and the lack of a detailed qualitative analysis of the reasons for the reported quantitative differences. The new empirical study was designed to evaluate effectiveness, efficiency and convergence of LIPS vs MOSA. Quite surprisingly, the findings of the new study differ remarkably from the original results. The new results show an undisputed superiority of the many-objective approach in all considered dimensions. The qualitative analysis of the results shows that MOSA makes a better usage of the available search budget by avoiding its allocation to a single target. Although the dynamic allocation of the search budget to a target presumably improves over its static allocation to the targets, according to our new study the many-objective approaches, which do not perform any kind of budget allocation, converge more quickly and on average achieve higher coverage.

2   Background

This section describes the two approaches being compared, LIPS and MOSA.

Linearly Independent Path based Search (LIPS). LIPS is a single-target approach proposed by Scalabrino et al. [11] for procedural languages. It uses single-objective genetic algorithms to optimise (cover) one branch (target) at a time. The fitness function for a branch is determined by the traditional approach level and branch distance [8]. In order to cover linearly independent paths to the targets, the branch selected as target is the last uncovered branch appearing in the path of the last test case that is added to the final test suite. Such a target is updated over the generations depending on whether (i) it is covered or (ii) the search budget allocated for the single target is consumed. In turn, the search budget allocated to each target is determined dynamically, as the total remaining search budget divided by the targets that are yet uncovered and that were never selected as single coverage targets in a previous generation. In this way, infeasible or difficult targets do not consume the overall search budget, because they are allocated only a fraction of the entire search budget. Moreover, even if they are not covered in the generation cycle allocated to them, they remain still coverable in successive generations thanks to collateral coverage (i.e., coverage achieved by a test case generated for a different target) or in case some residual budget remains at the end, due to easy to cover targets considered late in the process. For completeness, Algorithm 1 reports the pseudo-code for LIPS. It should be noted that no pseudo-code is available in the paper by Scalabrino et al. [11]. Moreover, the source code of the tool is also not available. Hence, we have elaborated the pseudo-code by trying to follow the specifications of LIPS available in the paper as strictly as possible. However, sometimes the description in the paper is not detailed enough for unambiguous interpretation and we had to make decisions on what to implement. While this might have produced differences between our and the original implementation of LIPS, we think that the key ideas behind LIPS, i.e., the ordering of the targets by execution path and the dynamic re-allocation of the search budget, are captured faithfully in our implementation. Moreover, by providing the pseudo-code for LIPS in our paper we contribute to the disambiguation of the minor, yet important, details behind the ideas described in the paper.

Algorithm 1. LIPS

Input: $B = \{b_1, \ldots, b_m\}$ the set of branches to cover in the program.
Population size M
Result: A test suite T

```
1  begin
2  |   tc_0 ⟵ randomly generated input vector
3  |   T ⟵ {tc_0}
4  |   worklist ⟵ uncovered branches ordered as in the path traversed by tc_0
5  |   target ⟵ pop last branch from worklist
6  |   START-CLOCK-FOR-TARGET(target)
7  |   budget ⟵ LOCAL-BUDGET()
8  |   t ⟵ 0 // current generation
9  |   P_t ⟵ RANDOM-POPULATION(M − 1) ∪{tc_0} // Initial population
10 |   while | worklist |> 0 AND not(overall search budget consumed) do
11 |   |   if t > 0 then
12 |   |   |   P_t ⟵ GENERATE-OFFSPRING(P_{t−1})
13 |   |   COLLATERAL-COVERAGE(P_t, worklist)
14 |   |   if target is covered then
15 |   |   |   T ⟵ T ∪ {test tc covering target}
16 |   |   |   worklist ⟵ UPDATE-WORKLIST(tc)
17 |   |   |   target ⟵ pop last branch from worklist
18 |   |   |   START-CLOCK-FOR-TARGET(target)
19 |   |   else if CLOCK-FOR-TARGET(target) ≥ budget then
20 |   |   |   target ⟵ pop last branch from worklist
21 |   |   |   START-CLOCK-FOR-TARGET(target)
22 |   |   budget ⟵ LOCAL-BUDGET()
23 |   |   t ⟵ t + 1
```

LIPS starts with an initial, randomly generated test case tc_0 (line 2 in Algorithm 1), which represents the input vector for the program under test [11]. Such a test is executed and the uncovered branches for all decision nodes in the execution path of tc_0 are added to a worklist (line 4 in Algorithm 1) in the order in which they are encountered. The worklist represents the queue of branches that can be potentially considered as search targets. Starting from tc_0, the genetic algorithm is initialised as follows [11]: (i) the initial search target is the last branch added to the worklist (line 5), and (ii) an initial population that includes tc_0 is randomly generated (line 9). In the evolutionary iterations, new tests are generated using crossover and mutation (GENERATE-OFFSPRING at line 12). Parents are selected using the tournament selection and according to the single fitness function of the current target [11]. Whenever a newly generated test tc covers the current target, (i) it is added to the test suite (at line 15), (ii) all the uncovered branches of decision nodes on the path covered by tc are added to the worklist in the order in which they are encountered (UPDATE-WORKLIST at line 16). If some of the uncovered targets in the path of tc were selected before as coverage targets, they are added at the front of the worklist, so that they are selected as current coverage targets only when all the other targets, which were never tried before, are covered, using the residual (if any) search budget. The last branch added to the worklist is selected as new target (line 17). The branches in the worklist that are covered (by chance) by the newly generated tests are removed from the worklist and marked as "covered" (COLLATERAL-COVERAGE at line 13). Since LIPS targets one branch at a time, it has to allocate a portion of the overall search budget for each uncovered and not previously selected branch. To account for collateral coverage, which could free some search budget, at each generation the budget is re-computed as SB/n, where SB is the budget that remained available after last target selection and n is the number of remaining uncovered branches that were never selected before (LOCAL-BUDGET at line 22). If the current target is not covered within the allocated *budget*, a new target is selected from the worklist (lines 19–20). The main loop at lines 10–23 is repeated until all the branches are covered or the total search budget is consumed [11].

LIPS has been defined for procedural programs written in C. Therefore, it does not address the problem of generating method sequences [14], which means it is not directly applicable to object-oriented programs. Moreover, the length of the chromosome used by LIPS is fixed, which means that data structures with variable size (e.g., arrays) are assigned a predefined, fixed size. This may prevent coverage of targets requiring a specific, special value of size (e.g., a condition that checks if an array has size zero). Finally, although not stated explicitly in the paper [11], we assume that LIPS uses elitism in GENERATE-OFFSPRING (line 11), given the fact the elitism has been shown to positively affect the convergence speed of GAs in various optimisation problems and it is also used (although in a different way) in MOSA.

Many-Objective Sorting Algorithm (MOSA). MOSA is a many-objective genetic algorithm proposed by Panichella et al. [10] for Java classes and implemented in EvoSuite[1]. A test case in MOSA is a method sequence (including input data) of variable length, which is evaluated against all uncovered branches. MOSA targets all uncovered branches at once by considering them as different (many) objectives to be optimised in parallel. It shares the same main loop with NSGA-II [4], which is one of the most popular multi-objective genetic algorithms. However, it differs on three key aspects: (i) it selects test cases according to a preference criterion suitably defined for the test case generation problem; (ii) it considers as objectives only the yet uncovered coverage branches (i.e., the set of optimisation objectives changes across generations); (iii) it uses an archive to store all test cases satisfying one or more previously uncovered branches. The pseudo-code of MOSA is shown in Algorithm 2 [10].

---

[1] https://github.com/EvoSuite/evosuite/tree/master/client/src/main/java/org/evosuite/ga/metaheuristics/mosa.

Algorithm 2. MOSA

Input: $B = \{b_1, \ldots, b_m\}$ the set of coverage targets of a program.
Population size M
Result: A test suite T

```
1  begin
2  │  t ←— 0 // current generation
3  │  Pₜ ←— RANDOM-POPULATION(M)
4  │  archive ←— UPDATE-ARCHIVE(Pₜ, ∅)
5  │  while not (search budget consumed) do
6  │  │  Qₜ ←— GENERATE-OFFSPRING(Pₜ)
7  │  │  archive ←— UPDATE-ARCHIVE(Qₜ, archive)
8  │  │  Rₜ ←— Pₜ ∪ Qₜ
9  │  │  F ←— PREFERENCE-SORTING(Rₜ)
10 │  │  Pₜ₊₁ ←— ∅
11 │  │  d ←— 0
12 │  │  while | Pₜ₊₁ | + | Fₐ |⩽ M do
13 │  │  │  CROWDING-DISTANCE-ASSIGNMENT(Fₐ)
14 │  │  │  Pₜ₊₁ ←— Pₜ₊₁ ∪ Fₐ
15 │  │  │  d ←— d + 1
16 │  │  SORT(Fₐ) //according to the crowding distance
17 │  │  Pₜ₊₁ ←— Pₜ₊₁ ∪ Fₐ[1 : (M− | Pₜ₊₁ |)]
18 │  │  t ←— t + 1
19 │  T ←— archive
```

MOSA starts with an initial set of randomly generated test cases (line 3 of Algorithm 2); then, new test cases (*offspring*) are created using *crossover* and *mutation* (GENERATE-OFFSPRING, at line 6 of Algorithm 2). Then, parents and offspring are selected to form the next generation according to their ranks, as determined by the PREFERENCE-SORTING routine [10] (line 9). Tests that satisfy the preference criterion are assigned to the first front $\mathbb{F}_0$ while all the remaining tests are ranked using the non-dominated sorting algorithm of NSGA-II [4]. The preference criterion prioritises test cases that are closer to one or more uncovered branches (according to the corresponding branch distance and approach level scores). When there are multiple test cases with the same objective scores, the preference criterion uses the test case length as secondary selection criterion [10], i.e., shorter tests are preferred. The population for the next generation is formed using the loop at lines 12–15: test cases are selected starting from those in front $\mathbb{F}_0$, then those in front $\mathbb{F}_1$, and so on. At the end of the loop (lines 16–17), the remaining test cases are selected from the current front $\mathbb{F}_d$ according to the descending order of crowding distance. Finally, MOSA uses an *archive*, to keep track of the shorter test cases that cover the branches of the program under test. Whenever new test cases are generated (either at the beginning of the search or when creating offspring), MOSA stores those tests that cover previously uncovered targets in the *archive* as candidates to form the final test suite (function UPDATE-ARCHIVE at lines 4 and 7).

MOSA has been defined for Java classes. Therefore, it addresses both test data and method sequence generation. Since it is implemented in EvoSuite, it can handle complex data structures as input, such as objects and arrays of objects. The encoding schema (the standard one in EvoSuite [6]) allows to create test cases (i.e., method sequences) as well as test inputs (e.g., arrays) with variable length. Finally, MOSA uses elitism: test cases closer to satisfying uncovered branches (or with minimum length at the same level of "closeness") are guaranteed to survive in the next generation [10].

3 Summary of the Replicated Empirical Study

This section summarises the empirical study published by Scalabrino et al. [11] comparing LIPS and their reimplementation of MOSA when generating test inputs for C functions. The empirical evaluation was performed on 35 C functions with number of branches ranging between 2 and 64 (15 branches per function on average). These C functions are taken from different open-source C libraries [11]: (i) 21 functions from `gimp`, an open source GNU image manipulation software; (ii) five functions from `GSL`, the GNU Scientific Library; (iii) three functions from *SGLIB*, a generic library for C; (iv) three functions from `spice`, an analogue circuit simulator; (v) one function from `bibclean`; and (vi) two functions from previous work on test data generation for the C language.

The comparison is performed on three different dimensions: (i) branch coverage (*effectiveness*), (ii) execution time (*efficiency*), (iii) number of tests in the final test suite (*oracle cost*). According to the results of the study, there is no difference in terms of branch coverage between LIPS and MOSA for the majority of the C functions. In ten out of 35 functions LIPS has a better branch coverage than MOSA and for these cases the average difference is 5.72%. In two out of 35 cases MOSA outperforms LIPS and the average difference in branch coverage for these cases is 5.61%. Notice that these average values are obtained from Table 2 of the LIPS paper [11]. LIPS is reported to be more efficient than MOSA for all C functions, with an average improvement around 66% in terms or running time. Scalabrino et al. [11] measure efficiency as the execution time required to perform 200,000 fitness function evaluations for the 27 functions with less than 100% coverage. Finally, they report that MOSA produces significantly shorter test suites compared to LIPS in 32 out of 35 functions. However, the differences are easily ironed out by greedy algorithms for test suite minimisation [11]. As reported in [11], the execution time for the minimisation is negligible given the small size of the functions under test and of the generated test suites.

3.1 Threats to Validity

We have identified the following threats to the validity of the original study and we believe that a replication of the study is very important to address them.

Threats to **external validity** affect the generalisation of the results. Among them, the number and size/complexity of the considered C functions affect the external validity of the reported findings to a major extent. *Size/complexity of the functions*: the selected functions are small and contain few branches. Only two functions have more than 50 branches (i.e., 56 and 64 branches) and 16 out of 35 functions (46%) have less than ten branches each. For comparison, MOSA was originally evaluated on Java classes with at least 50 branches each [10]. Therefore, it is not clear to what extent results are generalisable to functions with more than 50 branches. *Number of functions*: the empirical study considers only 35 small C functions. A larger sample is needed to extend the validity of the findings of the study.

Threats to **internal validity** regard internal factors that could have influenced the experimental results. Among them, the measurement of efficiency and the setting of some critical parameters of the algorithms might have affected the internal validity of the study. *Measurement of efficiency*: efficiency is measured as the execution time required by each algorithm to run until 200,000 fitness function evaluations are made and not as the execution time needed to reach maximum coverage. The chosen setting favours LIPS by design, since each generation of MOSA is more expensive to compute, due to the cost of the ranking procedure. Therefore, it is not clear whether the execution time needed by the two algorithms to reach maximum coverage differs or not.

Moreover, looking at the results reported in the original study in Table 2, we observed some inconsistencies in the execution time between LIPS and MOSA for simple C functions, where 100% of coverage is reached. For example, for function gimp_hsl_value_int LIPS required less than 10 ms to reach 100% coverage. Since this function is very simple, it can be presumably covered fully in the first generation (i.e., with no need for evolution). However, for MOSA the reported running time to reach full coverage on the same function is 10.23s. If the initial populations for MOSA and LIPS are the same (i.e., randomly generated), both algorithms should achieve full coverage within approximately the same time. We observed the same inconsistency in seven other very simple C functions used in the study [11].

3.2   Reasons to Replicate

In addition to the possibility of addressing some of the threats to the validity of the original study, there are further reasons for replicating the empirical study by Scalabrino et al. [11]. First, the study provides only a quantitative analysis of the collected results, without attempting to interpret them qualitatively. An in-depth qualitative analysis would allow us to better understand under which conditions one algorithm outperforms the other. Moreover, a further study is needed to better understand how LIPS and MOSA perform on programs with a large number of branches (>50). In fact, a recent study [9] involving classes with both low and high number of branches confirmed the higher effectiveness and efficiency of MOSA (and its improved variant DynaMOSA) for classes with high number of branches (high cyclomatic complexity) [9]. On the other hand, Scalabrino et al. [11] compared LIPS and MOSA on C functions with less than 20 branches on average (only one function has slightly more than 50 branches). Hence, there is a strong need for a larger study, with both small (<50 branches) and large (≥50 branches) programs.

3.3   How to Replicate

In principle, the simplest option to replicate the study would be to re-run LIPS and MOSA on a larger sample of C functions using OCELOT, i.e., the tool that implements LIPS [11]. However, this option is not viable since OCELOT and the code for LIPS are not publicly available at the time of this submission.

The viable alternative is to re-implement LIPS in EvoSuite. Differently from OCELOT, EvoSuite is publicly available on GitHub[2] and it already contains the original code of MOSA [10]. An important drawback of this choice is that Evo-Suite generates test suites for Java classes and not for C functions. Therefore, this option requires the conversion of the C functions used in the original study [11] into Java static methods. Fortunately, this conversion is straightforward since the selected C functions do not have complex input parameters with advanced C syntax (e.g., pointers to complex structures). Since EvoSuite supports the generation of test cases and input data (e.g., arrays) of variable length, as a side effect of using EvoSuite we also overcome one of the limitations of LIPS/OCELOT: the fixed chromosome size, discussed in Sect. 2.

4 Design of the New Study

We first describe our re-implementation of LIPS within EvoSuite. Then we describe the selected subjects, the research questions and the metrics we adopt to answer them.

Implementation of LIPS in EvoSuite: We have re-implemented LIPS based on the pseudo-code in Algorithm 1, within EvoSuite version 1.0.5, available from GitHub on March 12th, 2017. The main differences between the original version of LIPS [11] and our re-implementation regard the encoding schema and the genetic operators, for which we use the default settings in EvoSuite [5]. In EvoSuite [5], a test case is a sequence of statements, which is composed of method calls (i.e., call to static methods) and data inputs (e.g., arrays, strings). New test cases are generated by applying *single-point* crossover and *uniform mutation*. The latter can remove, change, or add statements from/in/to the test cases. While we allow the length of the test cases to vary during the GA search, so that the length of input arrays, strings, etc., can change, we only allow one method execution for the class under test, i.e., the execution of the static method under test, because we are interested in evaluating LIPS vs. MOSA for procedural, stateless methods only. Selection is *tournament selection*, the same operator originally proposed for LIPS [11]. The encoding schema and genetic operators are the same for MOSA [9,10], i.e., they work at test case level.

In the original LIPS implementation [11], the length of the chromosomes is fixed a priori, which might prevent coverage of specific branches. In addition, the original genetic operators [11] are *blend-crossover* (BLX) and *polynomial mutation*, which can be applied only to chromosomes with fixed length and containing only numerical values [3]. Since our re-implementation of LIPS in EvoSuite does not have such constraints, we deem it as superior to the original implementation and eventually able to cover more branches. We found this conjecture to be empirically true by comparing the results of our re-implementation with the results reported in the original study, considering the common subset of programs under test (see Sect. 5). It should be noticed that the core novelties of LIPS,

---

[2] https://github.com/EvoSuite/evosuite.

namely the order by which branches are selected as targets and the dynamic allocation of the search budget, are kept identical to the original formulation in our re-implementation. Our re-implementation of LIPS is publicly available for download on GitHub: https://github.com/apanichella/evosuite/tree/LIPS_replication.

Benchmark: Since LIPS was originally defined for procedural functions and not for object oriented programs, in our replication study we target only static methods with purely procedural behaviour. Our benchmark contains 70 static methods characterised as follows: (i) 33 static methods are the Java equivalent of the C functions used in the original study [11]; (ii) 37 additional static methods have been randomly selected from Java open-source libraries. Notice that we excluded two of the 35 functions used in [11], namely `Csqrt` and `triangle`, for which we could not find the source code. Our benchmark contains twice as many subjects as the original study [11]. Moreover, 14 subjects have more than 50 branches each, thus allowing to compare LIPS and MOSA on very large/complex functions. In general, the number of branches[3] in each static method ranges between 3 and 425. The characteristics of the Java static methods (i.e., name and number of branches) are detailed in Table 1.

Porting the Old Benchmark to Java. All C functions used in the original study take as input primitive data types, pointers to primitive data types and arrays. Therefore, porting such functions to Java was straightforward: for each function `f`, we create a corresponding Java class containing only one single static method with the same content and the same parameters of `f`.

New Subjects. To increase the size of the benchmark, we randomly selected 37 Java static methods from seven open-source libraries. In particular, we selected: (i) 17 methods from the `apache commons math` (*math* in Table 1); (ii) seven from `apache commons lang` (*lang*); (iii) two from `apache commons io` (*io*); (iv) three from joptimizer[4] (*IOpt.*); (v) two from nd4j[5] (*nd4j*); (vi) one from `google gson` (*Gson*); (vii) three from `apache commons imaging` (*imaging*) (viii) two from `apache commons bcel` (*Bcel*).

4.1 Research Questions and Performance Metrics

We investigate the following research questions:

- **RQ1**: *How do LIPS and MOSA perform in terms of effectiveness?*
- **RQ2**: *How do LIPS and MOSA perform in terms of efficiency?*
- **RQ3**: *Does the program size (number of branches) affect the performance of LIPS and MOSA?*

---

[3] The number of branches reported here is sometimes slightly different from that of the original study because EvoSuite performs the instrumentation and counts the branches at the byte code, not source code, level.

[4] http://www.joptimizer.com.

[5] http://nd4j.org.

To answer **RQ1**, we use the same measure of *effectiveness* used in the original study, i.e., the percentage of covered branches. For the efficiency (**RQ2**), we do not use the measure used by Scalabrino et al. [11]. This is because, as explained in Sect. 3, the execution time required by each approach to perform 200,000 fitness function evaluations penalises by design MOSA and does not consider the time actually needed to reach maximum coverage, independently of the number of fitness evaluations consumed to reach it. Instead, we use an overall maximum allowed execution time as stop condition, i.e., the two approaches are executed for the same amount of time (if full coverage is not reached; otherwise execution stops earlier). Then, we measure the *efficiency* as the execution time required by each approach to reach maximum branch coverage. Moreover, we consider *efficiency* as a secondary performance metric: we compare LIPS and MOSA in terms of efficiency only for those subjects with no statistically significant difference in effectiveness. Notice that we do not compare the length of the test cases since EvoSuite applies test minimisation by default.

For each subject, each search approach (LIPS or MOSA) is run 50 times to address the random nature of the genetic algorithms. In each run, we collect the percentage of covered branches (**RQ1**) as well as the elapsed time between the start of the search and the latest increment in branch coverage (**RQ2**). We report the average coverage and execution time achieved by LIPS and MOSA over these independent runs. To provide statistical support to the analysis of the results, we apply the non-parametric Wilcoxon Rank Sum test [2] with a significance level of $\alpha = 0.05$. We also measure the effect size (i.e., the magnitude) of the differences (if any) in effectiveness or efficiency using the Vargha-Delaney ($\hat{A}_{12}$) statistic [15]. Finally, to answer **RQ3**, we use the one-way permutation test [1] to verify whether there is any significant interaction between effectiveness/efficiency of the two approaches on one side and complexity of the static method under test, measured as the number of branches to cover, on the other side. In particular, we use the number of branches in the methods as independent variable and the $\hat{A}_{12}$ statistics (obtained from the comparison) as dependent variable. We set the test with a significance level of $\alpha = 0.05$ and a number of iterations equal to 10^8 (a number of iterations $>1,000$ is recommended for this test [1]). The one-way permutation test is a non-parametric test, thus, it does not make any assumption on data distributions.

Parameter Setting. We adopted the default parameter values used by Evo-Suite [5] for both LIPS and MOSA, with the only exception of those parameters explicitly mentioned in the original study [11]. Therefore, we set the population size to 100 individuals and the crossover probability to 0.90. For the search budget, we fix the same maximum execution time of one minute for both LIPS and MOSA. This value (60 s) corresponds to the largest running time observed in the original study. Therefore, LIPS and MOSA terminate either when 100% of branch coverage is reached or when the maximum search budget of one minute is consumed.

5   Experimental Results

Table 1 reports the mean branch coverage (**RQ1**) and mean execution time (**RQ2**) achieved by LIPS and MOSA for each Java static method over 50 independent runs. The table also reports the p-values of the Wilcoxon test as well as the corresponding $\hat{A}_{12}$ statistics (effect size). Notice that values of $\hat{A}_{12} > 0.5$ indicate that LIPS is more effective (higher branch coverage) or more efficient (lower execution time) than MOSA; values of $\hat{A}_{12} < 0.5$ indicate that MOSA is more effective or more efficient than LIPS.

Results for RQ1. From columns 4–7 of Table 1, we can observe that in 45 out of 70 subjects (64%) there is no statistically significant difference in terms of branch coverage between LIPS and MOSA. Among these 45 subjects, 26 (60%) are trivial subjects that are fully covered in few seconds and 20 come from the original study [11]. In none of the remaining subjects LIPS could outperform MOSA in terms of branch coverage. Instead, MOSA achieves statistically significantly higher branch coverage than LIPS in 25 out of 70 subjects (36%). In these cases, the average (mean) difference in branch coverage is 7.67%, with a minimum of 0.92% and a maximum of 22.94%. The subject with the largest difference is `NumberUtils.createNumber` from `apache commons math`, which contains 115 branches. For this method, LIPS achieved 65.43% branch coverage compared to 88.36% achieved by MOSA (+26 covered branches) within one minute.

To better understand whether the observed differences vary when increasing the search budget, Fig. 1-(a) shows the average branch coverage achieved by LIPS and MOSA over a larger search budget of five minutes for method `BasicCParser.preprocess` from `apache common imaging`. In the first generation (i.e., at time zero), the two approaches have the same average coverage since they both start with a randomly generated population. However, after the first 20s the scenario dramatically changes: MOSA yields a higher coverage for the rest of the search, leading to a difference of +25% at the end of the search. Figure 1-(b) depicts the fitness function values for the false branch b_{30} of the

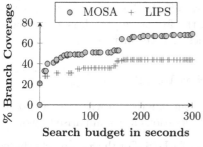
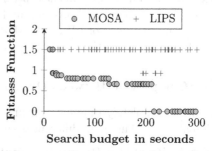

(a) Percentage of covered branches over search time

(b) Fitness values for one of the branches covered by MOSA but not by LIPS

Fig. 1. Comparison between LIPS and MOSA with a larger search budget of five minutes for method `BasicCParser.preprocess`

statement `if (c=='\r' || c=='\n')` at line 196 of class `BasicCParser` and placed inside multiple `if` statements within a `for` loop. MOSA takes around 205s to cover b_{30}, although this is one of the targets since the beginning of the search. Instead, LIPS selects this branch as its current target after 236s and only for 3s in total, which is not enough to cover it. Moreover, the fitness function curve is not monotonic in LIPS: it decreases between 194s and 200s but it increases in the next generations since b_{30} is not yet considered as the current target. A similar trend can be observed between 218s and 229s. Instead, in MOSA the fitness function curve is monotonic because the best test case for b_{30} is preserved (elitism) until a better test is found in the subsequent generations. Instead, in LIPS (as well as in any other single objective genetic algorithm), elitism holds only for the single fitness function being optimised (i.e., only for the current target).

Results for RQ2. For the 45 methods with no statistically significant difference in effectiveness, we compare the execution time required by LIPS and MOSA to achieve the highest coverage. The results of this comparison are reported in columns 8–11 of Table 1. Out of 45 methods, LIPS is significantly more efficient than MOSA in only one method, i.e., `MathArrays.sortInPlace`. For this method, LIPS required 1.36s on average to reach a coverage of 92% while MOSA spent 2.96s on average to reach the same branch coverage. On the other hand, MOSA is significantly more efficient than LIPS in 33 methods (73%). The minimum (yet significant) difference of 0.28s is observed for `gimp_cmyk_to_rgb` while the maximum of 13.55s is observed for `gimp_hsv_to_rgb`. For the remaining 11 methods, there is no significant difference between LIPS and MOSA.

Results for RQ3. For what concerns coverage, the one-way permutation test reveals that the $\hat{A}_{12}$ statistics is significantly influenced by the number of branches of the function/method under test (p-value < 0.01). In other words, MOSA achieves significantly higher branch coverage over LIPS especially for methods with high number of branches. For the execution time, the one-way permutation test reveals a marginally significant interaction between $\hat{A}_{12}$ statistics and the number of branches (p-value $= 0.06$). Thus, we can conclude that the size/complexity of the program under test affects the performance (coverage and execution times) of LIPS and MOSA: the former approach is less scalable than the latter when the number of branches to cover increases.

5.1   Comparison Between Old and New Results

We draw completely different conclusions from our results with respect to the original study. The main differences and observations are summarised below.

Superiority of Our Re-implementation of LIPS. For the 33 subjects shared with the original study, we observe that our re-implementation of LIPS could achieve 100% of coverage for 15 methods within 0.80s on average. Instead, in the original study LIPS reached 100% of coverage in only 8 cases [11]. This highlights the superiority of our re-implementation in EvoSuite compared to the original

Table 1. Average (mean) results for **RQ1 (effectiveness)** and **RQ2 (efficiency)**

Project	Method/Function Name	Tot. Branches	% Branch Coverage				Execution Time (ms)			
			LIPS	MOSA	p-value	Â₁₂	LIPS	MOSA	p-value	Â₁₂
bibclean	check_ISBN	47	89.36	89.66	0.16	0.48	511	313	<0.01	0.10
gimp	gimp_cmyk_to_rgb_int	3	100.00	100.00	1.00	0.50	248	217	<0.01	0.15
gimp	gimp_cmyk_to_rgb	7	98.86	100.00	0.16	0.48	348	320	<0.01	0.29
gimp	gimp_gradient_calc_bilinear_factor	9	94.00	100.00	<0.01	0.00				
gimp	gimp_gradient_calc_conical_asym_factor	9	100.00	100.00	1.00	0.50	500	295	<0.01	0.00
gimp	gimp_gradient_calc_conical_sym_factor	11	99.42	100.00	0.15	0.48	525	311	<0.01	0.00
gimp	gimp_gradient_calc_linear_factor	13	100.00	100.00	1.00	0.50	884	547	<0.01	0.24
gimp	gimp_gradient_calc_radial_factor	9	88.89	88.89	1.00	0.50	477	289	<0.01	0.09
gimp	gimp_gradient_calc_spiral_factor	11	100.00	100.00	1.00	0.50	552	289	<0.01	0.02
gimp	gimp_gradient_calc_square_factor	9	88.89	88.89	1.00	0.50	551	287	<0.01	0.04
gimp	gimp_hsl_to_rgb_int	5	100.00	100.00	1.00	0.50	478	236	<0.01	0.00
gimp	gimp_hsl_to_rgb	9	98.89	100.00	0.02	0.45				
gimp	gimp_hsl_value_int	11	100.00	100.00	1.00	0.50	501	260	<0.01	0.00
gimp	gimp_hsl_value	11	100.00	100.00	1.00	0.50	415	269	<0.01	0.05
gimp	gimp_hsv_to_rgb	23	99.83	100.00	0.16	0.48	19773	6223	<0.01	0.03
gimp	gimp_rgb_to_cmyk	13	99.08	100.00	0.04	0.46				
gimp	gimp_rgb_to_hsl_int	15	100.00	100.00	1.00	0.50	2167	1231	<0.01	0.23
gimp	gimp_rgb_to_hsl	17	93.77	94.12	0.16	0.48	791	339	<0.01	0.01
gimp	gimp_rgb_to_hsv_int	17	94.12	94.12	1.00	0.50	958	455	<0.01	0.10
gimp	gimp_rgb_to_hsv4	17	86.00	88.24	<0.01	0.31				
gimp	gimp_rgb_to_hwb	11	100.00	100.00	1.00	0.50	623	312	<0.01	0.00
gimp	gimp_rgb_to_l_int	3	100.00	100.00	1.00	0.50	341	166	<0.01	0.00
gsl	gsl_poly_complex_solve_cubic	23	86.96	86.96	1.00	0.50	623	350	<0.01	0.03
gsl	gsl_poly_complex_solve_quadratic	15	100.00	100.00	1.00	0.50	528	393	<0.01	0.06
gsl	gsl_poly_eval_derivs	13	100.00	100.00	1.00	0.50	1995	1472	0.07	0.40
gsl	gsl_poly_solve_cubic	21	85.71	85.71	1.00	0.50	723	353	<0.01	0.01
gsl	gsl_poly_solve_quadratic	15	100.00	100.00	1.00	0.50	406	357	0.01	0.34
sglib	sglib_int_array_binary_search	11	100.00	100.00	1.00	0.50	424	367	<0.01	0.31
sglib	sglib_int_array_heap_sort	18	100.00	100.00	1.00	0.50	1963	1222	<0.01	0.27
sglib	sglib_int_array_quick_sort	37	97.30	97.30	1.00	0.50	3778	2467	<0.01	0.25
spice	clip_line	47	78.47	80.21	<0.01	0.32				
spice	clip_to_circle	57	93.54	96.18	<0.01	0.12				
spice	cliparc	95	97.41	98.95	<0.01	0.10				
math	ArithmeticUtils.gcd	29	96.55	96.55	1.00	0.50	1410	439	<0.01	0.05
math	ArithmeticUtils.mulAndCheck	17	100.00	100.00	1.00	0.50	538	383	<0.01	0.01
math	CombinatoricsUtils.binomialCoefficient	21	100.00	100.00	1.00	0.50	3202	1845	<0.01	0.21
math	CombinatoricsUtils.binomialCoefficientLong	19	100.00	100.00	1.00	0.50	2588	1818	<0.01	0.31
math	CombinatoricsUtils.stirlingS2	29	86.14	96.55	<0.01	0.36				
math	MathArrays.checkOrder	25	96.00	96.00	1.00	0.50	380	337	<0.01	0.30
math	MathArrays.isMonotonic	21	95.14	95.24	0.33	0.49	400	384	0.22	0.43
math	MathArrays.safeNorm	21	100.00	100.00	1.00	0.50	9346	3931	<0.01	0.29
math	MathArrays.shuffle	15	93.33	93.33	1.00	0.50	567	517	0.60	0.47
math	MathArrays.sortInPlace	26	92.31	92.31	1.00	0.50	1357	2964	<0.01	0.79
math	MedianOf3PivotingStrategy	11	81.64	96.18	<0.01	0.34				
math	OpenIntToDoubleHashMap.findInsertionIndex	23	94.17	99.30	<0.01	0.28				
math	OpenIntToFieldHashMap.findInsertionIndex	23	94.00	99.30	<0.01	0.22				
math	FastMath.scalb	41	93.85	97.51	<0.01	0.26				
math	FastMath.exp	25	97.28	98.64	<0.01	0.34				
math	FastMath.atan	19	100.00	100.00	1.00	0.50	638	800	0.07	0.61
math	FastMath.atan2	69	74.58	81.16	<0.01	0.03				
lang	NumberUtils.isCreatable	121	71.97	89.69	<0.01	0.00				
lang	NumberUtils.createNumber	115	65.43	88.37	<0.01	0.00				
lang	Fraction.greatestCommonDivisor	33	96.97	96.97	1.00	0.50	697	370	<0.01	0.25
lang	RandomStringUtils.random	53	81.40	88.30	<0.01	0.12				
lang	DurationFormatUtils.formatPeriod	47	87.15	90.43	<0.01	0.08				
lang	DateUtils.modify	71	1.41	1.41	1.00	0.50	460	481	0.62	0.53
lang	WordUtils.wrap	27	100.00	100.00	1.00	0.50	1965	2547	0.93	0.51
IO	FilenameUtils.getPrefixLength	51	88.71	99.84	<0.01	0.02				
IO	FilenameUtils.wildcardMatch	37	93.19	96.86	<0.01	0.22				
JOpt.	ColtUtils.squareMatrixInverse	3	100.00	100.00	1.00	0.50	999	1042	0.70	0.48
JOpt.	ColtUtils.getMatrixScalingFactors	51	81.57	84.31	0.16	0.48	1056	1013	0.30	0.44
JOpt.	ColtUtils.calculateDeterminant	19	93.16	96.95	0.80	0.49	8576	9742	0.95	0.50
nd4j	BigDecimalMath.Gamma	15	94.13	92.78	0.10	0.59	32969	29776	0.21	0.43
nd4j	BigDecimalMath.zeta	21	100.00	100.00	1.00	0.50	23734	16530	<0.01	0.30
Gson	ISO8601Utils.parse	83	21.01	33.86	<0.01	0.03				
Imaging	BasicCParser.preprocess	109	31.63	45.91	<0.01	0.14				
Imaging	BasicCParser.unescapeString	71	22.11	36.48	0.02	0.36				
Imaging	T4AndT6Compression.compressT4_2D	39	100.00	100.00	1.00	0.50	4111	3251	0.17	0.37
Bcel	Utility.signatureToString	83	74.41	80.75	<0.01	0.05				
Bcel	Utility.codeToString	425	73.13	88.34	<0.01	0.00				
	Average (mean) results		89.18	92.06			7217	5380		

implementation, confirming our theoretical observations in Sect. 4. For example, for function `gimp_rgb_to_hwb` the original LIPS implementation reached only 50% coverage in 7.97s [11]. Instead, LIPS re-implemented in EvoSuite achieved 100% coverage in 0.62s.

MOSA is More Effective Than LIPS. Despite these improvements, LIPS could never achieve significantly higher coverage than MOSA. Instead, MOSA achieved significantly higher coverage on 36% of the subjects. To understand these results, let us consider `Utility.codeToString`, which has 425 branches. Given the high number of branches, LIPS can allocate a limited search budget to each branch, even in the presence of dynamic budget reallocation. As a consequence, LIPS can cover only the trivial branches that do not need many generations of test evolution. Instead, MOSA evolves test cases targeting all the branches at the same time, for the whole duration of the search budget.

MOSA is More Efficient Than LIPS. Our results contradict the results of the original study in terms of efficiency [11]. The main reason for such different conclusions is the different stop condition considered in the two studies: time required to perform 200,000 fitness evaluations (original study) vs. time needed to reach the same final coverage (new study). We believe the new stop condition provides a fair measurement of the respective time performance of the two algorithms, since 200,000 fitness evaluations are not necessarily required by both algorithms to reach the final coverage – indeed, they typically need a different number of fitness evaluations.

Most Subjects in the Original Study are Trivial. As reported in Sect. 5, the majority of the subjects (20 out of 35) used in the original study [11] can be fully covered in few seconds. We have run random search (RS) on the 33 subjects of the original study. In particular, we set RS with the same stop conditions used in LIPS and MOSA: either 100% of branch coverage is reached or the maximum budget of one minute is consumed. Results show that RS achieves 100% coverage in 18 out of 33 subjects (54%). It is also statistically equivalent to LIPS in other 9 subjects in terms of branch coverage. Thus, the large majority of subjects ($27/35 \approx 77\%$) used by Scalabrino et al. [11] are too easy to cover to draw any conclusion about the different performance of the two approaches. For this reason, we have extended the benchmark by adding more complex subjects.

5.2 Threats to Validity

Threats to construct validity. Since the tool OCELOT is not publicly available, we had to re-implement LIPS in EvoSuite. While our re-implementation may slightly differ from the original one, we strictly followed the descriptions provided by Scalabrino et al. [11] with particular attention to the key contributions of LIPS (target selection order and dynamic budget allocation). As discussed in Sect. 5.1, our re-implementation is superior to the original one on the benchmark programs of the original study. Another construct validity threat regards the conversion of C functions to Java static methods. As indicated in Sect. 4, this conversion was straightforward since the considered functions do not have complex input parameters and do not involve advanced C constructs.

Threats to Internal Validity. Compared to the original study, we have increased the number of repetitions for MOSA and LIPS from 30 to 50 runs, to increase the statistical power of the analysis. We used the same termination criterion for LIPS and MOSA in terms of execution time. We used a different metric to measure efficiency, defined so as to remove the arbitrary constraint that both algorithms should consume 200,000 fitness evaluations.

Threats to External Validity. To address the external validity threat of the original study, we have increased the size of the benchmark from 35 to 70 subjects by including methods with a larger number of branches (up to 425).

6   Conclusions and Future Work

We have replicated an empirical study comparing the test generators LIPS and MOSA. The former is a single-target approach with dynamic allocation of the search budget to each uncovered branch. The latter is a many-objective approach that targets all the branches at once. Our replication addresses several threats to external and internal validity of the preliminary study [11]. The new results differ remarkably from the original study: (i) MOSA is more effective than LIPS, especially for subjects with a large number of branches; (ii) MOSA is more efficient than LIPS, in terms of time needed to achieve the same, final coverage. Our implementation of LIPS together with the implementation of MOSA and a complete replication package are publicly available on GitHub as a fork of Evo-Suite at the following link https://github.com/apanichella/evosuite/tree/LIPS_replication.

Our future agenda includes extending this study to non-procedural Java code and considering DynaMOSA [9], a recent, more advanced version of MOSA.

References

1. Baker, R.D.: Modern permutation test software. In: Edgington, E. (ed.) Randomization Tests. Marcel Decker, New York (1995)
2. Conover, W.J.: Practical Nonparametric Statistics, 3rd edn. Wiley, New York (1998)
3. Deb, K., Deb, D.: Analysing mutation schemes for real-parameter genetic algorithms. Int. J. Artif. Intell. Soft Comput. **4**(1), 1–28 (2014)
4. Deb, K., Pratap, A., Agarwal, S., Meyarivan, T.: A fast elitist multi-objective genetic algorithm: NSGA-II. IEEE Trans. Evol. Comput. **6**, 182–197 (2000)
5. Fraser, G., Arcuri, A.: Whole test suite generation. IEEE Trans. Softw. Eng. **39**(2), 276–291 (2013)
6. Fraser, G., Arcuri, A.: A large-scale evaluation of automated unit test generation using EvoSuite. ACM Trans. Softw. Eng. Methodol. **24**(2), 8:1–8:42 (2014). http://doi.acm.org/10.1145/2685612
7. Juzgado, N.J., Vegas, S.: The role of non-exact replications in software engineering experiments. Empir. Softw. Eng. **16**(3), 295–324 (2011)
8. McMinn, P.: Search-based software test data generation: a survey. Softw. Test. Verif. Reliab. **14**(2), 105–156 (2004)
9. Panichella, A., Kifetew, F., Tonella, P.: Automated test case generation as a many-objective optimisation problem with dynamic selection of the targets. IEEE Trans. Softw. Eng. **PP**(99), 1 (2017). Pre-print available online

10. Panichella, A., Kifetew, F.M., Tonella, P.: Reformulating branch coverage as a many-objective optimization problem. In: 8th IEEE International Conference on Software Testing, Verification and Validation, ICST, pp. 1–10 (2015)
11. Scalabrino, S., Grano, G., Nucci, D., Oliveto, R., Lucia, A.: Search-based testing of procedural programs: iterative single-target or multi-target approach? In: Sarro, F., Deb, K. (eds.) SSBSE 2016. LNCS, vol. 9962, pp. 64–79. Springer, Cham (2016). doi:10.1007/978-3-319-47106-8_5
12. Shull, F., Basili, V.R., Carver, J., Maldonado, J.C., Travassos, G.H., Mendonça, M.G., Fabbri, S.: Replicating software engineering experiments: addressing the tacit knowledge problem. In: 2002 International Symposium on Empirical Software Engineering (ISESE 2002), 3–4 October 2002, Nara, pp. 7–16 (2002)
13. Shull, F., Carver, J.C., Vegas, S., Juzgado, N.J.: The role of replications in empirical software engineering. Empir. Softw. Eng. **13**(2), 211–218 (2008)
14. Tonella, P.: Evolutionary testing of classes. In: ACM SIGSOFT International Symposium on Software Testing and Analysis (ISSTA 2004), pp. 119–128. ACM (2004)
15. Vargha, A., Delaney, H.D.: A critique and improvement of the CL common language effect size statistics of Mcgraw and Wong. J. Educ. Behav. Stat. **25**(2), 101–132 (2000)

An Investigation into the Use of Mutation Analysis for Automated Program Repair

Christopher Steven Timperley[1]([✉]), Susan Stepney[2], and Claire Le Goues[1]

[1] Carnegie Mellon University, Pittsburgh, USA
christimperley@gmail.com
[2] University of York, York, UK

Abstract. Research in Search-Based Automated Program Repair has demonstrated promising results, but has nevertheless been largely confined to small, single-edit patches using a limited set of mutation operators. Tackling a broader spectrum of bugs will require multiple edits and a larger set of operators, leading to a combinatorial explosion of the search space. This motivates the need for more efficient search techniques. We propose to use the test case results of candidate patches to localise suitable fix locations. We analysed the test suite results of single-edit patches, generated from a random walk across 28 bugs in 6 programs. Based on the findings of this analysis, we propose a number of mutation-based fault localisation techniques, which we subsequently evaluate by measuring how accurately they locate the statements at which the search was able to generate a solution. After demonstrating that these techniques fail to result in a significant improvement, we discuss why this may be the case, despite the successes of mutation-based fault localisation in previous studies.

Keywords: Automated program repair · Mutation analysis · Fault localisation

1 Introduction

The worldwide cost of debugging and repairing software bugs is estimated to be \$312 billion per year; on average, programmers spend roughly 50% of their time finding and fixing bugs [1]. Research in *automated program repair* (APR) seeks to tackle this problem. Generate-and-validate (G&V) is one approach to APR, also known as search-based program repair, which uses meta-heuristics—such as random search [18] or genetic programming [2,8]—to discover patches that lead a program to pass a given set of test cases. At a high level, G&V begins with *fault localisation*, followed by continual processes of *generation* and *validation*. Fault localisation is typically performed using spectra-based fault localisation techniques (SBFL) [25]. SBFL assigns suspiciousness values to statements in the program, based on their dynamic association with the failing tests. Patches are generated by selecting statements according to their suspiciousness, and sampling *edits* at those statements from the repair space. This repair space

© Springer International Publishing AG 2017
T. Menzies and J. Petke (Eds.): SSBSE 2017, LNCS 10452, pp. 99–114, 2017.
DOI: 10.1007/978-3-319-66299-2_7

is defined by a set of transformation schemas, describing transformation shapes (e.g., insert statement, tighten if condition, replace call argument), and transformation ingredients, supplying the parameters necessary to complete shapes (e.g. a particular statement). Candidate patches are evaluated for correctness by running the patched program on the original test suite; repair is indicated by passing all of the tests.

Different G&V approaches vary in their mutation operators and traversal techniques. For example, GenProg [8] constructs patches that may append, replace or delete statements within the program, reusing existing statements within the program as fix ingredients. Other transformation schemas have been proposed based on human-produced patches [6] or a value search to reduce the cost of patch evaluation [10]. Search space traversal schemes employed include genetic programming [8], random search [18], and a deterministic walk [23].

Despite promising early results, most G&V techniques are currently limited to generating patches for a relatively small sub-set of single-line bugs [11,18,23]. To repair a wider variety of bugs, techniques will need to use richer, more granular transformation schemas, and to construct multiple-line patches. However, this produces a combinatorial explosion in the size of the search space. This motivates a need for methods to prune the exploded search space.

Inspired by recent work in mutation testing [14,16], we propose to use candidate test suite evaluations to identify suitable fix locations *online*. Mutation-based fault localisation show promising results when ranking statements as candidates for human modification; We explicitly evaluate their utility in assigning suspiciousness scores to candidate repair locations, the key concern in localisation for repair. To determine whether the results of candidate patch evaluations may be used to localise the fault, we first perform a mutation analysis on a sample of a particular G&V repair search space across 28 bugs in six real-world C programs. We use the same ground truth as previous studies on fault localisation, assuming the location(s) of the human-written repair or the injected fault to be a suitable fix location [14,16,25]. For the sake of convenience, we refer to these locations as "faulty"; non-modified statements are considered to be "correct".

We find that faulty locations exhibit a different average rate of passing-to-failing tests across their mutants than statements assumed to be correct. We also observe that an average of 30.07% of (compiling) mutants have no impact on the outcomes of the test suite, mirroring earlier findings by Schulte et al. [20]. Similarly, we find that, on average, 26.44% of mutants covered by at least one previously passing test fail all of their covering tests. These results suggest a largely all-or-nothing search space, in which most mutants either pass all of their (covering) tests, or none at all.

Based on the findings of our analysis, we evaluate a number of alternative fault localisation techniques in terms of their ability to localise statements at which a fix was found during the search (as opposed to assessing how well they localise the location of the human repair). We show that little benefit is gained by incorporating the results of candidate patch evaluations into the fault localisation, and that any gains are not particularly consistent. The best localisation approach using this information outperformed GenProg's default approach on just over half of the cases. To benefit from the knowledge of candidate evaluations, a more granular repair model is needed—to allow subtle faults to be detected—as well as a more effective means of aggregating different sources of fault localisation information. Overall, our primary contributions are:

- A detailed mutation analysis sampled from GenProg's search space, covering 28 bugs across six real-world C programs. Our results show that statement-level mutation operators used in many search-based program repair techniques can identify the code that humans modify to fix bugs.
- An evaluation of several alternative fault localisation techniques which use the test case outcomes of mutants produced during the search. Our results show that, although informative in terms of human-modified bug-fixing code, online mutation-based fault localisation does not definitively outperform existing offline SBFL approaches.
- An informed discussion of the limitations of GenProg's statement-level mutation operators in identifying faulty locations, and how these limitations might be addressed by alternative mutation operators.

2 Fault Localisation in Search-Based Program Repair

In this study, we examine the search space of GenProg, an established generate-and-validate APR technique, with a publicly-available implementation, based on genetic programming. We focus this discussion primarily on GenProg's approach to fault localisation, for illustration, but the principles generalise to most existing techniques in APR.

GenProg assigns suspiciousness values to each program statement based on their coverage by the failing and passing test cases. In the initial formulation, statements executed exclusively by the failing test cases are assigned a weight of 1.0; those executed by both failing and passing tests, 0.1; those not executed by a failing test, 0.0. Alternative weighting schemes have been explored since [9], including those that draw directly on advances in spectrum-based fault localisation [19]. Statements are sampled in proportion to their weight.

We now address Mutation-Based Fault Localisation (MBFL), a relatively new approach based on mutation analysis [14,16]. This analysis generates and evaluates a large number of mutants on the test cases. Each mutant is a variant of the original program, obtained by applying a traditional mutation testing operator (e.g., flip comparison operator) at a single location [16]. Two seminal approaches to MBFL are MUSE [14] and Metallaxis [16]. Both of these approaches share a common intuition: mutants generated at the fault location should exhibit different test suite outcomes to those generated at non-faulty locations. Despite sharing this intuition, each technique generates its suspiciousness values according to contradictory set of assumptions.

Prior to computing suspiciousness values for each statement $s \in S$, Metallaxis first computes explicit suspiciousness values for each mutant $m \in M$. The suspiciousness of a mutant is given by the similarity of its behaviour to that of the original, faulty program, measured using a variant of the Ochiai suspicious-ness metric [25], given below, where $\#K$ is the number of tests that "kill" the mutant (i.e., the tests which the mutant fails), $\#K_n$ is the number of previously failing tests that kill the mutant, and $\#K_p$ is the number of previously passing tests that kill the mutant:

$$\mu_{Metallaxis}(m) = \frac{\#K_n}{\sqrt{\#K \cdot (\#K_p + \#K_n)}} = \frac{\#K_n}{\#K} \tag{1}$$

To determine the suspicious of a statement, the set of mutants at that statement M_s is aggregated as follows:

$$\mu_{Metallaxis}(s; M) = \begin{cases} \max_{m \in M_s} \mu_{Metallaxis}(m) & M_s \neq \emptyset \\ 1.0 & \text{otherwise} \end{cases} \tag{2}$$

MUSE, on the other hand, computes statement suspiciousness directly, based on the average passing-to-failing rate $p2f$ and failing-to-passing $f2p$ rate of mutants at that statement. $p2f$ describes the fraction of previously passing tests that are failed by the mutant; $f2p$ describes the fraction of previously failing tests that are passed by the mutant. MUSE discards all of neutral mutants (i.e., mutants whose test outcomes are the same as the original program), and computes suspiciousness as:

$$\mu_{MUSE}(s) = \frac{1}{\#M_s} \cdot \sum_{m \in M_s} (f2p(m) - \alpha \cdot p2f(m)) \tag{3}$$

where α compensates for the greater likelihood that a previously passing test will fail than a previously failing test will pass:

$$\alpha = \frac{f2p_{all}}{\#M \cdot |T_{Pass}|} \cdot \frac{\#M \cdot |T_{Fail}|}{p2f_{all}} \tag{4}$$

where $f2p_{all}$ and $p2f_{all}$ give the number of tests, across all mutants, whose outcomes change, and T_{Fail} and T_{Pass} denote the set of initially failing and passing test cases, respectively.

One can treat the inner term of μ_{MUSE} as the suspiciousness of a particular mutant. From this perspective, we notice differing behaviours, and underlying assumptions, in the way that MUSE and Metallaxis aggregate mutant results, and how they treat failing-to-passing test outcomes:

– According to Metallaxis, a statement is suspicious as its most suspicious mutant. This behaviour assumes that the search landscape is mostly com-posed of non-neutral mutants. If the search space contains a large number of neutral mutants [20], Metallaxis assigns the maximum suspiciousness value to most statements. In contrast, MUSE actively discards its neutral mutants, and computes the suspiciousness of a statement as the average suspiciousness of its mutants, indicating a robustness to sampling noise.

– Whereas MUSE significantly increases the suspiciousness of statements containing mutants which pass previously failing test cases, Metallaxis implicitly decreases the suspiciousness of such statements. These behaviours highlight a contradiction between the techniques' underlying assumptions: MUSE sees partial solutions as signs of a repair, whilst Metallaxis views them as either irrelevant, or the result of overfitting.

Both techniques have demonstrated significant improvement over previous fault localisation approaches. However, evaluations have been limited to manually-seeded faults in small-to-medium sized programs, and use metrics that have been shown to be inappropriate for automated program repair [19], where the degree of difference in suspiciousness is more important than rank.

3   Analysis

The mutation-based fault localisation approaches described in the previous section suggest a natural overlap with search-based program repair, which effectively produces a large number of candidate mutants throughout the generate-and-validate process. This suggests a mechanism for *online* fault localisation that leverages the existing mutation approach presented by the underlying repair process. However, the raw suspiciousness scores produced by a fault localisation technique are more important than the ranks. Thus, the utility of this approach depends more on the discriminatory power of the $p2f$ and $f2p$ scores than on their raw accuracy (evaluated in the traditional way).

Thus, to determine whether such mutation analysis may be used to improve fault localisation in this context, we first analyse whether mutants at (assumed) faulty and correct statements exhibit different test suite outcomes to one another. Given the experimental parameters enumerated in Sect. 3.1, we begin by answering the following research questions (Sect. 3.2):

– **RQ1:** Can statements that were modified by the human fix be discriminated from those that were not, on the basis of the $p2f$ rates of their mutants?
– **RQ2:** Can human-modified statements be distinguished from non-modified statements, based on the fail-to-passing rates $f2p$ of their mutants?
  As a potential means of improving offline fault localisation, we also ask:
– **RQ3:** Are statements covered by the fewest number of previously passing tests the most likely to contain the fault?

Based on the results of this analysis, we propose and evaluate two new fault localisation strategies for search-based program repair (Sect. 3.3). However, we find that these new strategies do not offer significant improvement over previous SBFL strategies. We provide insight as to why not, as well as implications, supported by additional findings; these are detailed in Sect. 3.4.

3.1 Experimental Setup

We analyse test case results for a sample of single-edit mutants taken from 28 bugs across 6 real-world C programs. Some of these defects have been previously studied in the context of automated program repair; all are provided by the the RepairBox platform.[1] 15 of these bugs are artificial, injected into 3 small-to-medium sized programs sourced from the Software Infrastructure Repository [3]—the same source used to evaluate MUSE and Metallaxis. We include these bugs to determine whether GenProg's repair operators may be used to perform MBFL, rather than traditional mutation testing operators, used by existing approaches [14,16]. To determine whether MBFL remains effective when applied in the wild, we supplement this dataset with 13 real-world bugs across 3 large-scale, real-world programs. Table 1 summarises the studied programs.

Table 1. Subjects under study. "Source" indicates the benchmark source (SIR the Software Infrastructure Repository; RBX, RepairBox); "Scenarios" refers to the number of independent defective versions considered per program; "kLOC" measures the number of thousands of lines of C code in the program; "Tests" indicates the average number of tests over all scenarios for a program.

Source	Program	Scenarios	kLOC	Tests	Artificial?
SIR	gzip	6	6	104	✓
	grep	2	10	146	✓
	sed	7	14	255	✓
RBX	OpenSSL	5	248	77	✗
	Python	4	446	344	✗
	PHP	4	789	8597	✗

We use GenProg, a search-based program repair technique with well-established and commonly-used mutation operators, to focus this evaluation. However, we anticipate the results can generalise to any G&V technique following a similar paradigm. To collect the necessary data for the analysis, we first generated a list of all the single-edit patches within GenProg's search space, before randomly shuffling that list and evaluating as many patches as possible within a 12-hour window. This 12-hour random walk was repeated for each of the bugs within the dataset.[2] We restrict the generation of mutants to the sub-set of statements covered by at least one of the failing test cases. For historical reasons, and given its similarity to traditional mutation testing operators, we also ensured that a deletion was attempted at each statement. For the purposes of balancing replication with performance, we performed each run using a minimal, purpose-built Docker container, provided by RepairBox. We used a C4.Large instance on

---

[1] https://github.com/squaresLab/RepairBox.

[2] Source code and a Docker image for the version of GenProg used by this study is publicly available at: https://bitbucket.org/ChrisTimperley/gp3.

Table 2. Mutation analysis results for each bug scenario. "Mutants" shows number of mutants generated within the 12-hour random walk. "Sample Rate" is the average number of mutants per suspicious statement. "Compiling" shows the percentage of mutants that successfully compiled. "Neutral" shows the percentage of mutants with no effect on test outcomes, whereas "Lethal" shows the percentage of mutants that fail all covering tests.

Program	ID	Mutants	Sample Rate	Compiling	Neutral	Lethal
OpenSSL	0a2dcb6	377	2.48	100.00	14.06	50.66
	4880672	1971	4.82	90.72	22.27	35.51
	6979583	1097	13.06	99.18	26.62	51.23
	8e3854a	3028	4.69	93.66	38.14	25.59
	eddef30	2898	80.50	100.00	55.97	16.84
PHP	01c028a	28	0.06	96.43	7.14	0.00
	11bdb85	32	0.07	96.88	25.00	0.00
	1d6b3f1	741	8.72	88.66	14.57	25.78
	9fb92ee	217	0.51	100.00	28.11	37.33
Python	6c3d527	378	0.46	84.66	64.29	13.76
	a93342b	146	0.37	81.51	53.42	0.68
	b2f3c23	600	3.03	81.83	45.67	14.33
	f584aba	733	0.71	32.74	10.50	5.05
grep	v2-DG_1	628	1.00	98.73	39.17	35.99
	v3-DG_3	2353	10.14	67.06	31.92	31.19
gzip	v1-KL_2	1898	10.20	91.41	23.60	48.79
	v1-KP_1	2301	11.22	92.09	41.11	36.77
	v1-TW_3	2068	13.34	91.34	27.85	40.57
	v4-KL_1	2886	13.49	91.27	43.17	28.83
	v5-KL_1	6437	16.98	90.26	66.75	16.96
	v5-KL_8	1062	1.05	98.68	24.01	31.26
sed	v2-AG_17	1630	1.52	85.77	23.68	30.67
	v2-AG_19	3011	22.47	53.50	8.73	19.93
	v3-AG_11	2579	7.39	78.79	24.74	33.81
	v3-AG_15	1545	2.95	80.71	24.92	26.02
	v3-AG_17	1332	3.95	67.57	16.14	27.40
	v3-AG_18	1235	3.48	67.85	16.92	24.13
	v3-AG_6	2615	5.56	77.06	23.40	31.17
		1637	8.72	84.94	30.07	26.44

Amazon EC2 for the artificial bugs, and a DS1_V2 instance on Microsoft Azure for the real-world bugs.

3.2   Analysis

A brief summary of the results of the mutation analysis is given in Table 2. We observe that most mutants exhibit an all-or-nothing behaviour: either their test outcomes remain wholly unchanged, or all of their covering tests are failed. We also observe low sample rates (<1 mutant per suspicious statement) for most Python and PHP scenarios, because of substantial compilation overhead and, for statements covered by many tests, the cost of evaluating hundreds or thousands of test cases per mutant.

> **RQ1: Can statements that were modified by the human fix be discriminated from those that were not, on the basis of the $p2f$ rates of their mutants?**

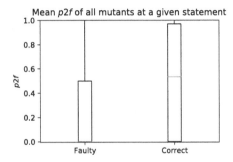

Fig. 1. We observe different mean $p2f$ distributions for faulty and correct statements ($KS2 = 0.301; p = 0.003, \hat{A} = 0.679$ [medium effect]).

To avoid misleading results, we omit mutants that do not compile, and those that are not covered by any of the passing tests. In line with our expectations and previous findings, we observe different mean $p2f$ rates between (assumed) faulty and correct statements, Fig. 1.

Using a two-way Kolmogorov-Smirnov test, we reject the null hypothesis ($p < 0.05$) that the samples for the faulty and correct statements are drawn from the same distribution. Between the $p2f$ distributions for correct and faulty statements, we find an effect size of 0.679 (measured by the Vargha-Delaney $\hat{A}$ measure [22]), indicating that correct statements tend to have a higher mean $p2f$ than faulty statements. This finding supports the intuition that modifications to correct statements are likely to result in a greater degree of functionality loss.

> **RQ2: Can human-modified statements be distinguished from non-modified statements, based on the fail-to-passing rates $f2p$ of their mutants?**

To answer this question, we first removed all non-compiling mutants from consideration. We then removed all mutants corresponding to acceptable solutions, giving us the most complete information possible without knowledge of a solution. Figure 2 compares the mean $f2p$ for faulty and correct statements.

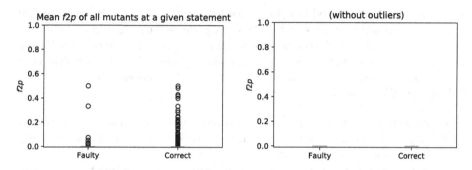

Fig. 2. We observe similar distributions of mean $f2p$ values for faulty and correct statements ($KS2 = 0.185; p = 0.177$). In both cases, more than half of the mutants at each statement did not pass any of the previously failing tests.

We find that the mean $f2p$ is zero for the majority of statements, regardless of whether or not they are assumed to be correct. On closer inspection we find that only 2.09% of mutants have any impact on the outcomes of the previously failing tests. This suggests that $f2p$ information may not be particularly effective at distinguishing faulty and correct statements.

> **RQ3: Are statements covered by the fewest number of previously passing tests the most likely to contain the fault?**

When the search is restricted to the sub-set of statements covered by all of the failing tests, most SBFL techniques become partly redundant, as the number of (non-)executed failing tests is no longer relevant. Instead, it may be preferable to measure statement suspiciousness as a function of the number of executed and non-executed passing test cases.

Using the results of the analysis, we measure the passing test coverage at each statement where a repair was found, and investigate whether (assumed) faulty statements are covered by fewer passing tests. Accounting for the varying sizes of the test suites, we measure the fraction of passing tests that cover each each statement, rather than the number. To determine coverage relative to other statements in the program, we compute the adjusted coverage as:

$$\text{AdjustedCoverage(s)} = \frac{\#T_{Pass}(s) - \text{MinCoverage}}{\#T_{Pass}} \tag{5}$$

where $T_{Pass}(s)$ is the set of passing tests covered by statement s, and MinCoverage is the number of passing tests that cover that least covered statement.

Measuring the adjusted coverage of each scenario, we find that 90% are covered by fewer than 2% of the previously passing tests, supporting our intuition and the intuition of the original suspiciousness metric used in GenProg.

3.3 Fault Localisation

Using the knowledge gained from our mutation analysis, we propose and evaluate two fault localisation strategies for G&V program repair, which may be aggregated. We aggregate localisations by computing their product. To use these layers in a noisy, online context, we ensure that each is numerically stable and that none assigns a suspiciousness of zero to any statement covered by a previously failing test. We consider:

- **Coverage, μ_{Cov}:** produces a 90% probability that a statement with less than 2% adjusted coverage will be selected, and a 10% probability that a statement with a greater level of coverage will be chosen.
- **Pass-to-Fail:** This layer assigns values between zero and one to each statement, based on the pass-to-fail rates $p2f$ of its mutants:

$$\mu_{p2f}(s) = \frac{1}{\#M_s + 1} \cdot \left[1 + \sum_{m \in M_s} (1 - p2f_m) \right] \tag{6}$$

To assess the effectiveness of the fault localisation approaches that combine these layers, we use the mutants of the analysis—excluding any solutions, to avoid potential biases—to generate a set of suspiciousness values μ for each of the bug scenarios. We then measure the accuracy of a fault localisation technique as the probability of selecting a statement that contains a fix found during the random walk.[3]

Table 3 compares the effectiveness of our proposed fault localisation strategies against a selection of existing strategies, across the 11 bugs for which solutions were found during the random walk. We find that no strategy, whether mutation- or spectrum-based, is dominant: Jaccard, the previously reported [19] best SBFL strategy for APR, is outperformed by GenProg's default strategy in 6/11 cases; our Adjusted Coverage strategy beats GenProg in 6/11 cases, but is also beaten by Jaccard in 6/11 cases. Neither Metallaxis nor MUSE dominate GenProg's default strategy: GP beats MUSE in 7 cases (and draws in 2) and Metallaxis in 8 cases.

---

[3] Note, we do not measure how well these techniques localise the statement modified in the human repair, since the patterns observed in this data were used to design these techniques.

Table 3. Comparison of fault localisation accuracies achieved by different approaches, where accuracy is measured by the probability of sampling a statement containing a fix from the resulting distribution. "Cov", "Jac.", "GP" and "MXS" refer to Adjusted Coverage, Jaccard, GenProg and Metallaxis, respectively.

Program	ID	Cov	p2f	Cov × p2f	GP	Jac.	MUSE	MXS
OpenSSL	0a2dcb6	0.14	0.91	0.05	1.23	1.82	1.38	0.53
	6979583	75.26	15.96	79.75	37.68	25.00	8.33	8.46
	8e3854a	0.11	1.01	0.10	0.71	0.61	0.95	0.73
	eddef30	76.04	45.92	77.58	66.67	54.55	41.67	41.67
gzip	v1-KP_1	4.46	4.67	6.49	6.63	4.63	2.44	2.60
	v1-TW_3	14.21	4.69	15.32	9.20	6.60	1.94	2.10
	v4-KL_1	2.73	1.72	3.08	2.69	3.03	0.94	0.99
	v5-KL_1	0.33	0.36	0.39	0.40	0.34	0.26	0.27
	v5-KL_8	6.59	0.34	4.67	2.17	4.08	0.30	0.89
sed	v2-AG_17	0.02	0.21	0.02	0.19	0.15	0.19	0.53
	v3-AG_11	6.95	0.61	3.09	0.57	1.92	0.57	0.81

Our $p2f$ strategy is beaten by GenProg in 8/11 cases, indicating that passing-to-information, when used alone, is not particularly effective at identifying suitable fix locations. When the Adjusted Coverage and $p2f$ strategies are aggregated by computing their product, the resulting hybrid beats GenProg and Jaccard in 6 and 8 cases, respectively. If the online modifications to μ_{p2f} are removed and $1 - p2f(s)$ is used to compute suspiciousness instead, the resulting localisation outperforms GenProg's fault localisation in all cases.

We experimented with ways of using $f2p$ information, but found the approach either attained near-perfect accuracy (since the only mutants to pass any of the previously failing tests were at statements where a solution was found), or substantially worse accuracy (since all mutants, other than the solutions at the faulty statements, failed all of the previously failing tests).

3.4 Discussion

From the results of our evaluation, we observe relatively little benefit in incorporating information learned from the evaluation of candidate patches into the fault localisation, in contrast to previous attempts to use mutation analysis to locate faults. We believe there may be a number of reasons for this result:

– **Lack of mutants:** for a number of bug scenarios, we find that excessively long test suite evaluation and compilation times prevent the search from producing an adequate sample of mutants at each statement. In previous research, Moon et al. [15] show that the performance of MUSE is sensitive to the number of samples—at low sample rates (i.e., the average number of samples per statement), MUSE is outperformed by offline SBFL techniques.

- **Lack of passing test coverage:** in cases where most statements are not covered by any passing tests, these statements will be assigned a suspiciousness score of 1.0 by $\mu_{P2F}(s)$; Metallaxis will also assign maximal suspiciousness to such statements. As a result, if the faulty statements are covered by any passing tests, they will be suppressed; if not, the fault localisation will fail to identify the faulty statements amongst the many statements that are not covered by the passing tests.
- **All-or-nothing $f2p$ response:** within GenProg's search space, we observe erratic negative test suite behaviour. In some cases, the only statements with mutants that passed a previously failing test were those where a repair was found. In other cases, previously failing tests were frequently passed, except at the statements where a repair was found. If one knew which type of $f2p$ response one was dealing with, a more accurate fault localisation might be possible. In the future, we plan to explore whether the rarity of passing previously failing tests might be used to determine whether a given failing-to-passing event is a coincidence or indicative of a potential repair at that statement.
- **Machine-generated repairs:** Across the random walk for each of the 28 bugs, we found fixes at a total of 48 different statements. Only 5 of these 48 statements were also modified by the original patch. This finding suggests that GenProg is crafting repairs unlike those that a human would make, supporting arguments made by Monperrus [13] that automated repair should consider alien-looking repairs, rather than restricting itself to producing human-like repairs. The disparity between the findings of RQ1, that faulty statements exhibit a different mean $p2f$ to correct statements, and the lack of improvement when mutant information is added to the fault localisation may suggest that locations patched by GenProg are less distinguishable by their mutants' behaviours.
- **Coarse-grained mutation operators:** one explanation for the relative lack of success from incorporating the results of the mutation analysis into the fault localisation may be due to the coarse-grained nature of the repair operators within GenProg's search space. With such actions, it may be difficult to expose subtle bugs within the statement, that might otherwise be identified using finer-grained mutation testing operators. In our analysis, we find that most repairs tend to either have no effect on the outcomes of the test suite, or to cause all of their covering tests to fail; this all-or-nothing behaviour may be a consequence of the granularity of the search operators.
- **Combining information:** to combine each of the proposed layers of fault localisation from our evaluation, we computed the product of each of the layers—a necessarily arbitrary decision. A meaningful and effective way of combining information from multiple sources, which may corroborate or conflict, is not immediately clear.

These results suggest a number of possibly fruitful directions to translate the potential of mutation analysis approaches such as MUSE into efficiency gains in automated program repair. Richer repair models, with lower-level repair operators (such as those traditionally used in mutation testing), may mitigate the all-or-nothing behaviour exhibited by mutants generated using GenProg's coarse-grained operators. Test outcomes for particular types of mutants may be informative in refining suspiciousness beyond the statement-level, and may even serve to predict the type of repair that might be needed. Finally, simple weighted averages or products, as we explored in Sect. 3.3, may be inadequate; it is possible that ensemble learning techniques could more effectively combine sources of information.

4   Related Work

In this section, we discuss previous research related to fault localisation within automated program repair, and other approaches to addressing the difficulties of scaling to larger repairs and search spaces.

Instead of tackling the problem of a growing search space by exploiting knowledge learnt online, several techniques have been proposed to learn the likelihood of candidate repairs based on their features by mining large collections of source code repositories [7,11,21]. A complementary approach to tackle the problem of the expanding search space is to reduce the cost of evaluating candidate patches, whether through test case prioritisation [17,18], test case sampling [4] or removal of redundant tests and (known) semantically equivalent mutants [23]. These approaches complement improved fault localisation for repair. In contrast to syntactic- or heuristic-based G&V repair, semantic repair techniques [5,12] infer partial specifications of desired behavior using test suites and then use synthesis to construct replacement code that satisfies them. These techniques also use test suites to localise faults and to validate patches, and thus could also benefit from improved fault localisation.

A large number of methods for automated debugging and fault localisation exist, including program slicing [24], delta-debugging [26] and various forms of spectra-based fault localisation [25]. To date, most automated repair techniques exclusively use SBFL; it is general and low-cost. SBFL approaches, to which GenProg's default fault localisation method belongs, use the test case coverage information for the program to assign suspiciousness values to each of its locations. Qi et al. [19] conduct a study of the effectiveness of various SBFL techniques when used with GenProg, finding that the Jaccard suspiciousness metric produced the best fault localisation information, as measured by the number of candidate repairs required to find a solution. In contrast to our study, we find no one approach to fault localisation is dominant.

Schulte et al. [20] conduct an empirical study of the robustness of 22 programs to mutation using GenProg's operators, finding that over 30% of generated mutants exhibit no change to the outcomes of their test suites. This behaviour may hinder the effectiveness of MBFL techniques. For instance, Metallaxis will assign maximal suspiciousness to statements with neutral mutants, causing the faulty statements to be suppressed.

5   Conclusions

Although mutation analysis can distinguish between human-modified and human-unmodified statements in a bug-fixing context, these results do not translate directly into clear gains as a fault localisation technique for the purposes of program repair. However, our results provide insight into why this may be the case, and suggest several possibly fruitful future directions for fault localisation for search-based repair. Given the previous successes of Metallaxis and MUSE with mutation testing operators, we believe GenProg's all-or-nothing search space, in which most edits are either neutral or fail all of their covering tests, may be partly responsible for the lack of clear gains. Low levels of passing test coverage may also preclude the use of mutation-based fault localisation techniques.

To benefit from the knowledge of test suite outcomes for candidate patches, we believe a set of more finely grained mutation operators are required—a requirement that will most likely allow a larger number of bugs to be solved at the same time.

To encourage further investigation, all results from this study, together with the files used to conduct it, are available at:

https://bitbucket.org/ChrisTimperley/ssbse-2017-data.

Acknowledgements. This research was partially funded by AFRL (#FA8750-15-2-0075) and DARPA (#FA8750-16-2-0042), and an EPSRC DTG; the authors are grateful for their support. Any opinions, findings, or recommendations expressed are those of the authors and do not necessarily reflect those of the US Government. The authors additionally wish to thank the anonymous reviewers, whose comments were especially insightful and constructive.

References

1. Cambridge University Study States Software Bugs Cost Economy $312 Billion Per Year. http://www.prweb.com/releases/2013/1/prweb10298185.htm. Accessed Apr 2017
2. Arcuri, A.: Evolutionary repair of faulty software. Appl. Soft Comput. **11**(4), 3494–3514 (2011)
3. Do, H., Elbaum, S., Rothermel, G.: Supporting controlled experimentation with testing techniques: an infrastructure and its potential impact. Empirical Software Eng. **10**(4), 405–435 (2005)
4. Fast, E., Le Goues, C., Forrest, S., Weimer, W.: Designing better fitness functions for automated program repair. In: Genetic and Evolutionary Computation Conference, GECCO 2010, pp. 965–972 (2010)
5. Ke, Y., Stolee, K.T., Le Goues, C., Brun, Y.: Repairing programs with semantic code search. In: Automated Software Engineering, ASE 2015, pp. 295–306 (2015)
6. Kim, D., Nam, J., Song, J., Kim, S.: Automatic patch generation learned from human-written patches. In: International Conference on Software Engineering, ICSE 2013, pp. 802–811 (2013)

7. Le, X.B.D., Lo, D., Goues, C.L.: History driven program repair. In: International Conference on Software Analysis, Evolution, and Reengineering, SANER 2016, vol. 1, pp. 213–224 (2016)

8. Le Goues, C., Dewey-Vogt, M., Forrest, S., Weimer, W.: A systematic study of automated program repair: fixing 55 out of 105 bugs for $8 each. In: International Conference on Software Engineering, ICSE 2012, pp. 3–13 (2012)

9. Le Goues, C., Weimer, W., Forrest, S.: Representations and operators for improving evolutionary software repair. In: Genetic and Evolutionary Computation Conference, GECCO 2012, pp. 959–966 (2012)

10. Long, F., Rinard, M.: Staged program repair with condition synthesis. In: Joint Meeting on Foundations of Software Engineering, ESEC/FSE 2015, pp. 166–178 (2015)

11. Long, F., Rinard, M.: Automatic patch generation by learning correct code. In: Principles of Programming Languages, POPL 2016, pp. 298–312 (2016)

12. Mechtaev, S., Yi, J., Roychoudhury, A.: Angelix: scalable multiline program patch synthesis via symbolic analysis. In: International Conference on Software Engineering, ICSE 2016, pp. 691–701 (2016)

13. Monperrus, M.: A critical review of automatic patch generation learned from human-written patches: essay on the problem statement and the evaluation of automatic software repair. In: International Conference on Software Engineering, ICSE 2014, pp. 234–242 (2014)

14. Moon, S., Kim, Y., Kim, M., Yoo, S.: Ask the mutants: mutating faulty programs for fault localization. In: International Conference on Software Testing, Verification and Validation, ICST 2014, pp. 153–162 (2014)

15. Moon, S., Kim, Y., Kim, M., Yoo, S.: Hybrid-MUSE: mutating faulty programs for precise fault localization. Technical report, KAIST (2014)

16. Papadakis, M., Le Traon, Y.: Metallaxis-FL: mutation-based fault localization. Softw. Test. Verification Reliab. 25(5–7), 605–628 (2015)

17. Qi, Y., Mao, X., Lei, Y.: Efficient automated program repair through fault-recorded testing prioritization. In: International Conference on Software Maintenance, pp. 180–189 (2013)

18. Qi, Y., Mao, X., Lei, Y., Dai, Z., Wang, C.: The strength of random search on automated program repair. In: International Conference on Software Engineering, ICSE 2014, pp. 254–265 (2014)

19. Qi, Y., Mao, X., Lei, Y., Wang, C.: Using automated program repair for evaluating the effectiveness of fault localization techniques. In: International Symposium on Software Testing and Analysis, ISSTA 2013, pp. 191–201 (2013)

20. Schulte, E., Fry, Z.P., Fast, E., Weimer, W., Forrest, S.: Software mutational robustness. Genet. Program Evolvable Mach. 15(3), 281–312 (2013)

21. Soto, M., Thung, F., Wong, C.P., Le Goues, C., Lo, D.: A deeper look into bug fixes: patterns, replacements, deletions, and additions. In: International Conference on Mining Software Repositories, MSR 2016, pp. 512–515 (2016)

22. Vargha, A., Delaney, H.D.: A critique and improvement of the CL common language effect size statistics of McGraw and Wong. J. Educ. Behav. Stat. 25(2), 101–132 (2000)

23. Weimer, W., Fry, Z.P., Forrest, S.: Leveraging program equivalence for adaptive program repair: Models and first results. In: International Conference on Automated Software Engineering, ASE 2013, pp. 356–366 (2013)

24. Weiser, M.: Program slicing. In: International Conference on Software Engineering, ICSE 1981, pp. 439–449 (1981)
25. Yoo, S.: Evolving human competitive spectra-based fault localisation techniques. In: Fraser, G., Teixeira de Souza, J. (eds.) SSBSE 2012. LNCS, vol. 7515, pp. 244–258. Springer, Heidelberg (2012). doi:10.1007/978-3-642-33119-0_18
26. Zeller, A., Hildebrandt, R.: Simplifying and isolating failure-inducing input. IEEE Trans. Software Eng. **28**(2), 183–200 (2002)

Short Research Papers

MuSynth: Program Synthesis via Code Reuse and Code Manipulation

Vineeth Kashyap[✉], Rebecca Swords, Eric Schulte, and David Melski

GrammaTech, Inc., Ithaca, NY 14850, USA
{vkashyap,rswords,eschulte,melski}@grammatech.com

Abstract. MuSynth takes a draft C program with "holes", a test suite, and optional simple hints—that together specify a desired functionality—and performs program synthesis to auto-complete the holes. First, MuSynth leverages a similar-code-search engine to find potential "donor" code (similar to the required functionality) from a corpus. Second, MuSynth applies various synthesis mutations in an evolutionary loop to find and modify the donor code snippets to fit the input context and produce the expected functionality. This paper focuses on the latter, and our preliminary evaluation shows that MuSynth's combination of type-based heuristics, simple hints, and evolutionary search are each useful for efficient program synthesis.

Keywords: Program synthesis · Evolutionary computation · Code reuse · Big code

1 Introduction

Software developers have collectively written an enormous amount of code. Availability of such "big code" in searchable archives has spurred recent research [12, 13], with the overarching theme of leveraging existing code to improve developer productivity. In this work, we use "big code" for program synthesis, to automatically generate programs that meet developer's requirements [7].

Code reuse [5] is widespread as it aids rapid prototyping with limited resources. It includes both as-is reuse and reuse involving code modification to fit a new context. As an example of the latter, to reduce time-to-market, developers adapt existing code to run on embedded devices with constrained resources—it may be infeasible to load whole image processing libraries, but code snippets implementing specific functionality from these libraries could be practically re-used and customized for the embedded device.

In many software development scenarios, the functionality that a developer is attempting to create already exists somewhere else, perhaps with minor differences. MuSynth is an automated program synthesis engine that (1) uses

This research was supported by DARPA MUSE award #FA8750-14-2-0270. The views, opinions, and/or findings contained in this article are those of the authors and should not be interpreted as representing the official views or policies of the Department of Defense or the U.S. Government.

© Springer International Publishing AG 2017
T. Menzies and J. Petke (Eds.): SSBSE 2017, LNCS 10452, pp. 117–123, 2017.
DOI: 10.1007/978-3-319-66299-2_8

partial specifications of the functionality being developed, (2) searches a large corpus for "donor" code that implements a similar functionality, and (3) reuses and modifies the donor code in the developer's context to produce desired functionality. In this paper, we focus on a research question regarding (3): given a partial specification via developer-provided tests and some donor code that potentially implements the functionality, how can we automatically manipulate the donor code to incorporate it into the developer's context? MUSYNTH combines type-based heuristics, developer hints, and evolutionary search to address this research question. Based on our preliminary results, we believe MUSYNTH is a novel and promising approach to program synthesis that can be effectively combined with traditional logic-based approaches [3] in the future.

2 Related Work

Program synthesis from partial programs. Syntax-guided synthesis [3] uses partial programs (sketches) and user specifications as input to generate programs. Specifications are logical predicates (pre- and post-conditions) describing the desired behavior of the program. Instead of using purely logical techniques to synthesize holes, our work exploits code reuse and evolutionary search.

Evolutionary search in program repair. Evolutionary search has been successful in the related field of program repair [10]. Although program repair can be viewed as synthesis of bug fixes, unlike program synthesis, program repairs are not expected to generate new functionality.

Program synthesis based on existing code. Recent techniques [4,12] have trained deep neural networks on existing code and used the generated models in program synthesis. MUSYNTH can augment these techniques. Program splicing [11] uses relevant donor code for synthesis but, unlike MUSYNTH, performs an exhaustive enumerative search over unmodified (except for variable renaming) donor code.

Evolutionary search and program synthesis. Evolutionary program sketching [6] modifies sketches until traditional techniques [3] can fill holes. Unlike MUSYNTH, the holes they consider are very simple, and can be filled only with constants or variables. Katz et al. [9] use genetic programming guided by model checking for program synthesis. Whereas their approach requires a formal specification of the functionality being synthesized, MUSYNTH works with partial specifications.

3 MuSynth Overview

Figure 1 provides an overview of MUSYNTH. It uses a similar-code-search engine to identify relevant donor code from a large corpus that may implement the required functionality. These donors are then mutated to fit the developer's problem context. The mutations are guided by evolutionary search. This paper

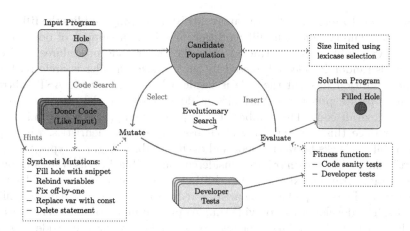

Fig. 1. MuSynth architecture. Gray boxes are the input, green box is the output. (Color figure online)

focuses on the donor code mutations and the evolutionary search in MuSynth, which are built on top of Clang [2] and Software Evolution Library [14].

The developer provides a draft program containing "holes" along with test cases and optional hints that specify the expected functionality of the completed program. MuSynth synthesizes code to appear in the holes and does not modify code outside of the holes. The program context surrounding the holes drives the search for similar functionality (i. e., the donor code) by using Source Forager (SF) [8], a similar-code-search engine. SF takes a C procedure as input—optionally with holes—and returns a list of C procedures from a large corpus that are the most input-similar and potentially relevant for subsequent synthesis. SF employs multiple code features from the surrounding context for code search, such as natural language (comments, variable and function names), abstractions of ASTs (Abstract Syntax Trees), types used and operations performed. Currently, SF can search over a million procedures in under two seconds.

MuSynth maintains a candidate population of program variants: each variant is derived by "filling" the holes in the draft program. At each step of the evolution, (1) a variant is selected, (2) a synthesis mutation is applied to the variant, (3) the variant is evaluated for fitness by compiling and running developer tests and various code sanity tests (i. e., tests finish within reasonable resource usage and time limits, and do not exit/abort early), and (4) based on the results of the evaluation, the mutated variant either re-enters population, or if good enough, is presented as the solution. MuSynth uses lexicase selection [15] over test cases and limits the size of the population to a pre-specified maximum. Evolutionary steps occur in parallel across threads. For successful synthesis, MuSynth requires the code search results to contain at least one relevant donor procedure, high-quality developer tests, and a correct (i. e., feasible to solve) draft program.

Figure 2 shows a simplified example sequence of synthesis mutations. The draft program declares an uninitialized array, a loop to iterate over the array, leaving a hole to zero-initialize the array. MUSYNTH always applies the **fill** mutation to any empty hole. The fill mutation first finds a snippet of donor code: various AST subtrees are extracted from the donor code procedures, and one of them is randomly selected, biased by subtree size (smaller is preferred) and the hole position (e. g., if the hole is inside a loop, donor code AST subtrees within loops are preferred). Variables in donor code are then mapped to the ones in the draft code. The number of such possible mappings is typically large, and to reduce this number, MUSYNTH uses type-based heuristics, i. e., type-compatibility checks between donor and draft variables. E.g, the types "array of `short`" and "pointer to `char`" are considered compatible, because the same operations (e. g., array indexing and bit shifting) can be applied on variables with either type. These type-based heuristics reduce the number of non-compiling variants. The developer can provide simple optional hints to MUSYNTH, such as (1) the superset of variables expected to be used in synthesized code, and (2) the subset of the variables that must be modified by the synthesized code. These hints help further reduce the number of possible mappings. Here, fill mutation maps the donor variables `x`, `index` to draft variables `array`, `j` respectively.

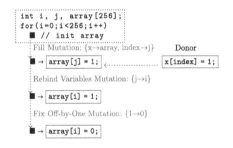

Fig. 2. Example sequence of mutations.

A **rebind** mutation attempts to find an alternate variable mapping for the hole, further exploring potential variable bindings. Here, `j` is renamed to `i` (of compatible type), and `array` is left unchanged. A **fix off-by-one** replaces a constant in the hole with an off-by-one constant: here, `1` is replaced by `0`. Finally, this change creates the correct zero-initialization. Other mutations frequently used by MUSYNTH are: **replace variable with a constant**, **delete statement**, **refill** (which throws away the current contents of the hole and refills with new donor snippet), and **insert new statement** (insert a new donor statement at random within the hole).

4   Evaluation

Our evaluation goal is to understand the effectiveness of MUSYNTH on a benchmark suite [1] of program synthesis challenges, openly available for review. The benchmarks consist of 3 algorithms: (1) image contrast enhancement using histogram equalization, (2) binary search, and (3) insertion sort. For each algorithm, we found an existing implementation online, removed code at different program points to create holes, and wrote test cases to specify the expected functionality. As it is not the focus of the paper, we cached the results (4–5 similar procedures [1] per algorithm) of running SF on these benchmarks—they constitute the donor code used in synthesis. The time taken by SF is *not* included in the reported times below. Table 1 summarizes our evaluation. Column 1 lists the various benchmarks—each is a draft program with a hole of different size and program location. Column 2 indicates a proxy for the expected complexity of the hole as a pair of numbers: (1) the number of n-ary operations expected to be in the hole (such as assignment, array indexing, bit shifting), (2) the number of variables expected to be used in the hole. These numbers were computed based on the original code that was replaced with corresponding holes.

We run MuSynth under 4 configurations to evaluate the research question outlined in Sect. 1. Evolutionary search is used by EVO^{NONE}, EVO^{SOME}, and EVO^{ALL}. EVO^{NONE} runs without any hints from the developer. EVO^{SOME} is provided the superset of the variables expected in the holes. In addition to these hints, EVO^{ALL} is provided the subset of the variables that must be modified by the hole. $RAND^{ALL}$ is the same as EVO^{ALL}, except that it uses random search instead (i.e., unguided search that always starts with a fill mutation, and then randomly applies a synthesis mutation, but restarts when uncompilable variants are produced). All 4 configurations use type-based heuristics—without which most benchmarks time out—and the same probabilities for all the synthesis mutations. An exhaustive enumerative search of the infinite solution space requires specifying an order for applying the synthesis mutations and variable bindings. Instead of hand-picking one such ordering, we avoid bias by using $RAND^{ALL}$ for comparison. The rightmost 4 columns in Table 1 provide the time taken (in seconds) for running MuSynth on different benchmarks until a correct solution is found. We run each experiment 10 times and the median time is reported. Experiments were run on an AMD ×64 machine (2.6 GHz, 4 cores, 16 GB main memory), with a population of maximum size 1000, 4 threads, and a 30 min timeout (∞ is used to indicate timeouts). The hole synthesized by running EVO^{ALL} on the benchmark contrast-enhance-4 is shown in Fig. 3 as an example of MuSynth's synthesis capabilities.

Table 1. Summary of evaluation results (fastest time highlighted in boxes).

Benchmark	Complexity	EVO^{NONE}	EVO^{SOME}	EVO^{ALL}	$RAND^{ALL}$
contrast-enhance-0	(2, 2)	239.97	5.18	4.88	4.40
contrast-enhance-1	(4, 4)	141.75	28.32	4.88	27.68
contrast-enhance-2	(7, 5)	1792.71	28.93	4.91	5.23
contrast-enhance-3	(10, 5)	∞	200.11	80.56	17.77
contrast-enhance-4	(10, 7)	∞	∞	576.17	∞
binary-search-0	(11, 5)	46.80	69.45	37.24	∞
binary-search-1	(8, 5)	661.06	72.46	12.52	15.05
binary-search-2	(12, 5)	26.32	11.35	12.91	10.97
insertion-sort-0	(16, 4)	19.66	9.65	9.74	9.81
insertion-sort-1	(5, 2)	34.70	13.74	8.18	14.70
insertion-sort-2	(19, 5)	4.96	4.43	4.26	3.55
insertion-sort-3	(4, 2)	5.27	5.66	5.16	3.93

```
for (i = 0; i < L; i++) {
  foo = ((unsigned long)histogram[i] << N);
  cdf += 255 * (foo/(unsigned long)pixels);
  gray_level_mapping[i] = ((unsigned long)(cdf>>N)) & 0xff;
}
```

Fig. 3. Synthesized code (indicated in red) for contrast-enhance-4, which required, among other things, finding the correct name bindings for seven variables and macros, and fixing an off-by-one error. The surrounding context has been elided for space. The donor code that gets adapted here uses a different image representation format and different amount of bit shifting than the synthesized code. This result shows that donor code can be adapted even when it uses different data structures or contains errors. (Color figure online)

Table 1 shows that in almost all cases, EVO^{ALL} is either the fastest, or is close to the fastest. EVO^{ALL} is also the only one to successfully complete (i. e., passes all test cases, with solutions manually verified afterwards) on all benchmarks within the time limit. This result indicates that *developer hints can significantly reduce synthesis time.* RAND^{ALL} is the fastest in a few cases because of the low overhead (i. e., no population to maintain). However, it times out in cases that require sequencing of multiple synthesis mutations. This result indicates that *evolutionary search is useful in navigating a large search space of synthesis mutations.* With these results, we believe that type-based heuristics, developer hints, and evolutionary search contributes to efficient program synthesis.

References

1. Program Synthesis Challenge Benchmark. https://github.com/ssbse-2017-submission/synthesis-challenges
2. The Clang Project. https://clang.llvm.org/
3. Alur, R., Bodik, R., Juniwal, G., Martin, M.M., Raghothaman, M., Seshia, S.A., Singh, R., Solar-Lezama, A., Torlak, E., Udupa, A.: Syntax-guided synthesis. In: FMCAD. IEEE (2013)
4. Balog, M., Gaunt, A.L., Brockschmidt, M., Nowozin, S., Tarlow, D.: DeepCoder: Learning to Write Programs. ArXiv e-prints., November 2016
5. Barr, E.T., Brun, Y., Devanbu, P., Harman, M., Sarro, F.: The plastic surgery hypothesis. In: FSE. ACM (2014)
6. Błądek, I., Krawiec, K.: Evolutionary program sketching. In: McDermott, J., Castelli, M., Sekanina, L., Haasdijk, E., García-Sánchez, P. (eds.) EuroGP 2017. LNCS, vol. 10196, pp. 3–18. Springer, Cham (2017). doi:10.1007/978-3-319-55696-3_1
7. Gulwani, S.: Dimensions in program synthesis. In: PPDP. ACM (2010)
8. Kashyap, V., Brown, D.B., Liblit, B., Melski, D., Reps, T.: Source Forager: A Search Engine for Similar Source Code. ArXiv e-prints (2017)
9. Katz, G., Peled, D.A.: Synthesis of parametric programs using genetic programming and model checking. In: INFINITY (2013)
10. Le Goues, C., Nguyen, T., Forrest, S., Weimer, W.: GenProg: a generic method for automatic software repair. IEEE Trans. Softw. Eng. **38**(1), 54–72 (2012)

11. Lu, Y., Chaudhuri, S., Jermaine, C., Melski, D.: Data-Driven Program Completion. ArXiv e-prints, May 2017
12. Murali, V., Chaudhuri, S., Jermaine, C.: Bayesian Sketch Learning for Program Synthesis. ArXiv e-prints (2017)
13. Raychev, V., Vechev, M., Krause, A.: Predicting program properties from "Big Code". In: POPL. ACM (2015)
14. Schulte, E.: Neutral networks of real-world programs and their application to automated software evolution. Ph.D. thesis, University of New Mexico, Albuquerque, USA, July 2014. https://cs.unm.edu/~eschulte/dissertation
15. Spector, L.: Assessment of problem modality by differential performance of lexicase selection in genetic programming: a preliminary report. In: GECCO. ACM (2012)

Human Resource Optimization for Bug Fixing: Balancing Short-Term and Long-Term Objectives

Elias Khalil, Mustafa Assaf, and Abdel Salam Sayyad[(⊠)]

Master Program in Software Engineering, Birzeit University, Ramallah, Palestine
eliasdkh@gmail.com, mustsaf@gmail.com, asayyad@birzeit.edu

Abstract. In software development projects, bugs are usually accumulated and technical debt gets bigger over time. Managers decide to reduce the technical debt by planning one or more iterations for bug fixing. The time required to fix a bug depends on the required skill and the resource skill level. Managers seek to achieve fixing the highest number of bugs during the iteration while at the same time fixing the highest possible number of high severity and high priority bugs. In this study, we optimize the human resource assignment to achieve the objectives above, using multi-objective evolutionary algorithms, and then we add a fourth objective, i.e. that the bugs left out of the iteration should require the least time to finish. We show that the additional objective can be optimized without the detriment of other objectives. The lesson is that complicating the multi-objective problem formulation can help with the overall quality of the solutions.

Keywords: Human resource allocation · Software project planning · Agile development · Search-based software engineering

1 Introduction

Software products should be delivered with high quality within time and budget. This requires spending high effort on testing and maintenance [2,11]. Statistics showed that 80% of development cost is spent on bug fixing [10]. Unfortunately, project budget is usually limited, where just 32% of software projects are completed on time and within budget [4]. These facts raise the need to balance the effort spent on testing and maintenance and the limited schedule and budget.

Prior studies showed that selecting bugs to fix within a target planning period, and the criteria of assigning bugs to developers are significant factors affecting time to fix bugs [1,7,11]. Additionally, assigning a bug to the right human resource has a significant impact on the maintenance period or on the amount or nature of the fixed bugs during this period.

Resource allocation is considered an NP-Hard complex problem [3]. The complexity of this problem arises from the high number of combinations of possible

© Springer International Publishing AG 2017
T. Menzies and J. Petke (Eds.): SSBSE 2017, LNCS 10452, pp. 124–129, 2017.
DOI: 10.1007/978-3-319-66299-2_9

allocation and the impact of the allocation on product development time, cost and quality, and overall project success.

This study focuses on human resource allocation for bugs within an agile process. Developing a product in an agile process passes through a sequence of iterations, each having a fixed period. By the end of the iteration, some bugs are moved to a backlog to be fixed in upcoming iterations. Hence, bugs accumulate in the backlog and the technical debt gets larger. At a certain point, management decides to plan one or more iterations dedicated to reducing the technical debit. The fact that resource allocation impacts the plan output raises the need to identify a close-to-optimal HR allocation using SBSE techniques.

The contribution of this paper is that it introduces and evaluates two formulations of the problem; one with three objectives (total bugs fixed, severe bugs fixed and high priority bugs fixed); and another where the time left to fix remaining bugs is added as a fourth objective. We show how adding the long-term quality objective does not hurt the quality of the three-objective case.

The rest of the paper is organized as follows: In Sect. 2 we describe experiment design and dataset. In Sect. 3 we show our results. And we provide a conclusion in Sect. 4.

2   Experimental Setup

In this section, we discuss the setup of our experiment, including the optimization method, chromosome structure, fitness evaluation, experiment configuration, and the dataset.

2.1   Multi-Objective Optimization

Multi objective algorithms provide a Pareto front of nondominated solutions. A solution $x^{(1)}$ is said to be dominating $x^{(2)}$ if $x^{(1)}$ is not worse than $x^{(2)}$ in all objectives and $x^{(1)}$ is better than $x^{(2)}$ in one or more objectives [9].

Many search-based algorithms have been studied in the past 20 years. Evolutionary algorithms has provided significant solutions for both single and multi objectives search based problem. For this study, we use Non-dominated Sorting Genetic Algorithm II (NSGAII)[5], which is the most widely used algorithm in Pareto-Optimal SBSE [8].

2.2   Chromosome Structure

A bug distribution plan is considered as an optimization solution where each bug is assigned to one developer. A list of bugs are assigned to a single developer. A binary solution is used to represent a bug distribution plan. It consists of a number of binary genes representing bugs to be fixed in the iteration as shown in Fig. 1. Each Chromosome contains n bugs (genes) and each gene consists of m bits representing the developer id, in addition to 5 bits as a sequence number.

This sequence number is used to handle the sequence that the developer will follow to fix bugs assigned to her.

Solutions usually have more than one bug assigned to a single developer. Thus two or more bugs may have the same sequence number. To solve this issue, a pseudo random number generator (PRNG) with this number as a seed is used to generate a list of unique numbers $gSeq_i$ where i is between 1 and number of bugs (n). Bug i with less $gSeq_i$ is planned to be fixed first.

Fig. 1. Chromosome structure.

2.3 Multi-objective Fitness Evaluation

Every bug has an estimated ETA set by a developer or manager. Usually this ETA is estimated based on an average skill level. A low skill level developer working on a medium or high skill level bug will spend more time to fix it. The opposite is also valid where a developer working on a bug requiring a skill level lower than the developer level, is expected to fix it in a time less than the bug ETA. Adjusted time for the developer to fix a bug ($Adjusted\,ETA$) depends on both the bug ETA, developer skill level ($Skill_i$) for the specific bug category and bug required skill level (Bug_iSkill)

$$Skill_i = f(dev_{id}, category(bug_{id}), Bug_iSkill) \tag{1}$$

Adjusted estimated time to fix a bug i can be estimated by the skill level of the developer $skill_i$ relative to the bug category

$$AdjustedETA = ETA\ f(\frac{skill_i}{requiredskill}) \tag{2}$$

Each solution is a sequence of bugs to be fixed:

$$dev_iList = \{B_{s_1}, B_{s_2}....B_{s_n}\} \tag{3}$$

A developer can fix number of bugs on the planned bugs list of the solution during iteration time T_{it}. This can be calculated by summing up the bugs fix time sequentially (Bs_i) until adding one more bug exceeds the iteration period.

$$BL_{it}(Dev_i) = \{B_{s_1}, B_{s_2}....B_{s_t}\}$$

$$where \sum_{j=1}^{t} adjustedETA(B_{s_j}) \leq IterationTime \tag{4}$$

Based on iteration time and bugs assigned to each developer, Total bugs fixed in an iteration $B - Fixed_{it}$ is defined as union of bugs assign to each developer.

$$Fixed_{it} = \cup_{i=1}^{d} BL_{it}(Dev_i) \tag{5}$$

An additional objective outside of the iteration scope is added to the optimization. This objective represents the time required to finish all bugs in the backlog which should be minimized. This time can be calculated by summing the time required to fix each developer bugs.

$$TotalTime = \sum_{i=1}^{n} adjustedETA\,(B_i) \tag{6}$$

In summary, the objective fitness are represented using the following values:

1. Total number of bugs fixed in the iteration
2. High severity bugs fixed in the iteration
3. High priority bugs fixed in the iteration
4. Total period to fix all bugs including the iteration planned bugs

2.4 jMetal Study

jMetal framework [6] is used to build and run the study for both three and four objectives. Default jMetal configuration is used as tunning the algorithms for better results is not the purpose of this study (Table 1).

Table 1. jMetal experiment configuration

Population size	100	Crossover type	Single point
Crossover probability	0.9	Mutation type	Bit flip
Mutation probability	0.01	Max evaluations	100,000

2.5 Dataset

The data provided for this study was extracted from a real bugs repository. Bugs were selected randomly for each set used in the study. For privacy reasons, the title, description, and other properties indicating any relation to the organization, industry or product were omitted. The remaining properties are the significant properties related to this study including ETA, severity, priority and required skill level. Additionally, a product category or module is added as a value between 1 to 5 representing 5 categories of the product where category name is removed for the same confidentiality reasons.

The trimmed dataset used by this study is hosted on the cloud[1]. It shows two employee files that include four or eight employees data. Skill level is ordered

---

[1] http://bzu.cloud:8080/BugsSBSE/resources/.

from lowest to highest as 1, 2, 3. Additionally, each employee is rated with a skill 1 to 3 on 5 product categories. In addition, two sets of 50 or 100 bugs and their properties are included.

3   Results

A jMetal experiment setup is used for both three and four objectives. jMetal is configured for 40 runs on 4 problem setups as follows: (1) 50 bugs, 4 developers. (2) 100 bugs, 4 developers. (3) 50 bugs, 8 developers. (4) 100 bugs, 8 developers.

The above setup was executed twice. Once on the three objectives (excluding total time objective from the fitness) and another time for the four-objective case.

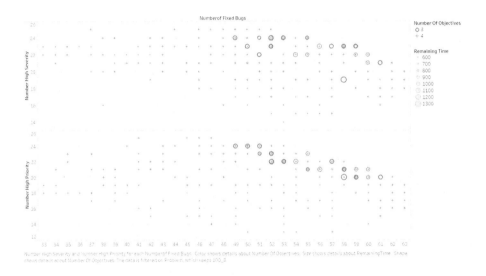

Fig. 2. Pareto front of three and four objectives displayed in 2D

Figure 2 is used to present the three and four objectives as a relation between total number of fixed bugs and each of number of fixed severe bugs and number of fixed priority bugs separately. This chart presents the 100-bug 8-developer setup. Three-objective Pareto points are represented as crosses while the four-objective points are presented as circles. In order to add a time dimension to this 2D chart, the size of circle or cross points is used to represent the time required to fix all bugs.

Figure 2 shows that the circles size is mostly big which reflects the bad achievement of this objective. Additionally, it is clear that there are more points in the four-objective Pareto front, providing more distribution of solutions while being able to achieve the same range achieved by the three objectives.

4   Conclusion

This study has adopted a search-based metaheuristic approach for human resource allocation for bug fixing iteration planning. Taking bugs severity, priority, ETA and required skill level in addition to developer skill level makes the choices more complicated for a manager planning such an iteration. We have showed that complicating the objectives by adding a long-term quality objective does not hurt the three objectives when compared with three-objective optimization results. In other words, complicating the problem formulation added quality to the recommended solutions.

References

1. Anvik, J.: Automating bug report assignment. In: Proceeding of ICSE, pp. 937–940 (2006)
2. Basili, V., Briand, L., Condon, S., Kim, Y.M., Melo, W.L., Valett, J.D.: Understanding and predicting the process of software maintenance release. In: Proceeding ICSE, pp. 464–474 (1996)
3. Bibi, N., Ahsan, A., Anwar, Z.: Project resource allocation optimization using search based software engineering a framework. In: Proceeding of ICDIM, pp. 226–229 (2014)
4. Chen, W.N., Zhang, J.: Ant colony optimization for software project scheduling and staffing with an event-based scheduler. IEEE TSE **39**(1), 1–17 (2013)
5. Deb, K., Pratap, A., Agarwal, S., Meyarivan, T.: A fast and elitist multiobjective genetic algorithm: NSGA-II. IEEE TEC **6**(2), 182–197 (2002)
6. Durillo, J.J., Nebro, A.J.: jmetal: A java framework for multi-objective optimization. Adv. Eng. Softw. **42**(10), 760–771 (2011)
7. Kang, D., Jung, J., Bae, D.H.: Constraint-based human resource allocation in software projects. S: Pract. Experience **41**(5), 551–577 (2011)
8. Sayyad, A.S., Ammar, H.: Pareto-optimal search-based software engineering (POS-BSE): a literature survey. In: Proceeding of RAISE, pp. 21–27 (2013)
9. Sayyad, A.S., Menzies, T., Ammar, H.: On the value of user preferences in search-based software engineering: a case study in software product lines. In: Proceeding of ICSE, pp. 492–501 (2013)
10. Tassey, G.: The economic impacts of inadequate infrastructure for software testing. NIST, RTI Project **7007**(011) (2002)
11. Zhang, F., Khomh, F., Zou, Y., Hassan, A.E.: An empirical study on factors impacting bug fixing time. In: Proceeding of WCRE, pp. 225–234 (2012)

Grammar Based Genetic Programming for Software Configuration Problem

Fitsum Meshesha Kifetew[1], Denisse Muñante[1(✉)], Jesús Gorroñogoitia[2],
Alberto Siena[3], Angelo Susi[1], and Anna Perini[1]

[1] Fondazione Bruno Kessler, Trento, Italy
{kifetew,munante,susi,perini}@fbk.eu
[2] ATOS, Madrid, Spain
jesus.gorronogoitia@atos.net
[3] Delta Informatica, Trento, Italy
alberto.siena@deltainformatica.eu

Abstract. Software Product Lines (SPLs) capture commonalities and variability of product families, typically represented by means of feature models. The selection of a set of suitable features when a software product is configured is typically made by exploring the space of tread-offs along different attributes of interest, for instance *cost* and *value*. In this paper, we present an approach for optimal product configuration by exploiting feature models and grammar guided genetic programming. In particular, we propose a novel encoding of candidate solutions, based on grammar representation of feature models, which ensures that relations imposed in the feature model are respected by the candidate solutions.

Keywords: Genetic programming · Grammar · Feature model · Software product line

1 Introduction

Software Product Line Engineering (SPL) follows the principles of product lines, originally introduced in mass markets, to enable product mass customisation. SPL rests on two key ideas: (1) to define a platform for the development of products in terms of components that maybe reusable, so as to reduce production costs and time to market; (2) to characterise the products in terms of the features they offer, and categorise them into common features that are part of each product and variable features that are only part of some products.

Feature modelling is recognised as an intuitive technique to represent and manage product variability in SPL. A feature model (FM) allows to hierarchically structure the set of features of a product in a tree-like graph representation, thus providing a compact representation of all possible products or configurations of an SPL. Features describe the functional as well as quality characteristics of the software product under consideration. The selection of the best and at the same time allowable combination of features that satisfy some objectives, which

© Springer International Publishing AG 2017
T. Menzies and J. Petke (Eds.): SSBSE 2017, LNCS 10452, pp. 130–136, 2017.
DOI: 10.1007/978-3-319-66299-2_10

can correspond to market segment needs or to specific users requirements or to desired quality attributes, is referred as the software configuration problem.

Several works in the literature have tackled the product configuration problem by applying search based techniques [7]. However, most of them employ an encoding of candidate solutions as a flat sequence of boolean variables, each representing a feature – indicating whether or not a feature is included in a particular product [3]. However, such encoding necessitates a subsequent check to make sure that the constraints imposed by the FM are respected by the candidate, resulting in further computational overhead merely as a result of the encoding. For instance, Oleachea *et al.* [9] compared an incremental exact algorithm called GIA with an approximate approach using Indicator-based Evolutionary Algorithm (IBEA). GIA produced optimal solutions in less than 2 hours for small models (≤44 features) and IBEA produced approximate solutions with an average of at least 42% accuracy in less than 20 min for more larger models (≤290 features). Hierons *et al.* [5] introduced a new promising method called *ShrInk Prioritise* (SIP). SIP combines a new encoding and reduces the number of invalid products removing core features of the representation and considering only leaf (concrete) features instead of exploring all features in the tree model. Henard *et al.* [4] enhanced IBEA by using the core encoding and also a SAT solver to implement new mutation and replacement operators used in an EMO algorithm. This approach, so-called SATIBEA, showed that it is not necessary to seed the search.

Our approach exploits the potential of Genetic Programming (GP) to evolve structurally valid individuals derived from a grammar, hence we first transform the FM to an equivalent grammar [1], then we apply grammar guided GP (GGGP) [8] to evolve candidate solutions towards ultimately finding the optimal set of product configurations. Each candidate solution (product configuration) is derived from the grammar, and hence by definition respects the constraints imposed by the FM. GGGP has proven effective in evolving structurally valid solutions fit for a specific purpose, for instance test case generation [6].

The main contributions of the paper are: (1) novel grammar based encoding of candidate solutions, and (2) a prototype tool that implements GGGP for optimal product configuration.

2   Feature Models and Grammars

In feature models (example shown in Fig. 1(a)), features are hierarchically organised by means of relations, which are so-called tree constraints or parent-child relations. The types of tree constraint relations are (see Fig. 1(b)): *Mandatory, Optional, Alternative,* and *Or.* If a feature has a *Mandatory* relation with its parent feature, it must be included in all products in which its parent feature appears. For example, 'Catalogue', 'Payment' and 'Security' in the example Fig. 1(a). If a feature has an *Optional* relation with its parent feature, it can be optionally included in products in which its parent feature appears. For example, 'Search' and 'Public report'.

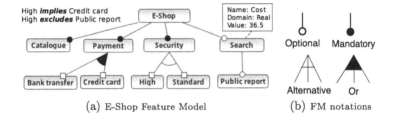

(a) E-Shop Feature Model   (b) FM notations

Fig. 1. Example feature model for E-Shop family products

```
# Grammar rules                          <High> ::= "High"
<E-shop> ::= <Catalogue> <Payment_or>    <Standard> ::= "Standard"
    <Security> <Search_opt>              <Search_opt> ::= <Public report_opt>
<Catalogue> ::= "Catalogue"              |
<Payment_or> ::= <Payment> <Payment_or>  <Public report_opt> ::= <Public report>
    | <Payment>                          |
<Payment> ::= <Bank Transfer>            <Public report> ::= "Public report"
    | <Credit Card>
<Bank Transfer> ::= "Bank Transfer"      # cross-tree constraints
<Credit Card> ::= "Credit Card"          #Const_0: -"High" V "Credit Card"
<Security> ::= <High>                    #Const_1: -"High" V -"Public report"
    | <Standard>
```

Fig. 2. Grammar and constraints corresponding to the feature model in Fig. 1(a)

A set of features are grouped as *Alternatives* if exactly only one of these feature should be included when their parent feature appears in the product. For example, 'High' and 'Standard' are grouped as alternatives. A set of features are grouped using an *Or* relation if one or more of these features can be included when their parent feature appears in the product. For example, 'Bank transfer' and 'Credit card' are grouped in a or relation.

In addition to the relations between features, a feature model may also include *cross-tree constraints* between features. The most common relations are: *Implies* and *Excludes*. If featureA *Implies* featureB, and featureA appears in a product, then featureB must be selected for the product. For instance in Fig. 1(a), 'High' *implies* 'Credit card'. If featureA *Excludes* featureB, and featureA appears in a product, then featureB must not be selected for the product. For instance, 'High' *excludes* 'Public report'.

Feature models can be mapped to grammars such that formal reasoning can be applied on them. In this work, we adopt a mapping similar to the one proposed by Batory [1]. However, while the grammar proposed by Batory is an *iterative* grammar, we use a *recursive* grammar which enables us to apply grammar based genetic programming for feature model optimisation. Consequently, the notations +, indicating *one or more* repetitions, and [], indicating *optional* elements present in Batory's grammar are not present in our grammar notation. Alternatively, we opt for a recursive grammatical notation with λ-*productions*, grammar rules that result in *empty* strings.

Tree constraints. Our mapping from tree constraints in feature models to grammars is summarised as follows:

1. *Optional*: OPIONAL(F) → <F_opt> ::= <F> | λ
2. *Alternative*: ALTERNATIVE(F1,F2) → <F> ::= <F1> | <F2>
3. *Or*: OR(F1, F2) → <F_or> ::= <F> <F_or> | <F> ; <F> ::= <F1> | <F2>
4. *And(*)*: AND(F1,F2) → <F> ::= <F1> <F2>
   (*) And relation was included to capture grouped features with the same parent but without alternative/or relations.

For the example (see Fig. 1(a)), the corresponding BNF notation grammar is presented in Fig. 2. Non-terminals are represented by names in angle brackets (*e.g.,* <Payment>) while terminals are represented by quoted strings (*e.g.,* "Credit Card"). For the sake of simplicity, λ rules are represented by a |.

Cross-tree constraints. Cross-tree constraints in FMs could be suffixed to the grammar so that they can be read and applied by a program. In our case, we adopt the propositional logic notation propose by Batory [1], as shown in the lower part of Fig. 2.

Attributes: are associated to each feature so that optimal product configurations could be derived using the values of the attributes, as shown in Fig. 1(a).

3   Search-Based Approach for Software Configuration

Given a feature model representing a family of features as well as a set of attributes of these features, the software product configuration problem involves the exploration and selection of the set of products representing optimal tread-offs among the various attributes. We propose to use GGGP for exploring the space of product configurations because it gives us a suitable representation of candidate solutions as trees that capture the relationships among features imposed by the FM. Such a representation facilitates the generation, manipulation, and evolution of candidates towards optimal solutions. Figure 3(a) gives an overview of the proposed approach. As shown in Fig. 3(a), the FM is first serialised into a grammar (as described in Sect. 2), which is then fed to the GGGP-based search module, which follows the evolution cycle of a typical evolutionary algorithm, resulting in a Pareto-optimal set of product configurations.

Given the nature of the problem at hand, we propose *multi-objective* optimisation, in particular we adopt the dominance-based approach as implemented in the NSGA algorithm [2].

Candidate encoding and initialisation. Each candidate solution is a set of features, represented as a *derivation tree* based on the given grammar. An example is shown in Fig. 3(b) based on the grammar presented in Sect. 2. Collecting the leaves of the tree, we get the set of features represented by the candidate solution. The population is initialised by randomly generating candidates from the grammar following the process of derivation [6]. Candidate solutions are by

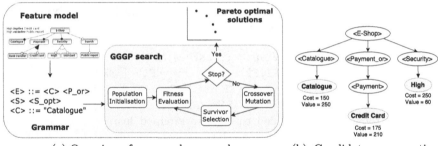

(a) Overview of proposed approach

(b) Candidate representing:
Catalogue, Credit Card, High

Fig. 3. Proposed solution and candidate encoding

definition valid with respect to the FM (grammar), i.e., constraints imposed by the FM are respected.

Fitness function. Fitness function is computed based on the values of quality attributes defined a priori. Given a candidate solution $C = \{f_1, f_2, ..., f_n\}$, the fitness value of C is composed of the aggregate values of each quality attribute in C. Each attribute is an *objective* to be optimised. For e.g., from Fig. 3(b), the sum of the *cost* of all features in C represents one objective, while the sum of the *value* constitutes the second objective.

Search operators. Since candidate solutions are encoded as *trees*, the operators we employ are *subtree crossover* and *subtree mutation* [6]. In *subtree crossover*, given two parents C_1 and C_2, subtrees of the same type (rooted at the same grammar non-terminal) are identified in each parent and swapped, producing *offspring*. In *subtree mutation*, an individual C is mutated replacing a subtree by a newly generated subtree from the grammar.

4   Preliminary Results and Discussion

We implemented our approach in a prototype tool[1] based on NSGAII [2]. We applied the tool to explore optimal configurations for **Drupal**, which has real attributes values [10]. The attributes we consider are [5]: (1) *Lines of code (LOC)* to be *minimised*, (2) *Cyclomatic complexity (CC)* to be *minimised*, (3) *Test Assertions* to be *maximised*, (4) *Number of installations* to be *maximised*, (5) *Number of developers* to be *minimised*, (6) *Number of changes* to be *minimised*, and (7) *Number of reported faults* to be *minimised*. The resulting multi-objective optimisation problem has 8 objectives, including the number of features to be maximised. Furthermore, to simulate a more realistic situation, we apply a *constraint* on one of the attributes – number of reported faults. That is, the owners of **Drupal** have imposed a constraint that products should not contain more than

---

[1] http://selab.fbk.eu/kifetew/downloads/ssbse17-replication-package.tar.

x number of faults reported in the features included. For the experiment, we set $x = 500$. As shown in Table 1, all the individuals in the final population represent unique optimal configurations. However, not all of them respect the constraint imposed, i.e., overall number of reported faults less than 500, hence the number of valid (respecting the constraint on total number of faults) reported in column *#ValidSolutions* is fewer than the total number of solutions (*#Solutions*).

Table 1. Results for Drupal FM

Search budget (sec)	#FitnessEvals	#Solutions	#ValidSolutions
60	33949	100	94
120	78280	100	97
240	96319	100	94

These preliminary results show that the approach is able to generate several Pareto-optimal configurations within a limited search budget. As future work, we intend to evaluate the approach on more realistic datasets and attributes, and compare it with other approaches from the literature.

Acknowledgements. This work is a result of the SUPERSEDE project, funded by the H2020 EU Framework Programme under agreement number 644018.

References

1. Batory, D.: Feature models, grammars, and propositional formulas. In: Obbink, H., Pohl, K. (eds.) SPLC 2005. LNCS, vol. 3714, pp. 7–20. Springer, Heidelberg (2005). doi:10.1007/11554844_3
2. Deb, K., Pratap, A., Agarwal, S., Meyarivan, T.: A fast elitist multi-objective genetic algorithm: NSGA-II. IEEE Trans. Evol. Comput. **6**, 182–197 (2000)
3. Guo, J., White, J., Wang, G., Li, J., Wang, Y.: A genetic algorithm for optimized feature selection with resource constraints in software product lines. J. Syst. Softw. **84**(12), 2208–2221 (2011)
4. Henard, C., Papadakis, M., Harman, M., Le Traon, Y.: Combining multi-objective search and constraint solving for configuring large software product lines. In: 2015 IEEE/ACM 37th IEEE International Conference on Software Engineering (ICSE), vol. 1, pp. 517–528. IEEE (2015)
5. Hierons, R.M., Li, M., Liu, X., Segura, S., Zheng, W.: Sip: Optimal product selection from feature models using many-objective evolutionary optimization. ACM Trans. Softw. Eng. Method. (TOSEM) **25**(2), 17 (2016)
6. Kifetew, F.M., Tiella, R., Tonella, P.: Generating valid grammar-based test inputs by means of genetic programming and annotated grammars. Empirical Softw. Eng. **22**(2), 928–961 (2017)
7. Lopez-Herrejon, R.E., Linsbauer, L., Egyed, A.: A systematic mapping study of search-based software engineering for software product lines. Inf. Softw. Technol. **61**, 33–51 (2015)

8. McKay, R.I., Hoai, N.X., Whigham, P.A., Shan, Y., O'Neill, M.: Grammar-based genetic programming: a survey. Genet. Program Evolvable Mach. **11**(3–4), 365–396 (2010)
9. Olaechea, R., Rayside, D., Guo, J., Czarnecki, K.: Comparison of exact and approximate multi-objective optimization for software product lines. In: Proceeding of the 18th International Software Product Line Conference vol. 1, pp. 92–101. ACM (2014)
10. Sánchez, A.B., Segura, S., Parejo, J.A., Ruiz-Cortés, A.: Variability testing in the wild: the drupal case study. Softw. Syst. Model. **16**(1), 173–194 (2017)

GPGPGPU: Evaluation of Parallelisation of Genetic Programming Using GPGPU

Jinhan Kim, Junhwi Kim, and Shin Yoo[✉]

Korea Advanced Institute of Science and Technology,
Daejeon, Republic of Korea
{jinhankim,junhwi.kim23,shin.yoo}@kaist.ac.kr

Abstract. We evaluate different approaches towards parallelisation of Genetic Programming (GP) using General Purpose Computing on Graphics Processor Units (GPGPU). Unlike Genetic Algorithms, which uses a single or a fixed number of fitness functions, GP has to evaluate a diverse population of *programs*. Since GPGPU is based on the Single Instruction Multiple Data (SIMD) architecture, parallelisation of GP using GPGPU allows multiple approaches. We study three different parallelisation approaches: kernel per individual, kernel per generation, and kernel interpreter. The results of the empirical study using a widely studied symbolic regression benchmark show that no single approach is the best: the decision about parallelisation approach has to consider the trade-off between the compilation and the execution overhead of GPU kernels.

1 Introduction

Genetic Programming has been widely adopted by the Search Based Software Engineering community: its application ranges from fault localisation [7,12,14], Genetic Improvement [5,9], and program repair [3,8]. Improving its efficiency and scalability would have a far reaching impact across the application domains.

Parallelisation is one of the most promising technique for scalability. Population based evolutionary computation has been described as 'embarrassingly parallel', because the fitness evaluation of each individual solution in the population is often completely independent from each other and, consequently, can be performed in parallel. This is particularly the case with Genetic Algorithms (GAs): GAs need to apply the same fitness function(s) to the entire population, which essentially consists of *input* data to the fitness function(s).

General Purpose Computing on Graphics Processor Units (GPGPU) exploits the Single Instruction Multiple Data (SIMD) architecture of graphics shaders to parallelise computation [4]. The SIMD architecture fits the parallel fitness evaluation of GAs naturally, and has provided significant speed-ups for search-based test suite minimisation [13].

Genetic Programming (GP), on the other hand, keeps a population of *programs*. Parallelisation at the GP population level is not possible, as it would not fit the SIMD architecture. Instead, GP can be parallelised at the training data level.

T. Menzies and J. Petke (Eds.): SSBSE 2017, LNCS 10452, pp. 137–142, 2017.
DOI: 10.1007/978-3-319-66299-2_11

Usually, a single candidate GP solution has to be evaluated against many data points in the training set, which can be done in parallel.

However, this GPGPU based fitness evaluation for GP requires the conversion of GP trees into GPGPU executable kernels. The conversion involves the kernel compilation, which is a time consuming process that is external to the GP. The cost of kernel compilation raises the issue of cost-benefit trade-off for GPGPU.

This paper evaluates different methods of amortising the cost of kernel compilation using CUDA[1] toolkit. Kernel per individual method converts each individual GP tree into a separate CUDA kernel. Kernel per generation aggregates all individuals in the population and performs a single compilation of all individuals. Finally, kernel interpreter method uses an expression interpreter: after a single compilation of the interpreter, GP can evaluate whatever GP tree without any further compilation. We use the CPU based GP as the baseline, and the Dow chemical data symbolic regression as the benchmark problem [10].

2   Evaluating GP Trees Using GPGPU

To achieve data level parallelisation using GPGPU, the kernel should be generated dynamically. Here, we introduce three different approaches.

- **Kernel per Individual:** The most intuitive approach to convert GP trees into CUDA kernel is to generate a single CUDA kernel for each candidate solution. Since the only difference between candidates is the expression they represent, kernel source code can be generated using templates: we only need to convert GP trees into infix expressions that conform to CUDA kernel syntax. While intuitive, a drawback of this approach is that we have to invoke CUDA compilers for each individual. If the population size is large, this may cause a significant overhead.
- **Kernel per Generation:** To reduce the kernel compilation overhead, we can generate one kernel source code file per generation: the single file will contain multiple kernels, each corresponding to the individual solutions in the GP population. While this results in much longer kernel source code files (and hence increased compilation time), we expect to save the overhead of invoking CUDA compilers multiple times.
- **Kernel Interpreter:** One technique that has been studied in the GP literature [1,11] is to use a single kernel that can *interpret* GP candidate solutions. Using an interpreter, the GP population is transferred to the GPU as *data*, which are then interpreted and evaluated against the data points in the training data. The kernel interpreter method requires only one compilation throughout the entire GP run. While this significantly reduces the kernel compilation time, it increases the complexity of the CUDA kernel, which in turn affects the performance of GPGPU. We implemented an RPN(Reverse Polish Notation) based CUDA interpreter kernel for this study.

---

[1] Compute Unified Device Architecture from NVIDIA.

3   Experimental Setup

3.1   Research Questions

Two major drivers of the computational load of GP fitness evaluation are the population size and the training dataset size. Both directly affects the number of fitness evaluations that have to be performed. We formulate our Research Questions around these two factors as follows:

- **RQ1.** Which approach performs best against different training dataset sizes?
- **RQ2.** Which approach performs best against different population sizes?

Our study uses the Dow Chemical symbolic regression benchmark [10] to investigate the performance of different parallelisation approaches: it contains a training dataset with 747 data points consisting of 57 independent variables and 1 dependent variable. We answer **RQ1** by artificially controlling the size of the training dataset and comparing the efficiency of different GPGPU approaches as well as the CPU baseline. Since the aim of our study is not to improve the accuracy of the evolved expression, we simply repeat each data point in the training dataset $10^0, 10^1, 10^2, 10^3$, and 10^4 times to generate datasets with different sizes. We answer **RQ2** by running GP with population size of 50, 100, and 200, and comparing the results. Every experiment is conducted 30 times.

3.2   Configurations and Environments

We use DEAP[2] to implement different approaches: we use the 57 independent variables in the Dow Chemical problem set as GP terminal nodes, and include addition, subtraction, multiplication, division, and negation. The GP uses a three-way tournament selection, a single point crossover with the rate of 0.6, and uniform mutation with the rate of 0.01. The tree depth is set to 4. We set the termination criterion as reaching 10 generations.

The experiments were conducted with an Intel i7-6700 CPU machine with 32 GB of RAM, running Ubuntu 14.04.5 LTS. The GPGPU has been performed on an NVIDIA TITAN X with 12 GB of GDDR5X using CUDA version 8.0. DEAP has been executed using Python 3.4.

4   Results

Figure 1 shows the execution time of GP using three parallelisation approaches as well as CPU, against five different training dataset sizes and the population size of 50. The lines connecting boxplots are merely visual aids for identifying the same approach: they connect the mean value of each boxplot. As the training data size increases, the efficiency of CPU based GP and kernel interpreter deteriorate sharply, whereas both kernel per individual and kernel per generation

---

[2] https://github.com/DEAP/deap.

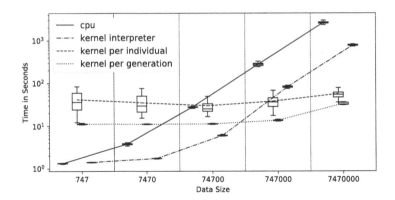

Fig. 1. Plot of three parallelisation approaches and CPU based GP on the fixed population size 50. The y-axis is shown on logarithmic scale.

approach show relatively stable performance. However, up to the dataset size of 74,700, the interpreter approach shows the best performance.

The performance deterioration of the interpreter approach is due to the overhead of RPN-based expression evaluation. When the size of the training dataset is relatively small, the savings in kernel compilation time compensate for this overhead. With larger dataset (i.e. more kernel execution), the interpreter overhead cancels out the savings in compilation time.

The interpreter overhead is mainly due to two factors. First, the interpreter uses CUDA registers to maintain a stack, increasing the I/O overhead compared to kernels that hardcode the expression (kernels per individual and kernel per generation). If the stack becomes too large to be contained within registers, we may have to rely on even slower memory, increasing the I/O overhead even further. Second, the interpreter makes more function calls internally, compared to the hardcoded kernels: the increased branching also deteriorates the performance of the kernel interpreter.

To answer **RQ1:** the best parallelisation approach is determined by the trade-off between compilation time and the computational overhead of the kernel interpreter. Above a certain number of kernel executions, the interpreter loses the savings from the fewer compilations.

To answer **RQ2**, we fixed the size of dataset and varied the population size. The results in Fig. 2a show that, for the data size of 74,700, the interpreter method outperforms all other approaches, regardless of the population size (i.e. its performance overhead is still being cancelled out by the savings in the compilation time). Note that the kernel per individual approach performs *worse* than the CPU. However, in Fig. 2b, kernel per generation performs the best. In fact, the relative order between approaches is the same as in Fig. 1 with dataset size of 747,000, regardless of the population size.

We note that the kernel per individual approach shows wider variances as the population size grows. Since the approach relies heavily on an external process

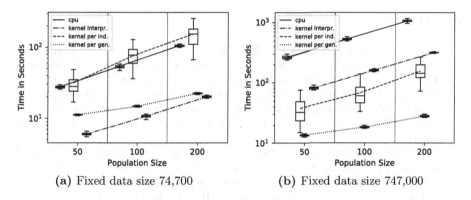

(a) Fixed data size 74,700   (b) Fixed data size 747,000

Fig. 2. Plot of three parallelisation approaches and CPU based GP on the fixed data size 74,700 and 747,000. Both y-axes are shown on logarithmic scale.

(i.e. CUDA compiler), we posit that it is more vulnerable to the external and environmental factors that can affect the execution time stochastically.

5   Related Works

The use of an interpreter has been suggested as a way to scale up GP on GPUs: Langdon and Banzhaf implemented an RPN-based interpreter for GP regression [1]. Wilson and Banzhaf implemented an entire Linear GP system on GPUs, parallelising not only the fitness evaluation but also the GP mutation [11]. Both approaches have been developed with earlier incarnations of GPGPU frameworks and do not benefit from the high level programming support of contemporary frameworks. Our work exploits the modern GPU development framework to compare approaches such as kernel per individual.

Other applications of GP in SBSE involves evolving not just expressions but arbitrary code [2,3,9]. To parallelise GP for these applications, we need to be able to execute arbitrary code on GPU. The existence of I/O operations or system calls prevents such use of GPGPU. However, there are ongoing works that attempt to overcome the limitations of GPU environment. For example, Silberstein et al. have tried to interface the host file system with GPU kernels [6].

6   Conclusion

This paper evaluates three different parallelisation approaches for GP fitness evaluation on GPU: kernel per individual, kernel per generation, and kernel interpreter. The empirical study using a symbolic regression benchmark problem shows that, while the kernel per generation performs best overall, the actual performance depends on multiple factors such as the size of the population and the volume of the training data. Consequently, we advise GP practitioners to choose their parallelisation approach carefully. Future work will investigate a wider range of benchmark problems.

References

1. Langdon, W.B., Banzhaf, W.: A SIMD interpreter for genetic programming on GPU graphics cards. In: O'Neill, M., Vanneschi, L., Gustafson, S., Esparcia Alcázar, A.I., Falco, I., Cioppa, A., Tarantino, E. (eds.) EuroGP 2008. LNCS, vol. 4971, pp. 73–85. Springer, Heidelberg (2008). doi:10.1007/978-3-540-78671-9_7

2. Langdon, W.B., Harman, M.: Genetically improving 50,000 lines of C++. Technical report, RN/12/09, Department of Computer Science, University College London (2012)

3. Le Goues, C., Dewey-Vogt, M., Forrest, S., Weimer, W.: A systematic study of automated program repair: fixing 55 out of 105 bugs for $8 each. In: Proceedings of the 34th International Conference on Software Engineering, pp. 3–13 (2012)

4. Owens, J.D., Luebke, D., Govindaraju, N., Harris, M., Krüger, J., Lefohn, A.E., Purcell, T.J.: A survey of general-purpose computation on graphics hardware. Comput. Graphics Forum **26**(1), 80–113 (2007)

5. Petke, J., Harman, M., Langdon, W.B., Weimer, W.: Using genetic improvement and code transplants to specialise a C++ program to a problem class. In: Nicolau, M., Krawiec, K., Heywood, M.I., Castelli, M., García-Sánchez, P., Merelo, J.J., Rivas Santos, V.M., Sim, K. (eds.) EuroGP 2014. LNCS, vol. 8599, pp. 137–149. Springer, Heidelberg (2014). doi:10.1007/978-3-662-44303-3_12

6. Silberstein, M., Ford, B., Keidar, I., Witchel, E.: GPUfs: integrating a file system with GPUs. SIGARCH Comput. Archit. News **41**(1), 485–498 (2013)

7. Sohn, J., Yoo, S.: FLUCCS: using code and change metrics to improve fault localisation. In: Proceedings of the International Symposium on Software Testing and Analysis, ISSTA 2017 (2017, to appear)

8. Weimer, W., Nguyen, T., Le Goues, C., Forrest, S.: Automatically finding patches using genetic programming. In: Proceedings of the 31st IEEE International Conference on Software Engineering (ICSE 2009), pp. 364–374. IEEE, 16–24 May 2009

9. White, D., Arcuri, A., Clark, J.: Evolutionary improvement of programs. IEEE Trans. Evol. Comput. **15**(4), 515–538 (2011)

10. White, D.R., McDermott, J., Castelli, M., Manzoni, L., Goldman, B.W., Kronberger, G., Jaśkowski, W., O'Reilly, U.M., Luke, S.: Better GP benchmarks: community survey results and proposals. Genet. Program Evolvable Mach. **14**(1), 3–29 (2013)

11. Wilson, G., Banzhaf, W.: Deployment of CPU and GPU-based genetic programming on heterogeneous devices. In: Proceedings of the 11th Annual Conference Companion on Genetic and Evolutionary Computation Conference (GECCO 2009), pp. 2531–2538. ACM Press, New York, July 2009

12. Yoo, S.: Evolving human competitive spectra-based fault localisation techniques. In: Fraser, G., Teixeira de Souza, J. (eds.) SSBSE 2012. LNCS, vol. 7515, pp. 244–258. Springer, Heidelberg (2012). doi:10.1007/978-3-642-33119-0_18

13. Yoo, S., Harman, M., Ur, S.: GPGPU test suite minimisation: search based software engineering performance improvement using graphics cards. Empirical Softw. Eng. **18**(3), 550–593 (2013)

14. Yoo, S., Xie, X., Kuo, F.-C., Chen, T.Y., Harman, M.: Human competitiveness of genetic programming in spectrum-based fault localisation: theoretical and empirical analysis. ACM Trans. Softw. Eng. Methodol. **26**(1), 4:1–4:30 (2017). doi:10.1145/3078840

Evaluating CAVM: A New Search-Based Test Data Generation Tool for C

Junhwi Kim[1], Byeonghyeon You[1], Minhyuk Kwon[2], Phil McMinn[3], and Shin Yoo[1(✉)]

[1] Korea Advanced Institute of Science and Technology,
Daejeon, Republic of Korea
shin.yoo@kaist.ac.kr
[2] Suresoft Technologies Inc., Seoul, Republic of Korea
[3] University of Sheffield, Sheffield, UK
p.mcminn@sheffield.ac.uk

Abstract. We present CAVM (pronounced "ka-boom"), a new search-based test data generation tool for C. CAVM is developed to augment an existing commercial tool, CodeScroll, which uses static analysis and input partitioning to generate test data. Unlike the current state-of-the-art search-based test data generation tool for C, Austin, CAVM handles dynamic data structures using purely search-based techniques. We compare CAVM against CodeScroll and Austin using 49 C functions, ranging from small anti-pattern case studies to real world open source code and commercial code. The results show that CAVM can cover branches that neither CodeScroll nor Austin can, while also exclusively achieving the highest branch coverage for 20 of the studied functions.

1 Introduction

We introduce and evaluate CAVM (pronounced "ka-boom"), a new search-based test data generation tool for C. CAVM is based on the Alternating Variable Method (AVM) [7]: however, unlike the existing AVM-based test data generation tool Austin [6], CAVM generates inputs consisting of dynamic data structures using purely a search-based technique: *growing* the appropriate shape of the dynamic data structure, as well as filling it with data, is part of the metaheuristic search performed. It also supports generation of string inputs (i.e., char arrays) for test data generation problems involving comparisons using the strcmp library function, using code rewriting.

We compare CAVM against a commercial test data generation tool, CodeScroll (developed by Suresoft Technologies), and Austin, with respect to their relative effectiveness for C code involving dynamic data structures. The empirical evaluation studies small anti-pattern case studies, known to be challenging for CodeScroll, as well as real world open source and commercial code. The results show that our new algorithms, which we implemented into CAVM, can cover branches that neither CodeScroll nor Austin can.

© Springer International Publishing AG 2017
T. Menzies and J. Petke (Eds.): SSBSE 2017, LNCS 10452, pp. 143–149, 2017.
DOI: 10.1007/978-3-319-66299-2_12

2 CAVM: A New C Test Data Generation Tool

CAVM is an open source byproduct of an industry collaboration, the aim of which is to augment CodeScroll with a search-based software testing technique so that it can deal with challenging branches more effectively.

Extending the basic AVM for primitive types, CAVM adopts different local search strategies for each input type. For primitive data types, CAVM uses Iterated Pattern Search (IPS) [4, 7]. In case of a struct type argument, CAVM applies AVM on each of its members: if the struct is nested, CAVM applies its AVM-based search algorithm recursively.

CAVM considers pointers to primitive types as arrays; CAVM initialises all pointers to NULL and applies IPS to each element of the current array, growing the size of the array by one if the search does not succeed. Note that the first "move" after failing to cover the given branch with NULL is to instantiate the pointer (i.e., *growing* it to a single element array) using a random value. CAVM grows dynamic data structures, such as linked lists or trees, by recursively growing nested pointers. For pointers to struct, if the current value is NULL, CAVM checks whether it can cover the current target branch simply by instantiating the pointer. CAVM randomly initialises primitive members of the instantiated struct. If the search does not succeed, CAVM subsequently tries to search for the values of the new instance (i.e., the members of the pointed struct) recursively. For more detailed description of CAVM and its algorithm, please refer to our technical report [5].

3 Experimental Setup

3.1 Subjects

Table 1 contains the list of subject functions that we study in this paper. The anti-pattern subject is a set of branches that CodeScroll is known to be unable to cover: these are the minimum working examples that contain only the problematic structural patterns. Line, Calendar, Triangle, and AllZeros examples are ported to C from McMinn and Kapfhammer [7] and constitute the baseline examples. LinkedList is a collection of utility function implementations for the singly linked list in C, taken from an on-line tutorial, whereas BinaryTree contains seven functions from the textbook by Horowitz et al. [3]. Finally, busybox-ls contains five functions from the open source implementation of ls utility for the busybox package, whereas decode.c contains 24 functions chosen from a name demangler module for C++ frontend, developed by the Edison Design Group. In total, we study 482 branches in 49 functions.

3.2 Configurations

We compare CAVM to Austin and CodeScroll based on the branch coverage they achieve. Since Austin and CAVM adopt stochastic approaches, we will report the average coverage over 20 runs. We only evaluate the deterministic heuristic of CodeScroll, and therefore do not repeat its runs.

Table 1. Subject C functions studied

Subject	Description	Branches	*	Rec. *	struct	strcmp
AllZeros	Examples from AVMf [7]	6	✓	-	-	-
Calendar		46	-	-	-	-
Line		14	-	-	✓	-
Triangle		16	-	-	-	-
CodeScroll Antipatterns	Set of branches that CodeScroll cannot cover	16	✓	✓	✓	✓
LinkedList	5 utility functions for singly linked list[a]	26	✓	✓	✓	-
BinaryTree	7 tree-related functions from a textbook by Horowitz et al. [3]	30	✓	✓	✓	-
busybox-ls	5 functions from ls in Busybox 1.2.0[b]	32	✓	-	-	-
decode.c	22 functions from decode.c[c]	296	✓	-	✓	-
Total	49 C functions	482				

[a] Taken from an on-line tutorial: http://milvus.tistory.com/17
[b] BusyBox is a collection of common UNIX utilities in a single small executable: https://busybox.net.
[c] https://www.edg.com/c

While CAVM allows the user to set the search range for each input parameter of the target function, Austin lacks such control. Consequently, we do not narrow down the input range and use the default range for each primitive type, so that both tools search in the same space. For both Austin and CAVM, we set the maximum number of fitness evaluations for each target branch to 1,000, and the timeout duration for each target function to five minutes. Note that both tools collect "collateral" coverage [1] (i.e., coverage of branches that are not the target but nonetheless covered by a test case generated by a tool[1]). Any collateral coverage achieved within five minutes counts in the final results. However, if a tool does not terminate within the five minute timeout, we record 0% coverage.

3.3   Environments

CAVM is written in C/C++ as well as Python. The target code instrumentation is written in C/C++ and depends on clang version 3.9.0 and GNU gcc version 4.9 or higher. The AVM search is written in Python 3 and depends on CFFI[2] as well as Python runtime version 3.5 or higher.

For the experiment, CAVM is executed on a machine with Intel Core i7-6700K 4.0 GHz and 32 GB RAM running Ubuntu 14.04 LTS. Due to specific dependencies, Austin is executed on the same machine running Ubuntu 12.04.5 LTS. CodeScroll only supports Microsoft Windows and consequently is executed on a machine with Intel Core i5-6600 3.9 GHz and 16 GB RAM running

---

[1] Here, we define collateral coverage as branches that are covered in addition to the original target by the final, generated test cases.
[2] C Foreign Function Interface: http://cffi.readthedocs.io.

Windows 7. We allow the different hardware environments because we are only interested in achieved coverage and success rates.

4 Results

Table 2 contains the coverage results from 20 repetitive runs of `Austin` and `CAVM`, as well as single runs of `CodeScroll`. Note that the functions in `decode.c` have been renamed in the table to save space: their full names, as well as their source code and the box plots of the coverage results will be available from the accompanying web page. For `Austin` and `CAVM`, we report mean (μ) and standard deviation (σ): the highest coverage is typeset in bold. Out of 49 functions, there are 5 functions for which `CodeScroll` alone achieves the highest branch coverage, and two functions for which `Austin` does the same. `CAVM` alone achieves the highest branch coverage for 20 functions. Notably, `Austin` fails to cover any branch of functions in `decode.c` within five minutes.

Table 2. Average branch coverage (μ) and standard deviation (σ) from single runs of `CodeScroll`, and 20 runs of `Austin` and `CAVM`: the highest coverage for each function is typeset in bold. `Br.` indicates the number of branches for each subject; CS stands for `CodeScroll`.

Function	Br.	CS	Austin μ	σ	CAVM μ	σ	Function	Br.	CS	Austin μ	σ	CAVM μ	σ
AVMf							AVMf						
allzeros□	6	0.00	0.00	0.00	**83.33**	0.00	line†	14	**100.00**	0.00	0.00	28.57	0.00
calendar*	46	**100.00**	0.00	0.00	0.00	0.00	triangle‡	16	**93.75**	0.00	0.00	89.06	5.32
Antipatterns							decode.c						
case1	4	0.00	**100.00**	0.00	**100.00**	0.00	func1	2	**100.00**	0.00	0.00	**100.00**	0.00
case2	4	75.00	**100.00**	0.00	**100.00**	0.00	func2	2	**100.00**	0.00	0.00	**100.00**	0.00
case3	2	50.00	**100.00**	0.00	**100.00**	0.00	func3	48	10.42	0.00	0.00	**29.90**	5.63
case4§	2	0.00	0.00	0.00	**100.00**	0.00	func4	14	21.43	0.00	0.00	**71.07**	6.34
case5	2	50.00	**100.00**	0.00	**100.00**	0.00	func5	14	**21.43**	0.00	0.00	0.00	0.00
case6	2	50.00	**100.00**	0.00	**100.00**	0.00	func6	16	18.75	0.00	0.00	**27.14**	9.44
LinkedList							func7	30	6.67	0.00	0.00	**11.56**	1.79
delete◊	6	**100.00**	**100.00**	0.00	16.67	0.00	func8	6	50.00	0.00	0.00	**75.83**	12.65
insert◊	8	87.50	**100.00**	0.00	50.00	0.00	func9	44	4.55	0.00	0.00	**69.66**	7.31
modify◊	4	75.00	**100.00**	0.00	38.75	12.76	func10	28	7.14	0.00	0.00	**62.32**	10.20
print_list	2	**100.00**	**100.00**	0.00	**100.00**	0.00	func11	2	**100.00**	0.00	0.00	**100.00**	0.00
search	6	**100.00**	0.00	0.00	**100.00**	0.00	func12	4	25.00	0.00	0.00	**27.50**	7.69
busybox-ls							func13	4	50.00	0.00	0.00	**73.75**	5.59
bold	2	50.00	**100.00**	0.00	**100.00**	0.00	func14	2	50.00	0.00	0.00	**52.50**	11.18
dnalloc	2	**100.00**	**100.00**	0.00	**100.00**	0.00	func15	2	50.00	0.00	0.00	**97.50**	11.18
fgcolor	2	**100.00**	**100.00**	0.00	**100.00**	0.00	func16	12	8.33	0.00	0.00	**22.50**	18.56
my_stat	10	0.00	0.00	0.00	0.00	0.00	func17	4	25.00	0.00	0.00	**27.50**	11.18
scan_one_dir	16	**6.25**	0.00	0.00	0.00	0.00	func18	4	50.00	0.00	0.00	**64.17**	6.11
BinaryTree							func19	28	3.57	0.00	0.00	**8.75**	3.57
inorder	2	**100.00**	**100.00**	0.00	**100.00**	0.00	func20	8	87.50	0.00	0.00	**100.00**	0.00
iter_inorder	4	0.00	0.00	0.00	**100.00**	0.00	func21	4	**100.00**	0.00	0.00	**100.00**	0.00
iter_search	6	**100.00**	0.00	0.00	**100.00**	0.00	func22	18	**100.00**	0.00	0.00	**100.00**	0.00
level_order	8	62.50	0.00	0.00	**100.00**	0.00	Section 4/**RQ1** discusses the following issues.						
postorder	2	50.00	**100.00**	0.00	**100.00**	0.00	□: indirect dependency. *: large search space.						
preorder	2	50.00	**100.00**	0.00	**100.00**	0.00	†: low success rates. ‡: infeasible branches.						
search	6	**100.00**	0.00	0.00	**100.00**	0.00	◊: imprecise dependency analysis. §: `strcmp`.						

We manually analysed the hard-to-cover branches in the smaller benchmarks and identified the following common issues (each issue can be cross-referenced to Table 2 through the symbols):

(1) Indirect control dependency (□): one of the branches in the `allzeros` function requires the number of zeros in the input array to be equal to the size of input: CAVM fails to cover this branch. CAVM does not receive any guidance through the fitness function because the counter for the number of zeros is changed in another branch that does not depend on the target branch, similar to the flag problem [2]. This results in CAVM repeating random restarts.

(2) Large search spaces (∗): a `for` loop in `calendar` consumes a large amount of time when inputs are initialised from a large range. Since the loop iterates over the range between two integer inputs, the number of iterations can be up to the range of integers in C. This leads to frequent timeouts and, consequently, 0% coverage. When the input variable range is set to $[-100, 100]$, CAVM consistently achieves 100% coverage.

(3) Low success rate (†): some branches in the `line` function are simply hard to cover under the given timeout and evaluation budget. While CAVM sometimes succeeds to cover all branches in `line`, the average coverage suffers from runs that failed to cover the hard branches.

(4) Infeasible branches (‡): the function `triangle` contains an infeasible branch. Consider the following code snippet from `triangle`:

```
if(a == b) { ... } else { if(a == b) { ... }}
```

The true branch of second predicate is logically infeasible because of the first one. Apart from this branch, CAVM and CodeScroll cover all branches in `triangle`.

(5) Use of `strcmp` (§): case4 in `Antipatterns` contains a call to `strcmp`, which neither CodeScroll nor Austin supports.

(6) Imprecise control dependency analysis (◊): currently CAVM suffers from imprecise control dependency analysis; it cannot detect implicit control dependencies between branches caused by, for example, a `return` in the middle of a function. Consider the following code snippet:

```
if(x > 42) return; if(y == 7)...
```

Both the true and the false branch of the second `if` statement depend on the false branch of the first one. However, this dependency is implicit, as it is not expressed as part of a nested structure. CAVM's current control dependency analysis fails to capture this. Consequently, CAVM cannot compute the fitness values correctly for these branches and cannot cover them. When we manually made the control dependency explicit (by inserting the appropriate `else` structure), CAVM achieves an average of approximately 60% branch coverage for functions `delete`, `insert`, and `modify` in the `LinkedList` subject, with some individual runs achieving 100% coverage. Precise control dependency analysis for the full set of C structural constructs is a part of future work.

Finally, let us discuss the performance of `Austin`. `Austin` requires an explicit pointer constraint in the source code of the target function in order to instantiate any pointer. If the code does not compare a given pointer to `NULL`, the pointer will not be instantiated. After confirming this behaviour to be intended with the main developer of `Austin`, we inserted explicit `NULL` checks to smaller benchmarks (`Antipatterns`, `AVMf`, `LinkedList`, and `BinaryTree`), but opted not to modify the real world subjects (`ls` and `decode.c`). This results in the consistent 0% coverage for functions in `decode.c`, as they all require pointer parameters.

Based on the results in Table 2, we answer RQ1: `CAVM` can cover branches that neither `CodeScroll` nor `Austin` can. In particular, `Austin` has a significant limitation regarding pointer instantiation. The accompanying webpage[3] contains results about efficiency of `CAVM`, including the number of required fitness evaluations and the average wall clock execution time.

5   Conclusion

We present `CAVM`, an AVM-based test data generation tool that handles dynamic data structures using a purely search-based approach. Unlike the current state-of-the-art tool, `Austin`, which determines the shape of the required data structure using symbolic analysis, `CAVM` simply grows the data structure by successive pointer instantiations. The empirical comparison of `CAVM` against `Austin` and a commercial test data generation tool, `CodeScroll`, shows that `CAVM` can cover many branches that neither of the other tools can. Future work include improvement of `CAVM` as well as its integration to `CodeScroll`.

Acknowledgement. This work was supported by the ICT R&D program of MSIP/I-ITP [Grant No. R7117-16-0005: A connected private cloud platform for mission critical software test and verification].

References

1. Harman, M., Kim, S.G., Lakhotia, K., McMinn, P., Yoo, S.: Optimizing for the number of tests generated in search based test data generation with an application to the oracle cost problem. In: Proceedings of the 3rd International Workshop on Search-Based Software Testing (SBST 2010), pp. 182–191, April 2010
2. Harman, M., Hu, L., Hierons, R., Wegener, J., Sthamer, H., Baresel, A., Roper, M.: Testability transformation. IEEE Trans. Softw. Eng. **30**(1), 3–16 (2004)
3. Horowitz, E., Sahni, S., Anderson-Freed, S.: Fundamentals of Data Structures in C. W. H. Freeman & Co., New York (1992)
4. Kempka, J., McMinn, P., Sudholt, D.: Design and analysis of different alternating variable searches for search-based software testing. Theoret. Comput. Sci. **605**, 1–20 (2015)
5. Kim, J., You, B., Kwon, M., McMinn, P., Yoo, S.: Evaluation of CAVM, Austin, and CodeScroll for test data generation for C. Technical report. CS-TR-2017-413, School of Computing, Korean Advanced Institute of Science and Technology (2017)

---

[3] http://coinse.kaist.ac.kr/projects/cavm/.

6. Lakhotia, K., Harman, M., Gross, H.: AUSTIN: a tool for search based software testing for the C language and its evaluation on deployed automotive systems. In: 2nd International Symposium on Search Based Software Engineering, pp. 101–110, September 2010
7. McMinn, P., Kapfhammer, G.M.: AVMf: an open-source framework and implementation of the alternating variable method. In: Sarro, F., Deb, K. (eds.) SSBSE 2016. LNCS, vol. 9962, pp. 259–266. Springer, Cham (2016). doi:10.1007/978-3-319-47106-8_21

Challenge Papers

Using Search-Based Test Generation
to Discover Real Faults in Guava

Hussein Almulla, Alireza Salahirad, and Gregory Gay[✉]

University of South Carolina, Columbia, SC, USA
{halmulla,alireza}@email.sc.edu, greg@greggay.com

Abstract. Testing costs can be reduced through automated unit test generation. An important benchmark for such tools is their ability to detect *real faults*. Fault databases, such as Defects4J, assist in this task. The Guava project—a collection of Java libraries from Google—offers an opportunity to expand such databases with additional complex faults. We have identified 11 faults in the Guava project, added them to Defects4J, and assessed the ability of the EvoSuite framework to detect these faults. Ultimately, EvoSuite was able to detect three faults. Analysis of the remaining faults offers lessons in how to improve generation tools. We offer these faults to the community to assist future benchmarking efforts.

Keywords: Search-based test generation · Automated test generation · Software faults

1 Introduction

With the growing complexity of software, the cost of testing has grown as well. Automation of tasks such as unit test creation can assist in controlling that cost. One promising form of automated test generation is *search-based* generation. Given a measurable testing goal, and a fitness function capable of guiding the search towards that goal, powerful optimization algorithms can select test inputs able to meet that goal [3].

When testing, developers ultimately wish to detect faults. Therefore, to impact testing practice, automated generation techniques must be effective at detecting the complex faults that manifest in real-world software projects [7]. By offering examples of such faults, fault databases—such as Defects4J [6]—allow us to benchmark generation tools against realistic case examples. Importantly, Defects4J can be expanded to include additional systems and example faults.

The Guava project[1] offers an excellent expansion opportunity. Guava is an open-source set of core libraries for Java, developed by Google, that include collection types, graph libraries, functional types, in-memory caching, and numerous other utilities. Guava is an essential tool of modern development, and is one of the most used libraries [8].

This work is supported by National Science Foundation grant CCF-1657299.

[1] https://github.com/google/guava.

© Springer International Publishing AG 2017
T. Menzies and J. Petke (Eds.): SSBSE 2017, LNCS 10452, pp. 153–160, 2017.
DOI: 10.1007/978-3-319-66299-2_13

Guava serves as an interesting benchmark subject for two reasons. First, much of its functionality is, naturally, related to the creation and manipulation of complex objects. Guava defines a variety of new data structures, and functionality related to those structures. Generation and initialization of complex input is an outstanding challenge area for automated generation [1]. Second, Guava is a mature project. Faults in Guava—particularly recent faults—are unlikely to resemble the simple syntactic mistakes modeled by mutations. Rather, we expect to see faults that require specific, difficult to trigger, combinations of input and method calls. Generation tools that can detect such faults are likely to be effective on other real-world projects. If not, then by studying these faults, we may be able to learn lessons that will improve these tools.

We have identified 11 real faults in the Guava project, and added them to Defects4J. We generated test suites using the EvoSuite framework [3], and assessed the ability of these suites to detect nine of the faults[2]. Ultimately, EvoSuite is able to detect three of the nine studied faults. Some of the issues preventing fault detection include the need for specific input values, data types, or sequences of method calls—generally factors that cannot be addressed through code coverage alone. We have made these faults available to provide data and examples that could benefit future test generation research.

2   Study

In this study, we have extracted faults from the Guava project. We have generated tests for the fixed version of each class using the EvoSuite framework [3], and applied those tests to the faulty version in order to assess the efficacy of generated suites. In doing so, we wish to answer the following research questions: (1) *can EvoSuite detect the extracted faults?*, and (2), *what factors prevented fault detection?*

In order to answer these questions, we have performed the following experiment:

1. **Extracted Faults:** We have identified 11 real faults in the Guava project, and added them to the Defects4J fault database (See Sect. 2.1).
2. **Generated Test Cases:** For nine of the faults, we generated 10 suites per fault using the fixed version of each class-under-test (CUT). We repeat this process with a two-minute and a ten-minute search budget per CUT (See Sect. 2.2).
3. **Removed Non-Compiling Tests:** Any tests that do not compile, or that return inconsistent results, are automatically removed (See Sect. 2.2).
4. **Assessed Fault-finding Efficacy:** For each budget and fault, we measure the likelihood of fault detection. For each undetected fault, we examined the report and source code to identify possible detection-preventing factors.

---

[2] Two faults were omitted from the case study as they require the use of JDK 7 (see Sect. 2).

2.1 Fault Extraction

Defects4J is an extensible database of real faults extracted from Java projects [6][3]. Currently, it consists of 395 faults from six projects. For each fault, Defects4J provides access to the faulty and fixed versions of the code, developer-written test cases that expose each fault, and a list of classes and lines of code modified to fix the fault.

We have added Guava to Defects4J. This consisted of developing build files that work across project versions, extracting candidate faults using Guava's version control and issue tracking systems, ensuring that each candidate could be reliable reproduced, and minimizing the "patch" used to distinguish fixed and faulty classes.

For inclusion in the final dataset, each fault is required to meet three properties. First, the fault must be related to the source code. For each reported issue, we attempted to identify a pair of code versions that differ only by the minimum changes required to address the fault. The "fixed" version must be explicitly labeled as a fix to an issue, and changes imposed by the fix must be to source code, not to other project artifacts such as the build system. Second, the fault must be reproducible—at least one test must pass on the fixed version and fail on the faulty version. Third, the fix to the fault must be isolated from unrelated code changes such as refactorings.

One property of all Defects4J faults is that the commit message for the "fixed" version reference a reported issue in the project's tracking system (i.e., "fixes #2345"). Fulfilling this property has not been a problem for the six existing projects, as the developers of those projects have used a standard commit message format. However, Guava commits do not follow a standard format—many "fixes" do not reference a reported issue. To maintain continuity with the other Defects4J projects, we restricted our search to fixes that do make an explicit reference. Following this process, we extracted 11 faults from a pool of 63 candidate faults that reference an explicit issue. In the future, we may allow commits without explicit references in order to mine additional faults.

One additional limiting factor is that particular Java Development Kit versions must be installed and used to build certain versions of Guava. Due to language changes, JDK 7 must be used to build faults 10 and 11. Faults 1-9 can be built using JDK 8. Recently, the decision was made to require that all new additions to Defects4J be compatible with JDK 8. Faults 10 and 11 will still be made available, but will not be included in the core Defects4J database or used in our case study.

The faults used in this study can be accessed by cloning the bug-mining branch of https://github.com/Greg4cr/defects4j. Additional data about each fault can be found at http://greggay.com/data/guava/guavafaults.csv, including commit IDs, fault descriptions, and a list of triggering tests. Later, these faults will be migrated into the master branch at http://defects4j.org. We plan to add additional faults and improvements in the future.

---

[3] Available from http://defects4j.org.

2.2   Test Generation and Removal

EvoSuite applies a genetic algorithm in order to evolve test suites over several generations, forming a new population by retaining, mutating, and combining the strongest solutions [7]. In this study, we used EvoSuite version 1.0.5 with a combination of three fitness functions—Branch, Exception, and Method Coverage—a combination recently found to be generally effective at detecting faults [5].

Tests are generated from the fixed version of the system and applied to the faulty version in order to eliminate the oracle problem. In practice, this translates to a regression testing scenario. Given the potential difficulty in achieving coverage over Guava classes, two search budgets were used—two and ten minutes, a typical and an extended budget [4]. To control experiment cost, we deactivated assertion filtering—all possible regression assertions are included. All other settings were kept at their default values. As results may vary, we performed 10 trials for each fault and search budget.

Generation tools may generate flaky (unstable) tests [7]. For example, a test case that makes assertions about the system time will only pass during generation. We automatically remove flaky tests[4]. First, non-compiling test cases are removed. Then, each test is executed on the fixed CUT five times. If results are inconsistent, the test case is removed. On average, 0.92 tests are removed from each suite.

3   Results and Discussion

In Table 1, we list—for each search budget—whether EvoSuite was able to detect each fault and, if so, the likelihood of detection (the proportion of suites that detected the fault). We also list the average Branch Coverage attained over the ten trials, the average number of tests in the generated suites, the average suite length (number of test steps), and the average number of tests removed.

From Table 1, we can see the three of the nine faults were detected (Faults 3, 4, and 8). Of these, Fault 3 was detected the most reliably (90% likelihood for both budgets). This fault, dealing with incorrect rounding[5], is a classic example of the types of faults that automated generation excels at. Branch Coverage drives the search towards the affected code and towards differing output between versions.

Fault 4[6] was also detected reliably. The faulty version uses a non-standard ASCII character in the `toString()` function for class `Range`. This is a relatively easy fault to catch—any call to *toString()* with a valid `Range` object will result in differing output between faulty and fixed versions. With the shorter search budget, EvoSuite is somewhat less likely to call the function and somewhat more

---

[4] This process is documented in more detail in [7] and [4].

[5] https://github.com/google/guava/commit/
1b1163b7e2c121d4a5b25b8966714201551976c4.

[6] https://github.com/google/guava/commit/
c6e21a35f3113a7a952a9615a0e92dcf1dd4bfb3.

Table 1. Test generation results for each fault and search budget—likelihood of fault detection, average achieved branch coverage (covered/total branches), average number of tests, average suite length, and average number of tests removed.

Fault	Budget	Fault detected	Likelihood of detection	Branch coverage (Covered/Total Goals)	Suite size	Suite length	Number of tests removed
1	2 min	X	0.00%	11.83% (22.60/191.00)	6.90	26.10	0.90
	10 min	X	0.00%	73.25% (139.90/191.00)	38.70	180.80	11.10
2	2 min	X	0.00%	92.47% (82.30/89.00)	26.10	65.60	0.00
	10 min	X	0.00%	93.60% (83.30/89.00)	26.90	70.00	0.00
3	2 min	✓	90.00%	96.64% (132.40/137.00)	65.90	114.90	0.00
	10 min	✓	90.00%	97.52% (133.60/137.00)	67.70	117.00	0.00
4	2 min	✓	60.00%	67.56% (83.10/123.00)	91.40	270.40	1.20
	10 min	✓	100.00%	92.03% (113.20/123.00)	130.40	424.20	1.60
5	2 min	X	0.00%	32.38% (13.60/42.00)	4.70	49.40	0.00
	10 min	X	0.00%	76.31% (30.70/40.20)	14.50	96.90	0.00
6	2 min	X	0.00%	3.10% (30.90/1008.00)	3.00	11.60	0.00
	10 min	X	0.00%	3.10% (31.10/1008.00)	3.40	13.00	0.10
7	2 min	X	0.00%	2.32% (23.30/1005.00)	3.40	20.50	0.00
	10 min	X	0.00%	1.91% (19.20/1005.00)	2.20	15.50	0.30
8	2 min	✓	10.00%	21.51% (11.40/53.00)	7.30	35.10	0.00
	10 min	✓	60.00%	91.89% (48.70/53.00)	42.40	214.90	1.20
9	2 min	X	0.00%	3.54% (5.60/158.00)	3.40	8.40	0.00
	10 min	X	0.00%	57.47% (90.80/158.00)	74.30	175.30	0.20

likely to set up an invalid range. However, the longer budget ensures that the fault is caught by all suites.

Fault 8 involves the computation of the intersection of `RegularContiguousSet` objects when one is a singleton[7]. One of the changes made to fix the fault is a shift from < in the return statement of the `isEmpty()` method to <=. Any test case where the two compared variables are the same will now detect the fault. A longer search budget increases the number of suites that detect the fault (10% to 30%), but this is still a clear case of a fault that requires not just coverage, but *picking specific input*.

EvoSuite failed to detect the other six faults. Therefore, our next step was to examine these faults to identify factors preventing detection. These factors include:

Specific Input Values are Required: As seen in Fault 8, it is not enough to simply cover a line. At times, specific input values are required to trigger and detect a fault. In the case of Fault 8, the generator is able to stumble on these

---

[7] https://github.com/google/guava/commit/
44a2592b04490ad26d2bc874f9dbd4c1146cc5de.

inputs given enough time. In other cases, such as with Fault 2^8, not enough context is offered to the generator. Because of this fault, splitting a string with a zero-width regular expression pattern would result in single-character strings on either end of the split being dropped. The fix to the code changes a $>=$ to a $>$, but unless input matching this particular corner case is used, the fault will not be discovered.

Specific Data Types are Required for Input: Guava includes functionality for iterating over lists that is intended to function regardless of the *type* of list used. Fault 9^9 illustrates the difficulty of verifying such functionality. Unlike sets, lists typically allow duplicate elements. This is not universally true, however. Therefore, if a list type is used that does not allow duplicates, then the affected code in Guava will throw an exception. This is another case that coverage cannot handle, as coverage can be obtained using any type of list. Detecting the fault requires choosing a specialized data type.

Inputs are Instances of Complex Data Types: Generating input for complex data types is still an open challenge for automated generation [1]. If the generator cannot produce and manipulate input of such types, it may not be able to cover code, reducing the possibility of triggering faults. Fault 6^{10} is one such example. This fault revolves around the wrong cause of removal being listed for items in a cache. To discover this fault, EvoSuite must generate and initialize an instance of the class `LocalCache`. In addition, this class is a generic type, further complicating automated generation [2].

A Specific Series of Method Calls Must be Generated: Each unit test consists of a series of one or more calls to methods in the CUT. Rather than specific input, at times, triggering a fault requires a specific sequence of calls. Fault 5^{11} is one such example. In this case, a long sequence of nested `Futures.transform(...)` calls on the same object will indefinitely hang because a `StackOverflowException` is thrown and swallowed. Detecting this fault requires not only input that triggers an exception, but a sequence of transformation calls on that input.

Fault 1^{12} offers a second example of this factor. `MinMaxPriorityQueue` fails to remove the correct object after a sequence of multiple **add** and **remove** calls—specifically, certain elements may be iterated more than once if elements are

---

[8] https://github.com/google/guava/commit/
55524c66de8db4c2e44727b69421c7d0e4f30be0.

[9] https://github.com/google/guava/commit/
1a1b97ee1f065d0bc52c91eeeb6407bfaa6cbea1.

[10] https://github.com/google/guava/commit/
0a686a644ca5cefb9e7bf4a38b34bf4ede9e75aa.

[11] https://github.com/google/guava/commit/
52b5ee640da780e0fd2502ec995436fcdc93e03e.

[12] https://github.com/google/guava/commit/
2ef955163b3d43e7849c1929ef4e5d714b93da96.

removed during iteration. It would not be unusual to see a sequence of calls in a generated test case. However, the example tests created by humans to reproduce this fault include relatively long sequences of calls. The suite minimization and bloat control mechanisms used to control suite size in automated generation are designed to avoid a long series of calls that do not contribute to code coverage—actively discouraging the generation of the very type of test cases that would detect this fault.

Many of these factors cannot be solved through increasing code coverage. Rather, they require context from the project. Methods of gleaning that context, either through seeding from existing test cases or data mining of project elements, may assist in improving the efficacy of test generation.

4 Conclusion

We have identified 11 real faults in the Guava project, and added them to the Defects4J fault database. To study the capabilities of modern test generation tools, we generated test suites using the EvoSuite framework. Ultimately, Evo-Suite is able to detect three of the nine studied faults. Some of the issues preventing fault detection include the need for specific input values, data types, or sequences of method calls—generally factors that cannot be addressed through code coverage alone. We have made these faults available to provide data and examples that could benefit future test generation research.

References

1. Feldt, R., Poulding, S.: Finding test data with specific properties via metaheuristic search. In: 2013 IEEE 24th International Symposium on Software Reliability Engineering (ISSRE), pp. 350–359, November 2013
2. Fraser, G., Arcuri, A.: Automated test generation for java generics. In: Winkler, D., Biffl, S., Bergsmann, J. (eds.) SWQD 2014. LNBIP, vol. 166, pp. 185–198. Springer, Cham (2014). doi:10.1007/978-3-319-03602-1_12
3. Fraser, G., Staats, M., McMinn, P., Arcuri, A., Padberg, F.: Does automated white-box test generation really help software testers? In: Proceedings of the 2013 International Symposium on Software Testing and Analysis, ISSTA, pp. 291–301. ACM, New York (2013). http://doi.acm.org/10.1145/2483760.2483774
4. Gay, G.: The fitness function for the job: search-based generation of test suites that detect real faults. In: Proceedings of the International Conference on Software Testing, ICST 2017. IEEE (2017)
5. Gay, G.: Generating effective test suites by combining coverage criteria. In: Menzies, T., Petke, J. (eds.) SSBSE 2017. LNCS, vol. 10452, pp. 65–82. Springer, Cham (2017)
6. Just, R., Jalali, D., Ernst, M.D.: defects4J: a database of existing faults to enable controlled testing studies for Java programs. In: Proceedings of the 2014 International Symposium on Software Testing and Analysis, ISSTA 2014, pp. 437–440. ACM, New York (2014). http://doi.acm.org/10.1145/2610384.2628055

7. Shamshiri, S., Just, R., Rojas, J.M., Fraser, G., McMinn, P., Arcuri, A.: Do automatically generated unit tests find real faults? an empirical study of effectiveness and challenges. In: Proceedings of the 30th IEEE/ACM International Conference on Automated Software Engineering (ASE), ASE 2015. ACM, New York (2015)
8. Weiss, T.: We analyzed 30,000 GitHub projects - here are the top. 100 libraries in Java, JS and Ruby (2013). http://blog.takipi.com/we-analyzed-30000-github-projects-here-are-the-top-100-libraries-in-java-js-and-ruby/

Optimising Darwinian Data Structures on Google Guava

Michail Basios[✉], Lingbo Li, Fan Wu, Leslie Kanthan, and Earl T. Barr

Department of Computer Science, University College London,
Malet Place, London WC1E 6BT, UK
{m.basios,lingbo.li,fan.wu,l.kanthan,e.barr}@cs.ucl.ac.uk

Abstract. Data structure selection and tuning is laborious but can vastly improve application performance and memory footprint. In this paper, we demonstrate how ARTEMIS, a multiobjective, cloud-based optimisation framework can *automatically* find optimal, tuned data structures and how it is used for optimising the Guava library. From the proposed solutions that ARTEMIS found, 27.45% of them improve *all* measures (execution time, CPU usage, and memory consumption). More specifically, ARTEMIS managed to improve the memory consumption of Guava by up 13%, execution time by up to 9%, and 4% CPU usage.

Keywords: Search-based software engineering · Genetic improvement · Software analysis and optimisation · Multi-objective optimisation

1 Introduction

Under the immense time pressures of industrial software development, developers tend to avoid early-stage optimisations, yet forget to do so later. When selecting data structures from libraries, in particular, they tend to rely on defaults and neglect potential optimisations that alternative implementations or tuning parameters can offer. This, despite the impact that data structure selection and tuning can have on application performance and defects [11]. For performance, examples include the selection of an implementation that created unnecessary temporary objects for the program's workload [13] or selecting a combination of Scala data structures that scaled better, reducing execution time from 45 to 1.5 min [10]; memory leak bugs exemplify data structure triggered defects, such as those in the Oracle Java bug database caused by poor implementations that retained references to unused data entries [14].

Optimisation is time-consuming, especially on large code bases. It is also brittle. An optimisation for one version of a program can break or become a de-optimisation in the next release. Another reason developers may avoid optimisation are development fads that focus on fast solutions, like "Premature Optimisation is the horror of all Evil" [6] and "Hack until it works" [4]. In short, optimisations are expensive and their benefits unclear for many projects. Developers need automated help.

© Springer International Publishing AG 2017
T. Menzies and J. Petke (Eds.): SSBSE 2017, LNCS 10452, pp. 161–167, 2017.
DOI: 10.1007/978-3-319-66299-2_14

Data structures are a particularly attractive optimisation target because they have a well-defined interface, many are tunable, and different implementations of a data structure usually represent a particular trade-off between time and storage, making some operations faster but more space-consuming or slower but more space-efficient. For instance, an ordered list makes retrieving a dataset in sorted order fast, but inserting new elements slow, whilst a hash table allows for quick insertions and retrievals of specific items, but listing the entire set in order is slow. A *Darwinian data structure* [9] is on that admits tuning and has multiple implementations, i.e. it is replaceable. The data structure optimisation problem is the problem of finding optimal tuning and implementation for a Darwinian data structure used in an input program.

In this paper, we aim to help developers perform optimisations cheaply, focusing solving the data structure optimisation problem. We present ARTEMIS, a cloud-based language-agnostic optimisation framework that identifies uses of *Darwinian data structures* and automatically searches for optimal combinations of implementations and tuning parameters for them, given a test suite. ARTEMIS' search is multi-objective, seeking to simultaneously improve a program's execution time, memory usage and CPU usage while passing the test suite. ARTEMIS is the first technique to apply multi-objective optimisation to the Darwinian data structure selection and tuning problem.

2   Proposed Solution

Darwinian Data Structure Selection (DS²) problem: given a program with a list of replaceable data structures, find the optimal combination of data structures and their arguments, such that the runtime performance of the program is optimised.

In order to solve the DS² problem, we proposed a language-agnostic optimisation framework, ARTEMIS. Figure 1 illustrates the architecture of ARTEMIS. It consists of three main components: the DARWINIAN DATA STRUCTURES STORE GENERATOR (DDSSG), the EXTRACTOR, and the OPTIMISER. ARTEMIS takes the language's Collection API library, the user's application source code and a test suite as input to generate an optimised version of the code with a new combination of data structures. A regression test suite is used to maintain the correctness

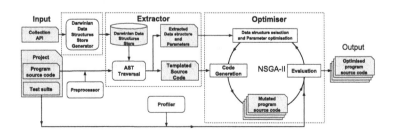

Fig. 1. System architecture of ARTEMIS.

of the transformations and to evaluate the non-functional properties of interest. ARTEMIS uses a built-in profiler that measures execution time, memory consumption and CPU usage.

DARWINIAN DATA STRUCTURE STORE GENERATOR (DDSSG): automatically builds a store of *Darwinian Data Structures* that can be exposed as tunable parameters to the OPTIMISER. DDSSG uses a hierarchy graph to represent the inheritance relations between classes, then it groups the replaceable classes together, as its output. ARTEMIS can automatically generate the hierarchy graph from the source code of the library (if provided) or from the library documentation.

To get the hierarchy graph from the source code, DDSSG traverses the AST of each file of the library and looks for class declaration expressions. It extracts the classes and stores them as points of a graph. Whenever it finds a special keyword, such as `extends` or `implements` in Java, it creates an edge in the graph that represents this relationship. After the graph construction is finished, a graph traversal is used to *automatically* generate a store of equivalent implementations for each interface; *e.g.,* {`List`, `ArrayList`, `LinkedList`}. Those implementations will be considered as replaceable during code execution and will be exposed as parameters to the OPTIMISER.

EXTRACTOR takes as input the program source code, identifies potential locations of the code that contain DARWINIAN data structures, and provides as output a list of parameters (*Extracted Data Structures and Parameters* in Fig. 1) and a templated version of the code which replaces the data structure with data structure type identifiers (*Templated Source Code* in Fig. 1).

In order to determine which parts of the code contain DARWINIAN data structures, the EXTRACTOR firstly generates an Abstract Syntax Tree (AST) from the input source code. It then traverses the AST to discover potential data structure transformations based on a store of data structures generated from DDSSG. For example, when an expression node of the AST contains a `LinkedList` expression, the EXTRACTOR marks this expression as a potential DARWINIAN data structure that can take values from the available `List` implementations: `LinkedList` or `ArrayList`. The EXTRACTOR generates a templated copy of the AST, with all discovered DARWINIAN data structures replaced by template identifiers (holes).

OPTIMISER is to find a combination of data structures that improves the performance of the initial program. Because we aim to optimise various conflicting performance objectives, we consider this as a multi-objective optimisation problem, thus the OPTIMISER uses a multi-objective Genetic Algorithm [2] to search for optimal solutions [1,7,8,12].

We use an array of integers to represent the tuning parameters. Each parameter may refer either to an equivalent data structure or a parameter of the data structure such as the initial size. Together with the templated AST generated from the OPTIMISER, ARTEMIS can rebuild the program with a different set of data structures. For each iteration of the algorithm, NSGA-II progresses by firstly applying tournament selection, followed by a uniform crossover and a uniform mutation operation. In our experiments, we designed fitness functions to capture execution time, memory consumption and CPU usage. After fitness evaluation, a standard NSGA-II non-dominated selection is applied to form the next generation. This process is repeated until the solutions converge. Finally, all non-dominating solutions in the final population are provided as solutions.

A program may contain a large number of data structures from which only some are DARWINIAN. Moreover, some of those DARWINIAN data structures can affect the performance of the program more than others. There are data structures that store only a few items and be called only a few times during program execution and, as a consequence, changing them will most probably not provide any significant improvement.

In our implementation, we have introduced a preprocessing step that *automatically* instruments the program to provide profiling details when it is executed the first time. The instrumented code is run before the optimisation begins and it generates a database with the most costly parts of codes worth optimising. This information is used by the EXTRACTOR to determine if a data structure is worth being considered as a DARWINIAN data structure. This preprocessing step is mostly useful for very large programs where there is a large number of data structures involved.

3   Experiments and Results

To assess how effectively ARTEMIS can improve a program's performance, we used Guava[1] as an instance of its application. Guava is an open-source set of common libraries for Java. It consists of 252,688 Lines of Code, which are tested by 1,674,425 test cases with 61.7% branch coverage. We conducted experiments with Oracle JDK 1.8 and Ubuntu 16.04 on top of machines featuring 8 cores and 14GB of DRAM. We used JVM profiling tools for performance measurements. To mitigate instability and incorrect results [3], we differentiate VM start-up and steady-state. We do repeated measurements for 30 times and record the measurements before and after doing the optimisations. Also we use Mann Whitney U test to examine if the improvement is statistically significant. For the settings of the optimisation algorithm, we used an initial population size of 30 and a maximum number of 900 function evaluations. These numbers were chosen after a few calibration experiments to ensure the best performance of the algorithm.

For the rest of this section, we asked four Research Questions and provided answers with supportive results in each of the following paragraphs.

RQ1. What is the improvement that ARTEMIS provides for each objective?

We ask this question to understand how much improvement ARTEMIS can achieve on each of the objectives and how the other objectives are affected. Firstly, we compute the mean response time and report the 95% confidence interval. We use effect size [5] for measuring the performance impact. To quantify the effects we use Cohen's d [5] strength values: small $(0.2 < d \leq 0.5)$, medium $(0.5 < d \leq 0.8)$ and large $(0.8 < d)$. In Fig. 2 we plot the mean values for the optimal solutions that contain at least one large improvement for one of the three

---

[1] https://github.com/google/guava.

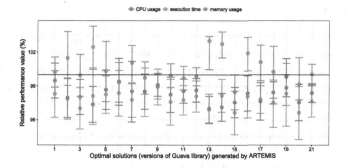

Fig. 2. Optimal solutions with large improvement in at least one measure.

measurements. The maximum improvement for each measure is 9% execution time, 13% memory usage and 4% CPU usage.

RQ2. How many provided solutions strictly dominate the original program?

A solution is said to strictly dominate another if it outperforms the other in all measures. If ARTEMIS can provide solutions that strictly dominate the original program, those solutions can be very valuable because they represent options to improve the program without sacrificing anything. The number of strictly dominating solution for Guava was 14 out of 51 final solutions. Those 14 solutions provide a wide range of options for users to choose depending on their favour of different objectives.

RQ3. What is the cost of using ARTEMIS?

This question asks about the computational cost of ARTEMIS. An extremely high computational cost may make the system impractical to use in real-world situations. Therefore we measured its cost on Guava subject in terms of machine hours. In this study, a Microsoft Azure D4-v2 machine, which costs £0.41 per hour[2], was used to conduct all experiments. This cost of using is negligible compared to a human software engineer. Moreover, ARTEMIS transforms the selection of data structure and sets the parameter on source code level, which means such optimisation does not need to be carried frequently.

RQ4. How many Darwinian data structures does ARTEMIS optimise?

We ask this question to understand what changes have been made to the program. To minimise the search space we applied ARTEMIS only to the most used code in Guava as identified by the preprocessor. As a result, ARTEMIS extracted only 6 Darwinian data structures in total from the Guava library. Across all the optimal solutions ARTEMIS produced, 1 to 6 data structures were changed in each, with a median of 3 data structures uses. For instance, ARTEMIS replaced HashMap with LinkedHashMap in 42 of the 135 changes across all optimal solutions.

---

[2] https://azure.microsoft.com/en-gb/pricing/.

4   Conclusions

In this paper, we introduced ARTEMIS, a novel multi-objective search-based framework that automatically selects and optimises the data structures and their arguments in a given program. ARTEMIS is language agnostic, meaning it can be easily adapted to any programming language. On a large real-world system, Guava, ARTEMIS found 9% improvement on execution time, 13% improvement on memory consumption and 4% improvement on CPU usage separately, and 27.45% of the final solutions provides improvement without sacrificing other objectives. Lastly, we estimated the cost of optimising Guava in machine hours. With a price of £0.41 per machine hour, the cost of optimising a real-world system such as Guava in this study is less than £7.85. Therefore, we conclude that ARTEMIS is a practical tool for optimising the data structures in large real-world programs.

References

1. Dan, H., Harman, M., Krinke, J., Li, L., Marginean, A., Wu, F.: *Pidgin Crasher*: searching for minimised crashing GUI event sequences. In: Goues, C., Yoo, S. (eds.) SSBSE 2014. LNCS, vol. 8636, pp. 253–258. Springer, Cham (2014). doi:10.1007/978-3-319-09940-8_21

2. Deb, K., Pratap, A., Agarwal, S., Meyarivan, T.A.M.T.: A fast and elitist multiobjective genetic algorithm: Nsga-ii. IEEE Trans. Evol. Comput. **6**(2), 182–197 (2002)

3. Georges, A., Buytaert, D., Eeckhout, L.: Statistically rigorous Java performance evaluation. ACM SIGPLAN Notices **42**(10), 57–76 (2007)

4. Hardin, B.: Companies with "hacking" cultures fail (2016). https://blog.bretthard.in/companies-with-hacking-cultures-fail-b8907a69e3d. Accessed 25 Feb 2017

5. Kitchenham, B.A., Pfleeger, S.L., Pickard, L.M., Jones, P.W., Hoaglin, D.C., El Emam, K., Rosenberg, J.: Preliminary guidelines for empirical research in software engineering. IEEE Trans. Softw. Eng. **28**(8), 721–734 (2002)

6. Knuth, D.E.: Structured programming with go to statements. ACM Comput. Surv. **6**(4), 261–301 (1974)

7. Langdon, W.B., Modat, M., Petke, J., Harman, M.: Improving 3d medical image registration cuda software with genetic programming. In: Proceedings of the 2014 GECCO, pp. 951–958. ACM (2014)

8. Li, L., Harman, M., Wu, F., Zhang, Y.: SBSelector: search based component selection for budget hardware. In: Barros, M., Labiche, Y. (eds.) SSBSE 2015. LNCS, vol. 9275, pp. 289–294. Springer, Cham (2015). doi:10.1007/978-3-319-22183-0_25

9. Michail, B., Li, L., Wu, F., Kanthan, L., Lawrence, D., Barr, E.: Darwinian data structure selection. arXiv preprint arXiv:1706.03232 (2017)

10. Nowling, R.J.: Gotchas with Scala Mutable Collections and Large Data Sets (2015). http://rnowling.github.io/software/engineering/2015/07/01/gotcha-scala-collections.html. Accessed 18 Feb 2017

11. Shacham, O., Vechev, M., Yahav, E.: Chameleon: adaptive selection of collections. In: ACM Sigplan Notices, vol. 44, pp. 408–418. ACM (2009)

12. Wu, F., Weimer, W., Harman, M., Jia, Y., Krinke, J.: Deep parameter optimisation. In: Proceedings of the 2015 Annual Conference on Genetic and Evolutionary Computation, pp. 1375–1382. ACM (2015)

13. Guoqing, X., Arnold, M., Mitchell, N., Rountev, A., Sevitsky, G.: Go with the flow: profiling copies to find runtime bloat. ACM Sigplan Not. **44**(6), 419–430 (2009)
14. Xu, G., Rountev, A.: Precise memory leak detection for Java software using container profiling. In: ACM/IEEE 30th International Conference on Software Engineering, ICSE 2008, pp. 151–160. IEEE (2008)

A Hyper-heuristic for Multi-objective Integration and Test Ordering in Google Guava

Giovani Guizzo[1]([✉]), Mosab Bazargani[2], Matheus Paixao[3], and John H. Drake[2]

[1] Federal University of Paraná (UFPR), Curitiba, Brazil
gguizzo@inf.ufpr.br
[2] Operational Research Group, Queen Mary University of London, Mile End Road, London, E1 4NS, UK
{m.bazargani,j.drake}@qmul.ac.uk
[3] CREST, Department of Computer Science, University College London, Gower Street, London WC1E 6BT, UK
matheus.paixao.14@ucl.ac.uk

Abstract. Integration testing seeks to find communication problems between different units of a software system. As the order in which units are considered can impact the overall effort required to perform integration testing, deciding an appropriate sequence to integrate and test units is vital. Here we apply a multi-objective hyper-heuristic set within an NSGA-II framework to the Integration and Test Order Problem (ITO) for Google Guava, a set of open-source common libraries for Java. Our results show that an NSGA-II based hyper-heuristic employing a simplified version of Choice Function heuristic selection, outperforms standard NSGA-II for this problem.

1 Introduction

The integration testing phase of a testing strategy combines and tests multiple units of a software system. As some units are dependent on others, stubs are used to mimic the behaviour of classes that are not available, are too expensive to use directly, or are not yet integrated and tested in the software. One drawback is that the stubbing process can also be expensive, and is potentially susceptible to errors. The Integration and Test Order Problem (ITO) is a search problem where the goal is to generate an order for units to be integrated and tested which minimises the cost of stub generation.

As there are a number of different ways of measuring stubbing cost, many previous approaches have considered ITO as a multi-objective problem. In multi-objective optimisation [3], where more than one objective is optimised at the same time, the aim is to find a set of solutions, known as the Pareto front, representing the best trade-off that exists between objectives. Assunção et al. [2] compared the performance of three well-known multi-objective evolutionary algorithms (MOEAs) for solving the ITO problem for eight software systems. Each of the MOEAs tested searched over a permutation of integers representing the order that units are integrated and tested, using two-point crossover and swap

© Springer International Publishing AG 2017
T. Menzies and J. Petke (Eds.): SSBSE 2017, LNCS 10452, pp. 168–174, 2017.
DOI: 10.1007/978-3-319-66299-2_15

mutation to modify solutions. Separate performance comparison was provided for the ITO problem using two objectives and four objectives.

Hyper-heuristics are high-level search methods which operate over a search space of low-level heuristics or heuristic components, rather than over a search space of solutions directly. Guizzo et al. [5] built on the work of Assunção et al. [2], introducing HITO, a Hyper-heuristic for the Integration and Test Order Problem. Operating within the well-known multi-objective Non-dominated Sorting Genetic Algorithm II (NSGA-II) [3], HITO uses a heuristic selection method to select which operators to apply at each step of an MOEA from a set of crossover and mutation operator combinations, optimising two objectives. Using three different heuristic selection methods, their experiments showed that hyper-heuristic selection of crossover and mutation operators within NSGA-II outperformed the traditional NSGA-II implementation (in terms of hypervolume) using only 2-point crossover and swap mutation presented by Assunção et al. [2]. A further performance comparison of using HITO within an SPEA2 framework was given in a later paper [6]. Guizzo et al. [7] provided another extension, formulating the problem as a many-objective problem with four objectives, comparing to a number of state-of-the-art MOEAs.

Google Guava [1] is a large open-source project, containing Google versions of a number of standard general purpose libraries for Java. In this paper, we use all three versions of HITO presented by Guizzo et al. [7], to search for an optimal ordering of units for integration testing of Guava. A performance comparison to the original NSGA-II method presented by Assunção et al. [2] is given.

2   Problem Description and Solution Methodology

The two first levels of tests in software testing are unit testing and integration testing. The unit testing level validates that each unit of the software performs as designed. Thereafter, integration testing is employed to expose faults in the interaction between integrated units. In this phase units are integrated into the software and then tested. When a unit is not yet integrated and tested, but its functionality is needed to integrate and test a dependent unit (an event which is known as dependency break), then a stub (emulation) must be created for such a unit. Generally speaking, units with a high number of calls (number of other units that are depending on them) should be integrated and tested prior to those units with a lower number of calls. If units are not tested in an optimised sequence, an extra cost for generating a greater number of stubs during integration testing will be imposed to the software testing process. Given n units to be integrated and tested, a solution to the problem is represented by a permutation of integers $[1, ..., n]$, denoting the order in which units are processed during integration testing.

This problem is a multi-objective optimisation problem, since several factors have an impact on the cost of stub construction, which makes it harder to find a good cost reduction. In this paper, we use the two objectives that are used by Guizzo et al. [5], i.e., number of attributes (A) and number of methods/operations (O); both need to be emulated in the stub if the dependencies between two modules are broken. Furthermore, this problem can be found in several development contexts. For example, in an object-oriented system units are classes, in component-based programming units are components, in aspect-oriented programming units are aspects, and in product line oriented systems units may be considered product features [2]. These characteristics make this problem suitable for the application of meta- and hyper-heuristics, since these kinds of algorithms are capable of optimizing several objectives at once [3], and are capable of being easily applied to different contexts without needing to have their implementation adapted for this end [7].

In order to extract the method/attribute dependencies of Google Guava we used the *Understand* tool, developed by scitools^{TM} [8]. As *Understand* can only work with Java 1.7 or older versions, we extracted the dependencies for Google Guava $v20.0$. We extracted two levels of dependencies, i.e., dependencies between units, and unit-method or unit-attribute dependencies. For each unit, *define*, *import*, *call*, and *override* features of that file are used for extracting its dependencies, and *define*, *use*, *set*, and *modify* features of each unit-method/unit-attribute are used for addressing dependencies of that method/attribute. Google Guava has 74530 lines of Java code, excluding comments and blank lines, written in 529 files. It has 2273 unit dependencies in total. This is bigger than all seven of the systems that HITO was applied to in previous work in the literature [5,7], where the maximum number of unit dependencies was 1592.

3   HITO

Hyper-heuristic for the Integration and Test Order Problem (HITO) is an NSGA-II based hyper-heuristic for the ITO problem. Three different versions of HITO have been introduced in the literature [5], namely HITO-R, HITO-MAB, and HITO-CF. These versions operate within the same hyper-heuristic framework, using different heuristic selection methods. While HITO-R selects low-level heuristics randomly, HITO-MAB and HITO-CF try to provide balance between exploration and exploitation during the search. HITO-MAB uses a Multi-Armed Bandit (MAB) strategy, selecting low-level heuristics based on their performance and number of executions in a given number of iterations. HITO-CF employs a simplified variant of the Choice Function (CF) [4], using only the performance of a low-level heuristic (f_1) and the elapsed time since a low-level heuristic has been executed (f_3). The performance of pairs of low-level heuristics (f_2) is eliminated from the Choice Function used in HITO-CF for simplicity [5], as pairwise performance between different types of operators is difficult to assess within the NSGA-II framework.

HITO uses nine low-level heuristics, consisting of pairwise combinations of 2-point crossover, uniform crossover, and partially-mapped crossover (PMX), with swap mutation, simple insertion mutation or no mutation. All of the crossover and mutation operators used in HITO are permutation-based, since this is the representation used when considering ITO as a combinatorial optimisation problem. For more information on the heuristic selection methods and low-level heuristics used, we refer the interested reader to the original HITO paper [5].

4   Experiments

This section presents the set of experiments to evaluate the performance of the three different versions of HITO in the Google Guava program. We also compare those results with standard NSGA-II using 2-point crossover and swap mutation. The next two subsections present the experimental set-up and the results.

4.1   Experimental Set-up

The experimentation encompasses four algorithms for solving the ITO problem: HITO-MAB, HITO-CF, HITO-R and NSGA-II. All parameters were set as in Guizzo et al. [7]. All algorithms were executed for 30 independent runs on the unit dependencies extracted from Google Guava. For all of these algorithms, population size is set to 300 and stopping criterion to 60,000 function evaluations. A crossover probability of 95% and mutation probability of 2% were used in NSGA-II experiments. HITO-MAB/CF/R dynamically select low-level heuristics as explained in the Sect. 3. A selected low-level heuristic is applied in HITO-MAB/CF/R with probability of 100%. The MAB parameters of HITO-MAB are size of the sliding window (W) and scaling factor (C) that are respectively set to 150 and 5. CF weight parameters of HITO-CF for f_1 and f_2 are set to $\alpha = 1.0$ and $\beta = 0.00005$, respectively.

The results were collected and evaluated using the hypervolume quality indicator [3]. Hypervolume is a measure of the volume of space dominated by the non-dominated set of solutions representing the approximation of the Pareto front, bounded by a given reference point.

4.2   Results

Table 1 shows hypervolume averages over 30 independent runs found from applying three different versions of HITO and NSGA-II to the Google Guava unit dependencies. Standard deviations of 30 independent runs are given in parenthesis. Hypervolumes are compared using the Kruskal-Wallis statistical test at 95% of significance, with the *p-value* reported alongside the hypervolume values in Table 1.

As shown in Table 1, for Google Guava, HITO-CF performs statistically significantly better than other algorithms with a *p-value* of *2.029E-15*. All HITO

Table 1. Hypervolume averages obtained from 30 independent runs.

System	NSGA-II	HITO-CF	HITO-MAB	HITO-R	p-value
Google Guava	0.309 (0.126)	**0.685 (0.108)**	0.586 (0.085)	0.537 (0.083)	2.029E–15

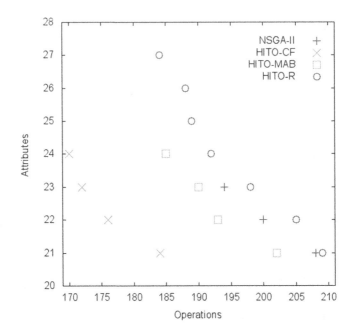

Fig. 1. Pareto fronts found after the 30 independent runs.

versions, even HITO-R, performed better than NSGA-II on average, which indicates the need and effectiveness of using combinations of several low-level heuristics in this problem. This performance is broadly in line with the observations of Guizzo et al. in [7] for seven other systems, with HITO-CF outperforming HITO-R and NSGA-II, however in that work HITO-CF did not show statistically significantly different performance to HITO-MAB. As those seven systems have fewer lines of code and unit dependencies than Google Guava, it might be that HITO-CF scales better to larger systems.

To give a better understanding of the behaviour of the HITO variants, we examined the number of times that each low-level heuristic was executed by each hyper-heuristic. We observed that HITO-CF applied the low-level heuristics with 2-point crossover roughly 2.85 times more than those using uniform crossover, and 3.35 times more than PMX crossover. This means that, for the Choice Function, low-level heuristics with 2-point crossover performed better overall during the search. On the other hand, HITO-MAB gave too much emphasis to the exploration of the search space. This resulted in it selecting all low-level heuristics almost the same number of times, with a slight preference to low-level heuristics with 2-point crossover (approximately 1.2 times more than uniform crossover and 1.18 times more than PMX crossover). This made HITO-MAB perform close to HITO-R. Of the other systems used in previous work [7], HITO-MAB behaved more similarly to HITO-CF in terms of low-level heuristic selection and obtained similar results overall.

Figure 1 depicts Pareto fronts of two objectives of the four algorithms for Guava. Each Pareto front has been generated by composing all the non-dominated solutions found in 30 independent executions. As we are minimising for both objectives, the lower the values, the better that front is. HITO-CF yields a Pareto front that dominates the approximation sets of all of the other algorithms. Even though NSGA-II obtained worse hypervolume results than HITO-R, its Pareto front only lacks diversity when compared to HITO-R. NSGA-II's Pareto front dominates almost half of HITO-R's front, whereas HITO-R could not find solutions that dominate any solution found by NSGA-II. This can be explained by the fact that hypervolume not only considers convergence, but also takes into account diversity in its computation.

As a 'sanity check', we also executed a Random Search algorithm, however it performed so poorly that the Pareto fronts of the other algorithms were unreadable when plotted on a graph. As a result we have omitted this algorithm from this section.

5   Conclusion

In this paper we applied a set of selection hyper-heuristics to the ITO problem for Google Guava. The Google Guava system and the number of unit dependencies it contains are larger than the systems previously used in the literature for this problem. The results obtained using hyper-heuristics for the Google Guava instance are coherent with previous results presented in the literature. The best variant, HITO-CF, was able to outperform other versions of HITO and also a well-known NSGA-II. This can be used as evidence that HITO-CF is capable of solving bigger and unseen instances of the ITO problem. Furthermore, we believe that this highlights the suitability of hyper-heuristics for further research in the field of Search Based Software Engineering (SBSE).

References

1. google/guava: Google Core Libraries for Java. https://github.com/google/guava. Accessed: 25 Apr 2017
2. Assunção, W.K.G., Colanzi, T.E., Vergilio, S.R., Pozo, A.: A multi-objective optimization approach for the integration and test order problem. Inf. Sci. **267**, 119–139 (2014)
3. Coello, C.C., Lamont, G.B., van Veldhuizen, D.A.: Evolutionary Algorithms for Solving Multi-objective Problems. Genetic and Evolutionary Computation, 2nd edn. Springer, Heidelberg (2007)
4. Cowling, P., Kendall, G., Soubeiga, E.: A hyperheuristic approach to scheduling a sales summit. In: Burke, E., Erben, W. (eds.) PATAT 2000. LNCS, vol. 2079, pp. 176–190. Springer, Heidelberg (2001). doi:10.1007/3-540-44629-X_11
5. Guizzo, G., Fritsche, G.M., Vergilio, S.R., Pozo, A.T.R.: A hyper-heuristic for the multi-objective integration and test order problem. In: Proceedings of GECCO 2015, pp. 1343–1350. ACM (2015)

6. Guizzo, G., Vergilio, S.R., Pozo, A.T.: Evaluating a multi-objective hyper-heuristic for the integration and test order problem. In: 2015 Brazilian Conference on Intelligent Systems (BRACIS), pp. 1–6. IEEE (2015)
7. Guizzo, G., Vergilio, S.R., Pozo, A.T., Fritsche, G.M.: A multi-objective and evolutionary hyper-heuristic applied to the integration and test order problem. Appl. Soft Comput. **56**, 331–344 (2017)
8. Scitools: Understand. https://scitools.com/features/. Accessed 25 Apr 2017

Hyperheuristic Observation Based Slicing of Guava

Seongmin Lee and Shin Yoo[⊠]

Korea Advanced Institute of Science and Technology, Daejeon, Republic of Korea
{bohrok,shin.yoo}@kaist.ac.kr

Abstract. Observation Based Slicing is a program slicing technique that depends purely on the observation of dynamic program behaviours. It iteratively applies a deletion operator to the source code, and accepts the deletion (i.e. slices the program) if the program is observed to behave in the same was as the original with respect to the slicing criterion. While the original observation based slicing only used a single deletion operator based on deletion window, the catalogue of applicable deletion operators grew recently with the addition of deletion operators based on lexical similarity. We apply a hyperheuristic approach to the problem of selecting the best deletion operator to each program line. Empirical evaluation using four slicing criteria from Guava shows that the Hyperheuristic Observation Based Slicing (HOBBES) can significantly improve the effeciency of observation based slicing.

1 Introduction

Program slicing aims to delete parts of the source code that does not affect the value of a specific variable at a point of interest [8]. While many applications, including testing [4], debugging [1], maintenance [5], and program comprehension [6], have been proposed, program slicing suffered from limitations in scalability and lack of support for multi-lingual systems: both due to the fact that traditional slicing techniques rely heavily on static dependency analysis.

Observation Based Slicing (ORBS) [2,3] is a new slicing technique that is purely dynamic and language independent. The intuition behind ORBS is that program slicing can be simply conceived as a series of deletions that preserves the behaviour of the program. The original ORBS iteratively considered deletions of consecutive lines. Recently, new deletion operators, based on lexical similairity, have also been introduced, increasing the pool of deletion operators for ORBS.

This paper evaluates a Hyperheuristic Observation Based Slicing (HOBBES). HOBBES applies deletion operators iteratively at each program line, but it uses a hyperheuristic approach to choose the next deletion operator. We formulate an online selective hyperheuristic approach using all available deletion operators as the lower level heuristic. The results of the empirical study using four slicing criteria from Guava project suggest that HOBBES can bring the best of both worlds: HOBBES can finish the given number of iterations sigficantly faster than Window-ORBS, while being able to delete comparable numbers of lines.

© Springer International Publishing AG 2017
T. Menzies and J. Petke (Eds.): SSBSE 2017, LNCS 10452, pp. 175–180, 2017.
DOI: 10.1007/978-3-319-66299-2_16

2   HOBBES: Hyperheuristic Observation Based Slicing

2.1   Observation Based Slicing

ORBS is not only language independent [2] but also can slice programs [3] or even graphics generated by Picture Description Languages [9] that traditional slicers cannot handle. This is because it decides whether to delete certain lines or not based on dynamic observation of executions using the given set of test data, rather than static dependency analysis.

The deletion operator used by the original ORBS is called a Window-deletion (we hereby call the original ORBS with Window-deletion as W-ORBS): if deleting a single line results in failure (in either compilation or preservation of execution trajectories), it incrementally attempts to delete up to n consecutive lines, n being a parameter to the operator. This way, W-ORBS can delete lines that can only be deleted together (such as openning and closing curly brackets in C.). While the W-ORBS can successfully slice various programs, one of its major limitations is the time efficiency. For each line, W-ORBS may attempt up to n compilations and executions before accepting its deletion.

2.2   Deletion Operators Based on Lexical Similarity

Recently, a new group of deletion operators, based on lexical similarity in the source code, have been introduced [7]. Vector Space Model (VSM) deletion operator (hereby called VSM-deletion) represents all source code lines in VSM, and attempts to delete the current line under consideration as well as all other lines that are within the distance δ from the current line. Latent Dirichlet Analysis (LDA) deletion operator (hereby called LDA-deletion) works similarly, but uses LDA-based topic modeling to measure distances between source code lines. With both operators, the intuition is that the lines, that are lexically similar with each other, are likely to have a dependency, so they should be deleted together. Both operators have been shown to provide an attractive cost-benefit trade-off: while they produce larger slices, they are also significantly faster than W-ORBS.

While ORBS using VSM- or LDA-deletion provide better time efficiency compared to W-ORBS, the new operators only delete about 25% of the lines deleted by W-ORBS. This is because neither VSM- nor LDA-deletion can delete lines that are not related by lexical similarity together.

2.3   Algorithm of HOBBES

Algorithm 1 presents HOBBES. It takes the source program $\mathcal{P}$, a slicing criterion (v: variable, l: line index, $\mathcal{I}$: a set of inputs), a set of deletion operators $D = \{D1, ..., DN\}$. After instrumenting the slicing criterion and establishing the original trajectory V, it initializes the selection probability of each deletion operator.

HOBBES iteratively attempts to delete the source code, choosing a deletion operator to apply at each line based on the corresponding selection probability.

Algorithm 1. HOBBES

input : Source program, $\mathcal{P} = \{p_1, ..., p_n\}$, slicing criterion, $(v, l, \mathcal{I})$, Set of deletion
        operators, $D = \{D1, ..., DN\}$
output: A slice, S, of $\mathcal{P}$ for $(v, l, \mathcal{I})$

```
1  O ← Setup(P, v, l)                                    /* Add trajectory extractor on P */
2  V ← Execute(Build(O), I)                              /* V is the original trajectory */
3  D ← InitOperator (D)                                  /* D is the set of (Dk, P(Dk)) */
4  repeat
5  │   deleted ← False
6  │   i ← 1
7  │   while i ≤ Length (O) do
8  │   │   Dcurr ← SelectOperator(D)
9  │   │   O' ← Dcurr(O)
10 │   │   compile, execute, line_cnt ← DeleteAttempt(O', V)
11 │   │   D ← UpdateScore(D, Dcurr, compile, execute, line_cnt)
12 │   │   if execute then
13 │   │   │   O ← O'
14 │   │   │   deleted ← True
15 │   │   end
16 │   │   i ← i + 1
17 │   end
18 until ¬deleted
19 return O
```

A chosen deletion operator creates a candidate slice: depending on the success of compilation and preservation of trajectories, HOBBES decides whether to accept the candidate slice (i.e. the chosen deletion) and updates the selection probability of the chosen deletion operator.

2.4 Studied Deletion Operators

The library of deletions operator consists of 12 different deletion operators. We break down the original Window-deletion operator to four individual deletion operators with fixed size deletion windows: this results in four fixed Window-deletion operators that delete one, two, three, and four consecutive lines respectively. The remaining operators are VSM- and LDA-deletion operators with $\delta = \{0.9, 0.8, 0.7, 0.6\}$. We fixed the topic size of the LDA-deletion operators to 500 based on previous results; the LDA approach also generates the topic model only once at the beginning (see the previous work [7] for more details).

2.5 Selective Hyperheuristic

The selection probability of a deletion operator D_K, $P(D_K)$ is initialized as $\frac{1}{|D|}$ by InitOperator. The function SelectOperator is a *roulette wheel selection* based on the probabilities.

The function UpdateScore updates $P(D_K)$ as follows:

$$newP(D_K) = \begin{cases} \omega_{comp} \cdot P(D_K) & \text{when compile fails} \\ \omega_{exec} \cdot P(D_K) & \text{when compile suceeds and execution fails} \\ (1 + \log_{10} l) \cdot P(D_K) & \text{otherwise} \end{cases}$$

The penalty values, ω, for the compilation or execution failures, are set as $\omega_{comp}, \omega_{exec} \in [0, 1)$, $\omega_{comp} \leq \omega_{exec}$. Here, l denotes the number of lines deleted by the chosen operator (note that $\log_{10} l > 0$). In this study, we set ω_{comp} as 0.8 and ω_{exec} as 0.9. UPDATESCORE linearly normalizes the selection probabilities so that $\Sigma_K P(\text{DK})$ is always 1.0.

3   Experimental Setup

3.1   Research Questions

We ask the following research questions:

RQ1: *How efficient is HOBBES compare to W-ORBS?* Previous work [7] showed that Window-deletion and the lexical similarity based deletion exhibit different cost-benefit trade-offs. RQ1 investigates whether using the selective hyperheuristic can improve the time efficiency of ORBS. We answer RQ1 by comparing the number of deleted lines, as well as the time the slicing took, between HOBBES and W-ORBS.

RQ2: *Does HOBBES actually use all deletion operators adaptively?* That is, does any single deletion operator exhibit dominant usage? We check whether HOBBES makes use of all operators adaptively by tracing the selection probabilities of each operator throughout the slicing operation.

3.2   Subjects, Configuration, and Environment

The slicing subjects have been chosen from the Guava library. We select two packages, `com.google.common.escape` and `com.google.common.net`, each with 590 and 1,569 LOCs. We choose 2 slicing criteria for each subjects. Since W-ORBS always produces the same slice for a deterministic program, we execute W-ORBS only once for each criterion. We repeat HOBBES 10 times to cater for the stochasticity in selection as well as in the LDA process.

The experiments have been performed on machines with Intel Core i7-6700K running Ubuntu 14.04.5 LTS. ORBS has been implemented in Python, whereas the subject programs have been built using Java version 1.8.

4   Results

RQ1. Efficiency of HOBBES: Fig. 1 shows the results of W-ORBS and HOBBES for the four slicing criteria. The x-axis represent the slicing iterations, going up to the number of iterations W-ORBS requires to terminate. The barplots and lines represent the cumulative numbers of deleted lines and execution time, respectively. The result shows that, on average, HOBBES can delete about 71% of the number of lines that W-ORBS deletes. However, HOBBES only takes about 30% of the time spent by W-ORBS.

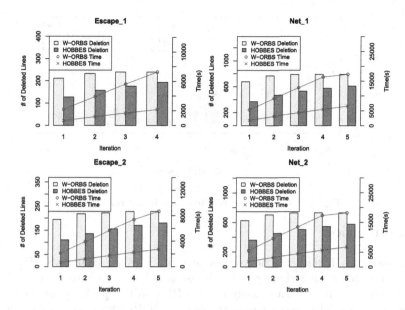

Fig. 1. Comparison between W-ORBS, HOBBES

Table 1. Result of Compile, Execute, Deletion per Time

Subject	Strategy	Iter1			Iter2			Iter3			Iter4			Iter5		
		C	E	D/T	C	E	D/T	C	E	D/T	C	E	D/T	C	E	D/T
escape1	HOBBES	502	66	0.20	926	104	0.13	1321	135	0.11	1699	165	0.09	2060	192	0.09
	W-ORBS	1711	183	0.10	3137	267	0.06	4523	342	0.04	5840	415	0.03	NA	NA	NA
escape2	HOBBES	1332	214	0.21	2424	309	0.15	3430	388	0.12	4384	455	0.11	5289	516	0.09
	W-ORBS	4179	655	0.13	7383	922	0.08	10436	1159	0.06	13460	1390	0.05	14116	1558	0.05
net1	HOBBES	513	70	0.17	955	114	0.11	1374	154	0.09	1771	189	0.08	2154	224	0.07
	W-ORBS	1759	189	0.09	3251	280	0.06	4707	364	0.04	6141	448	0.03	7174	517	0.03
net2	HOBBES	1341	222	0.20	2444	324	0.14	3460	402	0.11	4425	473	0.10	5346	536	0.09
	W-ORBS	4332	667	0.11	7781	963	0.07	11077	1237	0.05	14337	1504	0.04	14993	1672	0.04

Table 1 shows the detailed results of W-ORBS and HOBBES until their fifth iteration. HOBBES performs fewer compilations and executions than W-ORBS, while showing higher time efficiency (i.e. more deletions per time). Answering **RQ1**, we report that HOBBES can improve the time efficiency of W-ORBS.

RQ2. Participation of Deletion Operators: Fig. 2 shows how the selection probabilities of deletion operators change throughout the slicing of net_1. No deletion operator dominates the selection; also, there exist several peaks of different colours. We interpret this as each deletion operator being used at different stages by HOBBES. Note that the probabilities for both VSM- and LDA-deletion operators increased early in the slicing because these operators are not limited in the number of lines they can delete. However, we also observe that Window-deletion operators are also selected at different times.

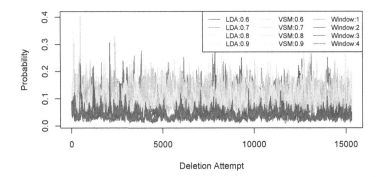

Fig. 2. Change of probability of deletion operators

5   Conclusion

We introduce a hyperheuristic version of ORBS, called HOBBES. HOBBES applies a selective hyperheuristic to choose a deletion operator iteratively at each source code line. A case study of HOBBES on two packages in the `Guava` library, using 12 deletion operators, shows that HOBBES can delete 71% of the number of lines deleted by W-ORBS, using only 30% of the time. Future work will investigate more diverse deletion operators as well as more sophisticated selective hyperheuristic algorithm.

References

1. Agrawal, H., DeMillo, R.A., Spafford, E.H.: Debugging with dynamic slicing and backtracking. Softw. Pract. Experience **23**(6), 589–616 (1993)
2. Binkley, D., Gold, N., Harman, M., Islam, S., Krinke, J., Yoo, S.: ORBS: language-independent program slicing. In: Proceedings of the 22nd ACM SIGSOFT International Symposium on the Foundations of Software Engineering, FSE 2014, pp. 109–120 (2014)
3. Binkley, D., Gold, N., Harman, M., Islam, S., Krinke, J., Yoo, S.: ORBS and the limits of static slicing. In: Proceedings of the 15th IEEE International Working Conference on Source Code Analysis and Manipulation (2015)
4. Binkley, D.W.: The application of program slicing to regression testing. Inf. Softw. Technol. Spec. Issu. Progr. Slicing **40**(11, 12), 583–594 (1998)
5. Gallagher, K.B., Lyle, J.R.: Using program slicing in software maintenance. IEEE Trans. Softw. Eng. **17**(8), 751–761 (1991)
6. Korel, B., Rilling, J.: Program slicing in understanding of large programs. In: 6th IEEE International Workshop on Program Comprenhesion (IWPC 1998), pp. 145–152. IEEE Computer Society Press, Los Alamitos (1998)
7. Lee, S., Yoo, S.: Using source code lexical similarity to improve efficiency of observation based slicing. Technical report CS-TR-2017-412, School of Computing, Korean Advanced Institute of Science and Technology, January 2017
8. Weiser, M.: Program slicing. In: 5th International Conference on Software Engineering, San Diego, pp. 439–449, March 1981
9. Yoo, S., Binkley, D., Eastman, R.: Observational slicing based on visual semantics. J. Syst. Softw. **129**, 60–78 (2016)

Student Papers

Diversity in Search-Based Unit Test Suite Generation

Nasser M. Albunian[(✉)]

The University of Sheffield, Sheffield, UK
nmalbunian1@sheffield.ac.uk

Abstract. Search-based unit test generation is often based on evolutionary algorithms. Lack of diversity in the population of an evolutionary algorithm may lead to premature convergence at local optima, which would negatively affect the code coverage in test suite generation. While methods to improve population diversity are well-studied in the literature on genetic algorithms (GAs), little attention has been paid to diversity in search-based unit test generation so far. The aim of our research is to study the effects of population diversity on search-based unit test generation by applying different diversity maintenance and control techniques. As a first step towards understanding the influence of population diversity on the test generation, we adapt diversity measurements based on phenotypic and genotypic representation to the search space of unit test suites.

Keywords: Search-based test generation · Population diversity · Genetic algorithm

1 Introduction

As software testing is a time-consuming, laborious, and error-prone task, developers can choose to generate tests automatically. In the context of unit testing object oriented software, where tests are sequences of calls on a class under test (CUT), Genetic Algorithms (GAs) have been successfully applied for generating tests achieving high code coverage [7].

The success of GAs is dependent on the diversity maintained in the search population [10]. If the individuals of the population all become too similar and lack diversity, then the search may converge on a local optimum of the objective function. This reduces the effectiveness of the GA, and in the case of search-based test generation, premature convergence would imply a reduced code coverage.

To avoid premature convergence and maintain diversity in the search population, different diversity techniques have been proposed at the genotype and the phenotype levels [19]. While the problem of maintaining the diversity has been extensively investigated within different domains of evolutionary algorithms (e.g., [3]), much less is known about diversity in whole test suite generation.

The aim of our research is to investigate the effects of population diversity on the generation of unit tests for Java programs. The attempt is to see whether the diversity of the search population helps in generating test suites that are capable

© Springer International Publishing AG 2017
T. Menzies and J. Petke (Eds.): SSBSE 2017, LNCS 10452, pp. 183–189, 2017.
DOI: 10.1007/978-3-319-66299-2_17

of achieving the search goal (e.g. higher code coverage) and, on the other hand, reducing the occurrence of premature convergence. To do so, different diversity maintenance and control techniques will be examined to determine their effects on the population diversity with the hope of proposing techniques that improve the diversity to generate better test suites. However, as a first step towards understanding the influence of population diversity on the test generation, we adapt diversity measurements based on phenotypic and genotypic representation to the search space of unit test suites.

2   Background

2.1   Search-Based Software Testing (SBST)

Search-Based Software Testing (SBST) describes the application of meta-heuristic optimisation techniques to the automation of various software testing tasks. In particular, SBST is frequently applied to generate test data [9]. When test data is numeric then local search algorithms such as hill climbing have been used successfully; in other domains, such as unit testing, GAs are more common.

In a GA, a population of candidate solutions is gradually evolved toward an optimal solution. The algorithm typically starts with a population of random individuals that will be iteratively evolved over many generations. In each generation, the processes of natural evolution are mimicked: Every individual in the population is evaluated by a fitness function, which determines how close this individual is to the desired solution. The fitter an individual, the more likely it is selected from the current population and used for recombination using crossover and mutation operators while building the next generation of the GA population. Higher selective pressure leads to a more biased selection of parent individuals and thus less diversity. Similarly, higher mutation rate can lead to more diverse individuals.

Although studies have shown the effectiveness of GAs for test generation [7], the application domain of unit testing seems to be special. In particular, Shamshiri et al. [18] recently showed that there are cases, in particular when the code coverage based fitness function hardly provides guidance, where random search is at least as effective as a GA. Shamshiri et al. hypothesise that in these cases the GA suffers from reduced diversity compared to the random search.

In the context of generating tests for object oriented programs, a common approach lies in evolving entire sets of unit tests [6]. The representation of a solution is a test suite, which is a set of test cases [6]. Each test case is a sequence of calls on the CUT. As the ideal test suite size is not known a priori, the number of tests in a test suite and the number of statements in a test case are variable and can be changed by the search operators.

The fitness function used to guide the search is based on code coverage. One of the most common coverage criteria in practice is branch coverage [6]. The overall fitness value of a test suite is the sum of normalised branch distance values (i.e., values estimating the distance to conditions evaluating to true and false), so that a test suite with 100% branch coverage has a fitness value of 0 [6].

2.2   Measuring Population Diversity

Maintaining population diversity during the evolution of EAs is widely believed to be crucial for avoiding premature convergence. Diversity measures are intended to quantify the variety of population's individuals in the base of structural or behavioural levels. These levels differ among different domains [19], e.g., the structure of an individual in the case of genetic programming (GP) is not similar to the one with other evolutionary algorithms (EAs).

In general, there are three different levels of diversity measurement [19]: Genotype level, Phenotype level, and Composite measures. The genotypic diversity measures the structural (i.e., syntactic) differences among the individuals of a population. In contrast, the phenotypic diversity is based on the behavioural (i.e., semantic) differences in the population's individuals. Finally, composite measures are a combination of genotypic and phenotypic measures. The genotypic and phenotypic diversity measures have been intensively applied for GPs, but have seen less attention in other EAs [19].

2.3   Maintaining Population Diversity

There are several techniques that have been used to maintain the diversity of a population during the evolution process. Črepinšek et al. [19] classified these techniques into non-niching and niching techniques.

The purpose of niching techniques is to alleviate the effects of genetic drift by segmenting the population into subpopulations to locate multiple optimal solutions [15]. Fitness sharing is the most popular and well-known approach among the niching techniques [15]. It aims to find multiple peaks in the solution space, where each subpopulation around a peak represents a niche where individuals share the same resource (i.e., fitness value). The idea behind fitness sharing is to decrease the value of the resource that is shared by the individuals of a niche when the number of individuals is high. In contrast, the resource value will be increased when there are few individuals in a niche, which gives these individuals higher probability to be selected for next generations.

On the other hand, the non-niching techniques include different approaches such as increasing population size, changing selection pressure, or applying replacement restrictions [19].

However, there are other diversity techniques (e.g., dynamic adaptation of crossover and mutation rates [14]) that rely on the feedback that is provided by the population diversity measures to steer the evolution towards better exploration and exploitation of the search space. These techniques are known by the diversity control techniques [19].

2.4   Diversity in Test Generation

In the context of test generation, there have been several studies on generating diverse test cases [16]. These studies adapt different evolutionary aspects to be based on diversity of tests. The aim of these studies is for the tests within the final test suite to be diverse, rather than the individuals in the search population (i.e., diverse test suites).

One aspect that can be modified to be based on diversity is fitness function. For example, Feldt et al. [4] modified the fitness function of their evolutionary algorithm to measure the fitness of a test case based on its similarity to other test cases. The measure is based on information distance (i.e., information about the actual execution of a test) between each two test cases.

Another approach that modifies the fitness function in a GA to be based on the diversity of black-box string test cases is presented by Shahbazi et al. [17]. The fitness function, in this case, measures the diversity of test cases as the distance between every test case and its nearest test case (i.e., higher fitness value indicates more diverse test cases). The authors examined different string distance functions including Levenshtein, Hamming, Cosine, Manhattan, Cartesian, and LSH distance functions and found that the LSH distance function performs better in measuring the distance.

Alshraideh et al. [2] defined a diversity measure that is used to rank individuals in the population (i.e., an individual with the highest distance from other individuals receives better rank). Their measure is enriched to their approach that directs the search when the fitness function at any test goal can not find scarce test inputs.

The selection of parents during the evolution is another aspect that can be adapted to be based on tests diversity. An approach that is applied by Palomba et al. [11] incorporated two metrics into the Many-Objective Genetic Algorithm (MOSA) within the selection mechanism as a secondary objective. One metric is to reduce the test coupling (i.e., higher diversity) and the other is to increase the test cohesion (i.e., lower test length).

Panichella et al. [13] proposed a novel many-objective GA that targets all branches in the software under test as different objectives to be optimised simultaneously. To maintain better diversity among test cases, the authors applied the crowding distance in the selection scheme; a test case has a higher probability to be selected if it has a higher distance from the other test cases.

3   Preliminary Work

Our goal is to analyse how test suite generation for Java programs is influenced by test case diversity, and whether maintaining diversity during the search can lead to better coverage results. We therefore started by applying three diversity measure techniques based on the phenotypic and genotypic levels. We measure the phenotypic diversity based on the fitness entropy and test execution traces, and we define a genotypic measurement based on the syntactic representation of test suites.

To maintain population diversity, we investigated the influence of five selection mechanisms (i.e., Roulette wheel, Tournament selection size 2 and size 7, and Rank selection bias 1.2 and bias 1.7) and five configurations of fitness sharing (i.e., using fitness values, predicate distance, normalised predicate distance,

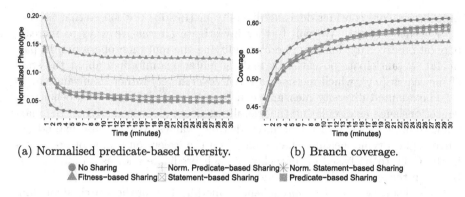

(a) Normalised predicate-based diversity.   (b) Branch coverage.

● No Sharing   ╂ Norm. Predicate-based Sharing ✳ Norm. Statement-based Sharing
▲ Fitness–based Sharing ⊠ Statement-based Sharing   ■ Predicate-based Sharing

Fig. 1. Diversity throughout the evolution using sharing algorithms.

statement distance, and normalised statement distance to define niches) on the diversity of the generated test suites.

To run our experiments, we used EvoSuite (version 1.0.3) with a "vanilla" configuration [5] with only branch coverage as target criterion, no test archive, and search budget of 30 min. We ran EvoSuite 10 times on 347 complex classes from the DynaMOSA study [12].

The results show that for selection mechanisms, the main constant across all types of diversity is that the roulette wheel selection leads to higher increase in the population diversity. If we compare tournament selection with tournament sizes 2 and 7, then the larger tournament size is expected to lead to less diversity, and indeed this is confirmed by the entropy measure. For rank selection, the higher rank bias of 1.7 results in less diversity than a bias of 1.2, as expected.

On the other hand, when comparing the five configurations of fitness sharing with the baseline without fitness sharing, the fitness sharing shows clear increase in diversity; fitness sharing based on fitness values shows the largest increase across all metrics. The normalised versions of the metrics are usually close to the non-normalised, except when normalised predicate-distance is used to drive fitness sharing, in which case it results in larger increase, as shown in Fig. 1a.

Figure 1b shows the average code coverage over time. Interestingly, all applications of fitness sharing lead to lower code coverage. Indeed the configuration that results in the highest diversity (fitness-based sharing) results in the lowest code coverage. Our conjecture for this observation is that diversity increases length. The likely reason for this lies in the variable size representation used in test suite generation, where higher diversity leads to larger individuals, and thus more expensive fitness evaluations.

4   Future Work

As our preliminary results indicate that increasing population diversity leads to an increase in the length of individuals rather than improving the coverage, we will therefore consider devising diversity metrics for test suites that are not influenced by length. We will further investigate alternative ways to increase population diversity, for example by modifying the mutation operators. In particular, we anticipate potential by making mutations informed about the state of the search (e.g., which methods are not covered yet) rather than random.

The adapted diversity measures can be extended and used with other configurations such as calculating the overall predicate diversity based on the maximum/minimum value of the resulted distance values. We will also extend our current phenotypic measure that is based on the execution profile of predicates in the CUT to be based on branches of each predicate and, as an alternative, based on the state of the object under test.

In addition, we aim to apply a generic modification of the search algorithms that improves the diversity such as adapting the Novelty search algorithm [8] to fit our diversity metrics and applying the Cellular form of GAs [1] to generate test suites.

References

1. Alba, E., Dorronsoro, B.: Cellular Genetic Algorithms. Operations Research/Computer Science Interfaces Series. Springer, US (2009)
2. Alshraideh, M., Bottaci, L., Mahafzah, B.A.: Using program data-state scarcity to guide automatic test data generation. Software Qual. J. **18**(1), 109–144 (2010)
3. Burke, E., Gustafson, S., Kendall, G., Krasnogor, N.: Advanced population diversity measures in genetic programming. In: Guervós, J.J.M., Adamidis, P., Beyer, H.-G., Schwefel, H.-P., Fernández-Villacañas, J.-L. (eds.) PPSN 2002. LNCS, vol. 2439, pp. 341–350. Springer, Heidelberg (2002). doi:10.1007/3-540-45712-7_33
4. Feldt, R., Torkar, R., Gorschek, T., Afzal, W.: Searching for cognitively diverse tests: towards universal test diversity metrics. In: Software Testing Verification and Validation Workshop, ICSTW 2008, pp. 178–186. IEEE (2008)
5. Fraser, G., Arcuri, A.: Evosuite: automatic test suite generation for object-oriented software. In: Proceeding of the 19th ACM SIGSOFT Symposium and the 13th European Conference on Foundations of Software Engineering, pp. 416–419. ACM (2011)
6. Fraser, G., Arcuri, A.: Whole test suite generation. IEEE Trans. Software Eng. **39**(2), 276–291 (2013)
7. Fraser, G., Arcuri, A.: A large-scale evaluation of automated unit test generation using EvoSuite. ACM Trans. Softw. Eng. Methodol. **24**(2), 8:1–8:42 (2014)
8. Lehman, J., Stanley, K.O.: Exploiting open-endedness to solve problems through the search for novelty. In: ALIFE, pp. 329–336 (2008)
9. McMinn, P.: Search-based software testing: past, present and future. In: 2011 IEEE Fourth International Conference on Software Testing, Verification and Validation Workshops (ICSTW), pp. 153–163. IEEE (2011)
10. Morrison, J., Oppacher, F.: Maintaining genetic diversity in genetic algorithms through co-evolution. In: Mercer, R.E., Neufeld, E. (eds.) AI 1998. LNCS, vol. 1418, pp. 128–138. Springer, Heidelberg (1998). doi:10.1007/3-540-64575-6_45
11. Palomba, F., Panichella, A., Zaidman, A., Oliveto, R., De Lucia, A.: Automatic test case generation: what if test code quality matters? In: Proceedings of the International Symposium on Software Testing and Analysis, pp. 130–141. ACM (2016)

12. Panichella, A., Kifetew, F., Tonella, P.: automated test case generation as a many-objective optimisation problem with dynamic selection of the targets. IEEE Trans. Software Eng. **PP**, 1 (2017)

13. Panichella, A., Kifetew, F.M., Tonella, P.: Reformulating branch coverage as a many-objective optimization problem. In: 2015 IEEE 8th International Conference on Software Testing, Verification and Validation (ICST), pp. 1–10. IEEE (2015)

14. Pellerin, E., Pigeon, L., Delisle, S.: Self-adaptive parameters in genetic algorithms. In: International Society for Optics and Photonics, pp. 53–64 (2004)

15. Sareni, B., Krahenbuhl, L.: Fitness sharing and niching methods revisited. Trans. Evol. Comp **2**(3), 97–106 (1998)

16. Shahbazi, A.: Diversity-based automated test case generation. Ph.D. thesis, University of Alberta (2015)

17. Shahbazi, A., Miller, J.: Black-Box string test case generation through a multi-objective optimization. IEEE Trans. Software Eng. **42**(4), 361–378 (2016)

18. Shamshiri, S., Rojas, J.M., Fraser, G., McMinn, P.: Random or genetic algorithm search for object-oriented test suite generation? In: Proceeding of the Conference on Genetic and Evolutionary Computation, pp. 1367–1374. ACM (2015)

19. Črepinšek, M., Liu, S.H., Mernik, M.: Exploration and exploitation in evolutionary algorithms: a survey. ACM Comput. Surv. **45**(3), 35:1–35:33 (2013)

Automated Controlled Experimentation on Software by Evolutionary Bandit Optimization

Rasmus Ros[(✉)], Elizabeth Bjarnason, and Per Runeson

Department of Computer Science, Lund University, Lund, Sweden
{rasmus.ros,elizabeth.bjarnason,per.runeson}@cs.lth.se

Abstract. Controlled experiments, also called A/B tests or split tests, are used in software engineering to improve products by evaluating variants with user data. By parameterizing software systems, multivariate experiments can be performed automatically and in large scale, in this way, controlled experimentation is formulated as an optimization problem. Using genetic algorithms for automated experimentation requires repetitions to evaluate a variant, since the fitness function is noisy. We propose to combine genetic algorithms with bandit optimization to optimize where repetitions are evaluated, instead of uniform sampling. We setup a simulation environment that allows us to evaluate the solution, and see that it leads to increased fitness, population diversity, and rewards, compared to only genetic algorithms.

1 Introduction

For companies developing internet-connected products, swift delivery of new value-adding features is a key competitive factor. User perception is an important factor in deciding which new features and software variants to include. This factor can be gauged through continuous experimentation [1], where users are exposed to different software variants, and decisions are made regarding which variant to release based on user responses. The de facto method [2] for this is iterative A/B testing, where the users are exposed to one of two or more variants of the software. Once enough data is collected a hypothesis test determines the winner of the controlled experiment, using a metric that aligns the software with business goals (e.g. fraction of satisfied users).

A/B testing has been formulated as an optimization problem of finding the optimal variants by parameterizing relevant variants in a software system [3], using genetic algorithms [4]. This automated A/B testing of software can test variants in quick succession, in this work we also evaluate multiple variants simultaneously, as in multivariate testing. The optimization context presents two challenges to evolutionary algorithms. Firstly, the fitness function is noisy, which is addressed by repeated sampling. Secondly, improvements should be made with as low cost as possible. Our proposed solution is to unify *evolutionary algorithms* and *bandit optimization* [5].

© Springer International Publishing AG 2017
T. Menzies and J. Petke (Eds.): SSBSE 2017, LNCS 10452, pp. 190–196, 2017.
DOI: 10.1007/978-3-319-66299-2_18

Bandit optimization is a technique for online experimental design, where the sizes of the groups in the experiment are changed dynamically, based on their performance. Bandit optimization has received attention from machine learning and statistical communities [5] and has been used in commercial tools for conducting controlled experimentation (e.g. in Google Analytics Content Experiments).

Controlled experimentation as a software engineering phenomenon, has been studied in search based software engineering (SBSE). There, controlled experimentation was first formulated as an optimization problem, by Tamburrelli and Margara [3], and our contribution builds on their work. They used genetic algorithms with repetitions on the fitness function to reduce variance, which spreads the experimentation evenly over the population. In knowledge discovery and data mining (KDD), Kohavi et al.'s seminal paper on the technical and practical considerations for large-scale web A/B testing [2] describes the context where our work can be applied. The research on controlled experimentation in evidence based software engineering (EBSE) uses the term *continuous experimentation* and takes a management and process perspective [1].

2   Solution Algorithm

We propose a novel algorithm for automated experimentation that combines the online experimental design of bandit optimization with the genetic operators crossover and mutation to expand the search. Our algorithm is tasked with continuously maximizing the performance of the software, as measured by some business value, a *reward* in bandit literature. The proposed algorithm is outlined in Algorithm 1 below. The design choices in the algorithm for bandit optimization, steps 1–3, and the evolutionary algorithm, steps 4–6, are explained in Sects. 2.1 and 2.2 respectively.

In bandit optimization a gambler is faced by multiple slot-machines (colloquially a one-armed bandit) with unknown reward distributions. The goal is to maximize rewards by using the bandits one at a time. Herein lies a trade-off between exploration of the bandits' reward distributions and exploiting the currently most rewarding bandit. For A/B testing, this non-uniform sampling can lower the total opportunity cost of experimenting, but is less robust to changes in bandit performance. Standard bandit algorithms use a fixed number of bandits, while in this work we propose to continuously change the set of available bandits by genetic algorithm operators.

The proposed algorithm has a population of variants $x_i \in X, i = 1 \ldots n$. Every time slot $t = 1 \ldots T$ a user of the system arrives and requests a software variant. The variant is selected from X, according to the bandit policy, to maximize the expected reward. Rewards $r_{t,i} \in R$ from experimentation are continuously used to update beliefs about reward distributions θ_i. Any variant can be eliminated if they are performing significantly worse than the best variant in X. The standard genetic operators – crossover and mutation – are then used to generate new variants in the population.

Algorithm 1. Proposed evolutionary bandit algorithm.

$X =$ initial population of software variants, rewards $R = \varnothing$.
for $t = 1, \ldots, T$ **do**
    `// A user arrives in the system.`
    1. Select variant x_i from X according to bandit policy.
    2. Observe reward $r_{t,i}$ from experiment with x_i, $R = R \cup r_{t,i}$.
    3. Update belief about θ_i with $r_{t,i}$.
    4. Evaluate fitness on all variants in X based on R.
    5. Select most-fit variants from X, eliminating the rest.
    6. Add new variants to X through crossover and mutation.
end

Example problem. We use the visual layout of web pages as an example problem to validate our algorithm. This is a commonly used example for A/B testing [2]. Representing the layout as a grid allows easy definitions of the genetic operators. The scalar value of each grid cell defines which layout component to use on that cell. The grid can be transformed into a minimal set of rectangles in polynomial time, using results from computational geometry [6].

The number of variations in the problem is $C^{n \times m}$, where C is the number of different layout components, and $n \times m$ is the size of the grid. The reward is either success or failure of the layout in performing its task (e.g. sell a product in an e-commerce web-site).

2.1   Bandit Optimization Policies

From the many heuristic methods of solving the bandit problem we have tested upper confidence bound (UCB) and Thompson sampling [5]. Both UCB and Thompson sampling are asymptotically optimal heuristics; they achieve an expected *regret* of $O(\log T)$ for binary rewards. Regret is defined as $T\mu - \sum_{t=1}^{T} r_t$, where μ is the expected reward of the best possible bandit and r_t is the reward at time t. We found that probability matching performed the best and therefore restrict our discussion to this method.

Thompson sampling. A conceptually simple Bayesian method of solving the bandit problem is to match the probability of selecting a bandit with the probability of it being the optimal bandit. This is achieved by sampling from a posterior distribution once for each bandit and selecting the bandit with the highest sampled value. The posterior distribution $P(\theta_i|r_i)$ of variant x_i is updated as experiments are completed.

Example bandit policy for the layout problem. The bandit policy for the layout problem is Thompson sampling, and since the rewards are binary, they are modelled by a Bernoulli distribution. The Beta distribution is a conjugate prior to the Bernoulli distribution, and so to sample a value from the posterior it is sufficient to take a single sample from the $\text{Beta}(\alpha_i + a, \beta_i + b)$ distribution, where α and β

are the number of successes and failures in experiments involving variant x_i. Selecting $a = b = 1$ as the prior successes and failures yields a non-informative prior.

2.2 Evolutionary Algorithm Design

The design of our evolutionary algorithm is influenced by the iterative process imposed by bandit optimization, since selection is performed in steps instead of in batches. As a consequence we use an additional selection as mating strategy. The population size n is kept fixed, and as variants are eliminated, the population is expanded through crossover and mutation. The number of variants eliminated per time slot are dynamic, and depends on the fitness of the variants. Fitness is evaluated based on the feedback observed from experiments with users.

Selection. When there is sufficient evidence that a variant is under performing it is removed from the population. Any variant whose fitness confidence interval is non-overlapping with the best fitness confidence interval is eliminated from the population, this is effectively a dynamic version of truncation selection.

Mating strategy. Since breeding is performed in small steps there is a risk of mating the most-fit variants frequently, leading to pre-mature convergence. Hence selecting mates through either uniform sampling, tournament selection or proportional selection [4] is appropriate. Fitness proportional selection with rejection sampling [7] worked best in the simulation, where a variant x_i is selected uniformly at random and then accepted with probability f_i/f_M, where f_i is the fitness of the variant x_i and f_M is the fitness of the most-fit variant, evaluated through maximum *a posteriori* estimation of reward distributions $P(\theta_i|r_i)$.

Example genetic operators for the layout problem. The genetic operators for the layout problem are defined as follows. Crossover between two parents is done by selecting a horizontal or vertical line in the grid, and using the values from either parent from each side of the line respectively. Mutation is performed by changing the value of a randomly selected rectangle in the grid.

3   Simulation

The proposed algorithm is evaluated in a simulation of the visual layout problem, see the results in Fig. 1 and Table 1. A simulation provides a highly controlled environment for evaluating the solution, but is not as realistic as a real world implementation. The code and all simulation results are available in Github[1]. As a baseline for comparison we use a genetic algorithm with repetitions, implemented using the different options in the Matlab Optimization Toolbox.

To get as realistic simulation as possible we need a fitness function with multiple local optima, this function would be unknown in a real scenario. Solutions with high number of rectangles are ranked lower, since those are hypothesized to

---

[1] https://github.com/rasros/evolutionarybandit

be less visually appealing. This is motivated by popular design guidelines that promote minimalistic design (e.g. material design[2]). Following this reasoning, the distance between two grids is defined as the fraction of cells in the grid that are non-equal. To punish complex solutions we add $\max(R_p - R_t, 0)/(n \cdot m)$ to the distance, where R_t and R_p is the number of rectangles in the target and proposed grid respectively. Finally, since there can be multiple solutions of various quality we take the weighted harmonic mean between the distances from the proposed grid to multiple target grids. The mean is then the probability for a proposed grid to receive a reward. We believe this presents a challenging and somewhat realistic target fitness function.

The conditions for the simulation are as follows. The grid size is 8×10 with 4 possible values, thus there are approximately 10^{48} unique combinations and 80 variables, this is sufficiently large to encode complex layouts with multiple software components. The initial population is generated to have fitness between 0.1–0.2. The simulation proceeds over $T = 4000$ experiments, which is based on the number of samples needed for an A/B test with 70% power and 0.05 confidence, with an effect of 0.02. The simulation is repeated 1000 times.

Both algorithms have multiple hyper-parameters, which we tune using random search with linear regression, with some interaction factors. The response variable is the mean population fitness at end time T. Important parameters are population size, number of repetitions for the baseline algorithm, and cut-off threshold for the evolutionary bandit algorithm. Lowering the number of repetitions increases selection pressure, leading to short term gains in fitness, but decreases diversity which can lead to getting stuck in local optima. A similar effect with cut-off threshold is observed for the evolutionary bandit algorithm.

From the results in Table 1 and Fig. 1, we see that the evolutionary bandit algorithm is better in the relevant measures, fitness and diversity. Both algorithms improve significantly upon the starting conditions, although neither are close to converging. There is no asymptotic optimality of $O(\log T)$ regret seen in Fig. 1b. This is not surprising as it would be contingent on observing the optimal variant, and evolutionary algorithms provides no such guarantees.

Table 1. Simulation results at end time, $T = 4000$, with 1000 repetitions. Group fitness is the mean fitness over the population, top fitness is maximum fitness obtained in the group, duplication is the number of non-unique genomes. $\hat{A}$ is the Vargha-Delaney effect-size, calculated between the two algorithms.

Algorithm	Rewards		Group fitness		Top fitness		Duplication
	Median	IQR	Median	IQR	Median	IQR	
Baseline	624	143	0.185	0.061	0.247	0.061	25%
Bandit	721	192	0.219	0.071	0.295	0.075	0%
Effect-size $\hat{A}$	0.722		0.700		0.765		

---

[2] https://material.io/guidelines.

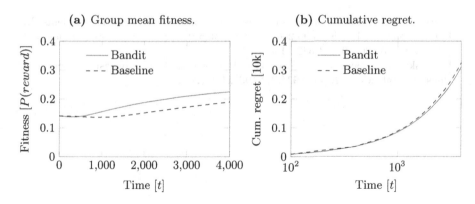

Fig. 1. Simulation results comparing the proposed bandit evolutionary algorithm against baseline genetic algorithm with repetitions. Results are averaged over 1000 simulation runs.

4   Conclusions

By formulating controlled experimentation of software systems as an optimization problem many more variants can be tested and evaluated than with manual experimentation under given resource constraints. Based on simulations, we show that adding bandit optimization to genetic algorithms increases both long-term fitness, rewards, and population diversity for this problem. An additional finding is that there are trade-offs in hyper-parameter tuning between short-term gains and long-term fitness, practitioners should make an active choice there. Future work includes additional overall realistic evaluation, and further investigation of the effect of time delays in rewards or dynamic changes of reward probabilities.

Acknowledgment. This work was conducted within the Wallenberg Autonomous Systems and Software Program (WASP) (http://wasp-sweden.se).

References

1. Fagerholm, F., Guinea, A.S., Mäenpää, H., Münch, J.: The RIGHT model for continuous experimentation. J. Syst. Softw. **123**, 292–305 (2017)
2. Kohavi, R., Henne, R.M., Sommerfield, D.: Practical guide to controlled experiments on the web: listen to your customers not to the HiPPO. In: Proceedings of the 13th ACM SIGKDD International Conference on Knowledge Discovery and Data Mining, pp. 959–967 (2007)
3. Tamburrelli, G., Margara, A.: Towards automated A/B testing. In: Goues, C., Yoo, S. (eds.) SSBSE 2014. LNCS, vol. 8636, pp. 184–198. Springer, Cham (2014). doi:10. 1007/978-3-319-09940-8_13
4. Melanie, M.: An Introduction to Genetic Algorithms. MIT Press, Cambridge (1999)
5. Burtini, G., Loeppky, J., Lawrence, R.: A Survey of Online Experiment Design with the Stochastic Multi-Armed Bandit. ArXiv e-prints (2015). arXiv:1510.00757v4 [stat.ML]

6. Eppstein, D.: Graph-theoretic solutions to computational geometry problems. In: Paul, C., Habib, M. (eds.) WG 2009. LNCS, vol. 5911, pp. 1–16. Springer, Heidelberg (2010). doi:10.1007/978-3-642-11409-0_1
7. Lipowski, A., Lipowska, D.: Roulette-wheel selection via stochastic acceptance. Phys. A: Stat. Mech. Appl. **391**(6), 2193–2196 (2012)

Author Index

Printed in the United States
By Bookmasters

Printed in the United States
By Bookmasters